MEDICAL TOURISM

Selected Titles in ABC-CLIO's
CONTEMPORARY
WORLD ISSUES
Series

For a complete list of titles in this series, please visit
www.abc-clio.com

Books in the Contemporary World Issues series address vital issues in today's society, such as genetic engineering, pollution, and biodiversity. Written by professional writers, scholars, and nonacademic experts, these books are authoritative, clearly written, up-to-date, and objective. They provide a good starting point for research by high school and college students, scholars, and general readers as well as by legislators, businesspeople, activists, and others.

Each book, carefully organized and easy to use, contains an overview of the subject, a detailed chronology, biographical sketches, facts and data and/or documents and other primary-source material, a directory of organizations and agencies, annotated lists of print and nonprint resources, and an index.

Readers of books in the Contemporary World Issues series will find the information they need to have a better understanding of the social, political, environmental, and economic issues facing the world today.

MEDICAL TOURISM

A Reference Handbook

Kathy Stolley and Stephanie Watson

CONTEMPORARY
WORLD ISSUES

 ABC-CLIO

Santa Barbara, California • Denver, Colorado • Oxford, England

Library of Congress Cataloging-in-Publication Data

Stolley, Kathy S.
    Medical tourism : a reference handbook / Kathy Stolley and Stephanie Watson.
        p. cm. — (Contemporary world issues)
    Includes bibliographical references and index.
    ISBN 978-1-59884-540-2 (hardback) — ISBN 978-1-59884-541-9 (ebook)   1. Medical tourism—Handbooks, manuals, etc.   I. Watson, Stephanie.   II. Title.
    RA793.5.S76   2012
    362.1—dc23   2012004133

ISBN: 978-1-59884-540-2
EISBN: 978-1-59884-541-9

16 15 14 13 12   1 2 3 4 5

This book is also available on the World Wide Web as an eBook.
Visit www.abc-clio.com for details.

ABC-CLIO, LLC
130 Cremona Drive, P.O. Box 1911
Santa Barbara, California 93116-1911

This book is printed on acid-free paper ∞

Manufactured in the United States of America

Contents

Preface

Throughout recorded history, people have traveled for health-related reasons. In the past decade, however, "medical tourism"—the new moniker for this type of travel—has become big business, involving millions of travelers annually. Once considered an industry niche, medical tourism has "gone mainstream," and it has done so in a major way (HNN Team 2009). Medical tourism is a rapidly growing global multi-billion dollar industry, now the fastest growing segment of the tourist market in several countries (Bookman and Bookman 2007).

Today's medical travelers visit some of the same destinations, and for some of the same reasons, that have drawn travelers for centuries. They still travel to spas on the Mediterranean for relaxation and recuperation, seek traditional Ayurveda treatments in India, and pilgrimage to Lourdes in France in search of miracle healings. However, modern technologies and tourism have also brought new destinations, options, and concerns. Mediterranean tourists now trek to Turkish hospitals that are equipped with the latest medical technologies. Travelers get high-tech heart surgery in India. In France, they now find a health system ranked number one in the world by the World Health Organization (WHO 2000). They venture around the globe in search of specialized care, shorter waiting times, costs savings, or adventure. And, sometimes, they hope for miracles from unproven treatments or even from illegal procedures.

More and more countries are joining the list of destinations for medical tourists. China, for example, has become one of many destinations for travelers seeking experimental, and sometimes controversial, stem cell therapies. World-renowned fertility clinics draw travelers to Israel and Barbados, among other countries. The adventurous can have both cosmetic surgery and a safari sightseeing trip in South Africa. Even the cruise industry is "on board" in adding medical tourism to its offerings (Lambier 2010).

A variety of forces are driving this growth in medical tourism. Part of the impetus is age demographics. Aging populations in many of the richer countries around the world have increased the demand for health care in those countries. Older medical tourists can find some relief from lengthy waiting lists as well as cheaper care for chronic ailments by crossing borders. A growing emphasis on youth culture and in staving off the effects of time on both aging bodies and what the mirror reflects influence those seeking cosmetic procedures and other rejuvenation therapies.

Cost is also a major driving force in medical tourism. Even after factoring in travel expenses, and depending on the procedure and destination, cost savings can be significant for those willing to travel for health care. This makes medical tourism an especially attractive option for those who are under-insured, uninsured, or have large deductibles. Similarly, those who seek treatments or procedures that must come "out-of-pocket" because they are un-approved or not covered by insurance (e.g., experimental therapies, cosmetic surgery) increasingly find traveling abroad an option to meet their needs (Jenner 2008). For less money, patients may also get more attentive service than they would at home, including well-appointed accommodations for both them and their travel companions, making the option of undergoing a medical procedure away from home a more attractive option.

Medical tourism has also seen a huge growth in media attention (Eades 2010), suggesting that people are increasingly aware of such options. While there were no items about medical tourism appearing in major English language news media in 1990, and only eight items by 1992, there were more than 2,300 such items in 2007 (Erfurt-Cooper and Cooper 2009). The bulk of that increase occurred after 2003. Researchers investigating the increasing attention to medical tourism on the Internet observed that the online search engine Google returned 1,100,100 results for an Internet search using the term "medical tourism" on July 29, 2007. Repeating the identical search just 62 days later, they found that number had increased by 300,000 results in just two months (Horowitz, Rosensweig, and Jones 2007). By mid-January 2012, the same search returned 7,370,000 results.

Additionally, travel is more accessible now than it has ever been. Discounted airfares mean travel is no longer the exclusive opportunity of the rich. In this age of globalization, people are also more informed about the world and accordingly more willing to travel.

But what does the global picture of medical tourism actually look like? And what does this all mean? Medical tourists often do receive excellent care, at a good value. Their money feeds the tourism and health care sectors as well as local economies, and arguably may even advance public health in countries that are travel destinations. Medical tourism's importance in the world health and economic arenas is clearly established. Simply put, medical tourism seems here to stay. Yet, while providing new and innovative options for health care, it also raises new questions and concerns.

Medical tourism is inseparably woven into complex issues of globalization. Ongoing debates examine medical tourism's role in exacerbating or reducing systemic inequalities in a global marketplace. This includes not only impacts on patients and facilities, but also the global health care workforce already straining to meet demand. What impact will medical tourism have on poor, under-resourced areas vying to become destinations for these travelers' business? Will a focus on tourist dollars mean even less attention is paid to the needs of the poor? And will catering to medical tourists annihilate local culture? Or will medical tourism actually raise the standard of care for everyone? Is it sustainable in terms of benefits for various stakeholders and cultures? Other unsettled questions surround the sometimes-competing interests of international trade and regulatory oversight.

The vast growth in the medical tourism industry has occurred with arguably little oversight, and has been evaluated with little methodologically rigorous research. Not only is there a lack of solid, empirically-based data on the medical aspects and outcomes of medical tourism, even basic information such as the annual numbers of medical travelers remains unclear. Potential patients often find themselves sifting through copious amounts of information on medical tourism, much of which intermingles marketing literature with medical information. This can mean they have much challenging "homework" to do in ascertaining the credentials of medical staff, health care facilities, and even medical tourism companies. Liability, privacy issues, and financial responsibility can all be uncertain. Some countries allow treatments to be offered that are considered experimental or even banned as dangerous elsewhere. In a world where health is increasingly treated like other commodities, travelers' money sometimes buys illegal "merchandise" (such as transplant organs).

The picture that emerges of medical tourism, captured in these pages, is rapidly changing, complicated, and multi-faceted. Health-related travel may indeed be a practice as old as recorded history, but it is also a thoroughly modern industry on a global scale. It is rich in the possibilities and opportunities brought about by new technologies ranging from medical advances to social media. But it is also subject to cultural lag, as practices have raced ahead of regulatory guidelines and standards that are still in process. The way ahead is still being charted. The destination is global. The outcomes will help shape the future of health care for us all.

References

Bookman, Milica Z., and Karla R. Bookman. *Medical Tourism in Developing Countries.* New York, NY: Palgrave Macmillan, 2007.

Eades, Jerry S. "Sun, Surgery, and Cyberspace: The Role of the Internet in the Rise of Medical Tourism." In *Biomedical Knowledge Management: Infrastructures and Processes for E-Health Systems,* edited by Wayne Pease, Malcolm Cooper, and Raj Gururajan. Hershey, PA: IGI Global, 2010, 217–231.

Erfurt-Cooper, Patricia, and Malcolm Cooper. *Health and Wellness Tourism: Spas and Hot Springs.* Bristol, UK: Channel View Publications, 2009.

HNN Team. "Medical Tourism and Global Healthcare: Where Are You Going?" Health WorldNet, Inc., May 11, 2009. http://healthworldnet. com/articles/heads-or-tails/medical-tourism-and-global-healthcare-where-are-you-going.html (accessed January 15, 2012).

Horowitz, Michael D., Jeffrey A. Rosensweig, and Christopher A. Jones. "Medical Tourism: Globalization of the Healthcare Marketplace." *Medscape General Medicine.* 2007. 9(4): 33. www.ncbi.nlm.nih.gov/pmc/articles/PMC2234298/ (accessed September 29, 2011).

Jenner, Elizabeth Anne. "Unsettled Borders of Care: Medical Tourism as New Dimension in America's Health Care Crisis." *Care for Major Health Problems and Population Health Concerns: Impacts on Patients, Providers and Policy.* Edited by Jennie Jacobs Kronenfeld. Bingley, UK: Emerald Group Publishing Limited, 2008, 235–249.

Lambier, Cayla. "Smooth Sailing: Cruise Lines and Medical Tourism, a Budding Relationship." *Medical Tourism Magazine.* December 7, 2010. http://www.medicaltourismmag.com/article/smooth-sailing-

cruise-lines-and-medical-tourism-a-budding-relationship.html
(accessed January 15, 2012).

World Health Organization (WHO). *The World Health Report 2000.
Health Systems: Improving Performance.* Geneva, Switzerland: WHO,
2000. www.who.int/whr/2000/en/index.html (accessed March 5, 2011).

1

Background and History

People have long felt the urge to escape from their everyday lives and venture off to distant shores for a little hard-earned rest and relaxation. Centuries ago, only the wealthy could afford to travel. The working class didn't have the time or the means to travel very far from their homes.

Those who were affluent enough to travel sought out more than just sunnier climates and relaxation. They also wanted a cure for what was ailing them. The ancient Greeks and Egyptians journeyed to the Mediterranean to take advantage of the healing hot springs and baths. In the 18th and 19th centuries, Europeans and Americans sought out spas to cure tuberculosis and other deadly diseases.

The idea of traveling for health reasons isn't new, but the name associated with it—*medical tourism*—is. Experts predict that by the year 2012, medical tourism will be a $100 billion industry, with more than 780 million people looking abroad for their medical care (Davis 2008).

What Is Medical Tourism?

In his 2005 bestseller, *The World Is Flat, New York Times* reporter Thomas Friedman (2005) described a new global economy in which technology is erasing geographical boundaries, and companies are taking advantage of the lower costs and greater efficiency they can find abroad. Today when people call their Internet service providers for technical support, they are often speaking with someone in Mumbai, or other parts of India. When American students go online for homework help, they are also likely connecting to a tutor in India.

The same principles—cost and availability—that have driven outsourcing have fueled the growth of medical tourism. The need for quality health care is growing exponentially. The world's population is estimated to reach 9 billion by 2050, and the fastest growing segment of that population in developed nations is people age 60 or older (United Nations 2007). As the Baby Boomers retire, they are demanding better quality care for their more active lifestyles.

No longer do developed nations like the United States have a monopoly on top-notch health care to meet those needs. Developing nations such as India and the Philippines are now home to hospitals and medical facilities that rival those in the West for state-of-the-art technology and highly trained staff, and they can offer those services far less expensively than in the United States.

The balance has also shifted when it comes to travelers themselves. Travel is no longer just for the wealthy. People of all socioeconomic backgrounds have the ability to buy a plane ticket and take advantage of medical care abroad. In fact, bargain hunters can find real cost savings by looking for health care services in other countries.

Medical tourism is the idea of traveling for the purposes of obtaining health care or wellness services. It can range from driving to a hospital in a neighboring state to take advantage of discounted foot surgery, to flying to Costa Rica for a tummy tuck, or to India for an artery bypass. People in less-developed nations may travel to the West for a highly specialized procedure they cannot find at home, or residents of the United States or Europe may travel to a less-developed country to take advantage of lower-cost medical services.

People can travel to save money on necessary surgeries (such as open-heart surgery) that are much cheaper abroad, or on elective procedures (such as cosmetic surgery or dental implants) that are not covered by medical insurance. Medical tourism also encompasses travel for services that improve people's general well being, such as vacations to spas or retreats.

What really puts the "tourism" in medical tourism is what often happens after the medical procedure. Travelers can take advantage of their visit abroad by sightseeing, taking day trips to the beach, or participating in other traditional tourism activities in the country they're visiting. Unlike other forms of tourism, in which travelers first choose a destination that appeals to them and then plan out their activities, with medical tourism the availability of a particular procedure determines the destination, and the vacation revolves around the medical care.

Why Do People Travel Abroad for Medical Care?

Medical tourism is driven by a number of factors, including health care quality, social factors, and political issues. But, as with so many other industries, its main driver is economics. People want the best medical care, and they want it at the lowest cost. "Medical tourism is about patients making educated decisions on where they can go to achieve the best possible healthcare outcomes at an affordable price," said Jonathan Edelheit, Chief Executive Director of the Medical Tourism Association (Davis 2008).

Cost

Getting medical care is an expensive endeavor, especially in the United States. Health care spending in this country reached $2.5 trillion in 2009—which works out to around $8,160 per person (Kaiser Family Foundation 2009). For the more than 47 million Americans who don't have any health insurance, finding inexpensive care is essential (U.S. Census Bureau 2007). Having a medical procedure performed abroad does add the costs of airfare, hotel, and transportation, but given that a single heart surgery in the United States can cost more than $100,000, finding that same operation for $12,000 in a country like India more than justifies the added travel costs (Riczo and Riczo 2009). Overall, traveling abroad can save American patients anywhere from 15 to 85 percent in medical costs (Woodman 2008).

One big incentive for medical travelers is to take advantage of lower-cost procedures that aren't typically covered by insurance, such as cosmetic surgery, some dental procedures, infertility treatments, and other nonemergency care. An estimated 40 percent of American medical tourists travel for elective treatments (Woodman 2008).

Quality

Another goal in medical tourism is to find higher quality care. In the past, stepping up to a higher standard of health care meant traveling from a less-developed country to Europe or the United States, but today that is no longer true. Countries like India and Thailand have spent billions of dollars improving their health care infrastructure, building state-of-the-art medical centers, and providing their doctors with the best training available. These countries also have adopted a patient-centric approach that far exceeds what is available in many U.S. hospitals. Patients get access to VIP facilities and services, one-on-one nursing care, and highly accessible doctors.

Shorter Wait Times

Patients in countries with socialized medicine programs enjoy free health care, but at a cost. In Great Britain and Canada, patients on free government-run health care plans may have to wait for up to a year or more to receive needed procedures (Woodman 2008). Some people die before they are ever able to make it into the operating room.

Even in the United States, waiting for health care is sometimes an unfortunate reality. Nearly one-third of injured veterans have to wait more than 30 days for an appointment at a VA medical center, according to one study (*Medical News Today* 2007). People who are in need of a replacement organ must put their names on a national organ donor list. As of February 12, 2010, there were more than 114,000 people in the United States waiting for a new kidney, liver, or other organ—waits that, for thousands of people, can exceed five years (U.S. Department of Health and Human Services, Health Resources and Services Administration 2010).

Unavailable Procedures

Despite its high overall quality of health care, the United States can sometimes lag behind other nations in adopting new medical techniques and technologies, in part because of its societal mores and rigorous approval processes. For example, India offers embryonic stem cell treatments that are still considered too controversial and experimental in the United States. Doctors in Europe, Canada, India, and Australia have been performing hip-resurfacing—a longer-term alternative to total hip replacement—since the late 1990s. The U.S. Food and Drug Administration (FDA) did not approve the same technology until 2006.

Anonymity

Traveling halfway around the world is one way for patients to ensure that no one at home will find out about their surgery. Anonymity is especially appealing to patients who are undergoing more-sensitive procedures, such as cosmetic or gender reassignment surgery.

Vacation

Finally, medical tourism offers patients the chance to escape for a few days or weeks. They can recuperate from their procedure in relaxing surroundings, far from the stresses of their everyday lives. Once they feel up to it, travelers can sunbathe, scuba dive, visit historical sites, or take advantage of other tourist attractions in their destination. Today, medical tourism facilitators make vacationing after surgery easy because they bundle medical care into packages with accommodations, transportation, and sightseeing tours.

Inbound vs. Outbound Medical Tourism

In the United States, medical tourism is broken into two distinct groups: inbound and outbound. With *outbound medical tourism,* American patients travel to another country to receive medical care. In 2007, an estimated 750,000 Americans participated in outbound medical tourism (Deloitte 2009). *Inbound medical tourists* travel from other countries to receive health care services in the United States that they can't get or have to wait too long to receive in their own country. Each year, an estimated 250,000 people travel to the United States for treatment (Bookman and Bookman 2007). Sometimes, Americans might also be considered inbound medical tourists when they travel from their home in one state to a hospital in another state to take advantage of a specialized procedure that is not available in their area, or a lower-cost surgery than they can receive in their local hospitals.

Many health care providers in the United States have increased incentives to attract more inbound travelers. They have been marketing aggressively to foreign patients, not only to drive business, but also because inbound medical tourists who come to the United States for care often pay in cash. Hospitals can charge foreign tourists more for the same procedures Americans receive, because U.S. health insurance plans often refuse to pay the full amounts.

As an example of this aggressive marketing effort, in the 1990s, Methodist Healthcare System in San Antonio, Texas, launched a campaign to attract more Mexican patients, in part by implementing bilingual and culturally sensitive services. In 2007, the marketing effort paid off when Mexico awarded five of Methodist Healthcare's hospitals the designation of accredited Hispanic Healthcare Hospitals.

Shady Grove Fertility Center in the Baltimore/Washington area established a partnership with fertility clinics in the UK to woo British patients. Even though Britain's National Health Service (NHS) covers fertility treatments, some patients don't qualify, and it's hard to find an egg donor in Britain, because they aren't paid like they are in the United States. Plus, wait times for fertility treatments in the UK can stretch as long as three years. Thanks to its incentives, in 2008, Shady Grove administered IVF treatment to more than five-dozen British patients, an increase of 350 percent from the previous year (Vequist and Valdez 2009).

Types of Medical Tourism

Patients can travel for just about every type of health care procedure and, accordingly, there are many branches of medical tourism to represent each kind of available medical care. The following are some of the best-known forms of medical tourism:

Dental Tourism

Dental care is one of the easiest medical services to receive abroad, because it is usually performed on an outpatient basis and the recovery is quick. That may be why about 40 percent of medical tourists go abroad for dental work (Pickert 2008). Patients can visit a dental clinic for a root canal in the morning, and go sightseeing the very same afternoon. The UK and Ireland are two of the biggest users of dental tourism services (Kumar 2009).

Reproductive Tourism

In many American states, fertility treatments (such as in vitro fertilization or donor egg transfers) for couples that are struggling to conceive are not covered by health insurance. In other countries, donor eggs may be difficult to find, or waiting lists may be prohibitively long. Reproductive medical tourism, which has been nicknamed the "procreation vacation," enables couples to travel to other countries to conceive, and then return home to give birth. (In some cases, the opposite occurs, and mothers deliver in another country to give their baby dual citizenship.)

Another aspect of reproductive tourism is pregnancy termination. Pregnant women may travel abroad when laws in their own home country make abortion a difficult, or even impossible, proposition.

Transplant Tourism

Transplant organs are hard to come by in the United States. The demand for kidneys, hearts, and other life-saving organs far exceed their availability. People who are in need of a transplant often have to spend years on a waiting list. Some never receive the organ they need. In 2007, nearly 6,000 people in the United States died while on the organ waiting list (*Medical News Today* 2008). Traveling to a country with less-stringent rules about organ distribution can reduce that wait.

Sometimes, to circumvent the wait time, patients can receive organs from a foreign donor. Wealthy patients in the United States or Europe can pay upwards of $150,000 for an organ through an international broker. Donors are often found in the poorest slums and are paid a few thousand dollars for their organs. This practice, known as organ trafficking, has been on the rise. The World Health Organization estimates that one-fifth of the kidneys transplanted worldwide each year come from the black market (Interlandi 2009). This situation is covered in more depth in chapter 2.

Lifestyle Tourism

Travelers have been visiting warm springs and spas for centuries to receive wellness therapies. Today, the practice of lifestyle tourism has expanded to include massage, yoga, anti-aging, meditation, weight loss, stress reduction, and many other pampering services. Spas in India, Thailand, Malaysia, and the Philippines have created vacation programs that cater to both visitors' minds and bodies. Many spas also offer holistic and preventive medicine services, which blur the distinction between hotels and hospitals.

Sometimes, patients travel not to receive a medical procedure, but to recover from a treatment they've already had at home.

Other Medically Related Forms of Tourism

People also travel to receive medical care for other, perhaps less widely recognized, reasons. Some of these reasons overlap the categorizations above. In their book, *Medical Tourism in Developing Countries*, Bookman and Bookman (2007) identify several of these additional reasons for travel. Obese people may go on *fasting tours*. Patients dealing with alcoholism who wish to receive treatment discreetly, such as patients from Islamic countries where alcohol is prohibited, may take *detoxification (detox) tours*. Countries with liberal euthanasia laws even sometimes attract *suicide tourists*. There is even *science tourism*, in which scientists travel to countries that provide more latitude in conducting research than U.S. laws allow, such as medical therapies using stem cells. (Chapter 2 discusses issues surrounding suicide tourism and stem cells in more depth.) A growing tourism niche increasingly connected with medical issues is *MICE tourism* (Connell 2011), also called *conference tourism*. The acronym "MICE" stands for meetings, incentives, conferences, and exhibitions. These events target special issues or interests, such as a disease or healing approach.

What Factors Drive the Growth of Medical Tourism?

Despite significant downturns in the global economy in recent years, medical tourism continues to be an industry that enjoys consistent growth. In fact, the medical tourism industry is growing at a rate of about 35 percent a year (Deloitte 2009). The following factors are driving that rapid expansion.

Cost

Among the incentives to medical tourism, cost reigns supreme. Health care costs in the United States are rising at a rate of about 9 percent each year for employers who offer coverage (*USA Today* 2009). Employers have to pass those higher costs on to their employees in the form of higher premiums, deductibles, or co-pays.

Because of the availability of lower-cost procedures abroad, medical tourism could potentially save employers (and subsequently, their employees) 50 to 90 percent on medical claims (*USA Today* 2009).

When the Patient Protection and Affordable Care Act (ACA) was signed into law in the United States in March 2010, health insurers became fearful of increased regulation and lower profit margins, while small businesses worried about having to cut further into their profits in order to insure their employees. Both insurance companies and employers could get behind medical tourism in an effort to keep their costs down. Meanwhile, consumers might look abroad for procedures, such as hip replacements and cosmetic surgery, which health insurers deem nonessential.

Demand

Baby boomers are aging, and they want to stay active by keeping on top of their health. They are demanding all kinds of elective surgical procedures, from knee replacements to cosmetic surgeries. Between 1996 and 2006, the number of outpatient procedures performed in the United States tripled. Americans spent more than $13 billion on cosmetic procedures alone in 2007 (Deloitte 2009). Often these procedures aren't covered by medical insurance. That may be why outpatient surgeries make up almost 75 percent of medical tourism procedures (Deloitte 2009).

Availability

The wait for surgeries in countries such as Great Britain and Canada that have government-run health care can stretch to a year or more (Kumar 2009). Rather than waiting for a procedure, patients in these countries can pay a small price to have their surgery scheduled immediately in another country.

Ease of Travel

Frequent flier miles, hotel rewards programs, and Internet-based last-minute and off-peak travel services are just a few of the innovations that have made international travel easier and less expensive. Tourism facilitators are also making medical tourism an affordable reality. They bundle surgery, airfare, accommodations, transfers, and everything else medical tourists will need during their stay into convenient, reasonable travel packages.

Quality

Patients demand high-quality medical care and personalized service, which are often not available in their native countries. Emerging medical tourism destinations such as India and Thailand provide state-of-the art, high-quality, safe medical care, combined with personalized VIP services that are highly attractive to tourists.

Higher Standard of Living

In the 20th century, few people in developing nations, such as India, could afford high-end health care. Today, India has a thriving middle class, made up of people who are demanding a higher standard of care. That demand has helped spur the growth of top-notch medical centers staffed with highly trained doctors (many of whom were educated in the West).

Who Are the Medical Tourists?

Anyone can theoretically be a medical tourist, provided that they have the need, the desire, and the means to travel abroad for care. Medical tourists represent all ages, nationalities, cultures, and races. Travelers can come from just about everywhere in the world, but more than 90 percent are from developed nations such as the United States, Canada, Great Britain, Western Europe, Australia, and the Middle East (Bookman and Bookman 2007).

Following is a brief snapshot of the types of people who seek their health care in other countries.

The Uninsured

In the past, many of the people who traveled for treatment did so because they had no medical insurance, and they wanted to find the procedures they needed at the lowest possible cost. Today, many medical tourists are insured, but are looking to lower their out-of-pocket costs. With prices for surgery in countries like India, Thailand, and Singapore as little as 10 percent of what they are in the United States (including the travel costs), having a procedure in one of these countries can cost less than the insurance deductible alone. Patients also can get bargains on procedures that aren't covered by insurance (including cosmetic and dental surgery, fertility treatments, and gender reassignment surgery).

The Hopeful

People who have been diagnosed with life-threatening or debilitating illnesses will do anything possible to extend their prognosis. Often, the treatments they seek are not available in the United States, particularly controversial therapies, such as stem cell treatments. Experimental procedures in other countries can provide hope for patients when every other treatment at home has failed. In countries with a national health service, such as Great Britain, traveling abroad means not having to wait months—or even years—for a necessary medical procedure.

The Accidental Tourist

Sometimes in the middle of a vacation, travelers may have the need for medical services. Either they become ill from being exposed to bacteria and viruses that are not common in their home country (diarrhea is a typical ailment among tourists), or they become injured while skiing, scuba diving, or participating in another leisure activity at their destination. These accidental tourists usually will use emergency services for their care. Although travelers who receive medical care while on vacation are not technically considered medical tourists, they are taking advantage of medical services in their host country.

The Traveler

For some medical tourists, travel is a necessity to save money. For others, it's an adventure. People who live in societies that value travel (such as the United States and Japan) may have a procedure abroad just so they can experience a new culture. This is especially true with nonessential, elective procedures, such as cosmetic surgery.

The Luxury Seeker

In the United Stats, medical care is all about practicality. Patients go to the hospital, have their procedure, recuperate, and then leave the hospital as soon as possible (often because their insurance company mandates it). In other countries, health care for foreigners is a far more luxurious and relaxing experience. At Bumrungrad Hospital in Thailand, for example, patients recover in accommodations that look more like luxurious hotel suites than sterile hospital rooms. They receive 24-hour personalized service, and they can order room service from Starbuck's, Au Bon Pain, or one of the many other Western restaurants on the premises.

The Expatriate

An estimated 5.26 million Americans live in more than 160 different countries around the world (Association of Americans Resident Overseas 2010). Likewise, residents of virtually every other country also live abroad. These expatriates may be studying, working, or simply enjoying their retirement years. When they need medical care, they can either receive it where they are living, or travel back home to their native country, both of which can be considered forms of medical tourism.

The Health Conscious

Health care today is focused on not only getting people better once they are sick, but also on preventing them from becoming sick in the first place. A number of hotels and hospitals around the world are jumping on the wellness bandwagon by offering health screenings, spa services, and other health-improvement programs to their foreign guests.

The Wealthy

A well-stocked bank account is not a necessity for medical tourism in this age of frequent flier miles and discount travel services. However, the wealthy travel abroad in search of a higher standard of care—and they are willing to pay a lot to get it. As the baby boomer generation ages, they have more disposable income, and a greater understanding of illness and how to prevent it. Wealthy patients may travel to a country like Argentina or Costa Rica for discreet cosmetic surgery, and follow it up with a luxury recuperative vacation at a five-star resort. Or, they may seek out the world's leading specialist in a particular treatment. When cost is no object, virtually any level of medical care is achievable, and the distance patients will travel to receive that care is immeasurable.

The Poor

People without means travel for a very different reason—to find the best possible care at the lowest prices. Bargain hunters can save up to 90 percent by seeking out health care in another country's public health system. Many people in poor nations go to neighboring countries to get a higher quality of care than they could find at home. While caring for wealthy foreigners in their state-of-the-art hospitals, countries like Thailand and India also treat many impoverished patients who cross their borders. Even in developed nations, patients cross the border looking for discounted medical care. Thousands of people in California get their medical check-ups and treatments in Tijuana, because the cost is so much lower than at home.

The Informed

With the click of a few buttons, every consumer has the ability to learn about any health condition—no medical degree required. The Internet has made information about conditions, tests, and treatment options readily accessible, and that means consumers are now becoming active players in their own health care decisions. Thanks to the Internet, consumers can also compare surgical costs and options, and plan trips abroad, without the help of a travel agent.

Top Medical Tourism Destinations

As mentioned earlier in the chapter, medical tourism is unique among other types of tourism in that travelers do not choose a destination for its weather or attractions. They first decide which treatment they want to have, and then pinpoint the country (or countries) that offers the treatment they seek.

Once patients have narrowed potential destinations by treatment, secondary factors that play into the decision include the country's climate, distance from home, availability of English-speaking tourism and hospital staff, and attractions.

Below are some of the leading medical tourism destinations, and their specialties.

Asia

Asia is one of the fastest growing regions of the world for medical tourism. By 2013, its medical tourism industry is expected to reach $8.5 billion (Renub Research 2009). Singapore, Thailand, and India have led the Asian nations, and are now the hubs of medical tourism within the region.

More than 1.3 million medical tourists flock to Asia each year (Chew and Norzilawati 2007), drawn to the area's high-tech hospitals, well-trained health care providers, emphasis on hospitality, and gorgeous scenery. Asia has encouraged this influx of health care visitors with its low-cost labor, open government cooperation in medical tourism, history of complementary and alternative medicine, and already well-established tourism industry.

India

Just as it has become the go-to country for American tech call centers, the second-most populous country in the world has also become the destination for inexpensive, high-quality medical procedures (CIA 2010). In 2003, the country's then-Finance Minister Jaswant Singh called for India to become a "global health destination" (Kumar 2009). It seems Singh got what he requested. Medical tourism has become a $35 billion industry in India, and it is expected to reach $150 billion ($US) by 2017 (Madhok 2009). It's no wonder that India's medical tourism industry is booming, considering that that country has 15 hospitals accredited by the Joint Commission International (JCI) (the accreditation agency that ensures the quality standards of hospitals around the world), and its prices for medical care are about one-tenth the cost of the United States and Europe.

People travel to India for a variety of complex procedures, including cardiovascular surgery, knee and hip replacements, eye procedures, dentistry, and cosmetic surgery. Today, India's highly educated doctors are leading the world in cutting-edge treatments, as well as in genetic, diagnostic, and stem cell research. In addition to offering traditional medical therapies, the country has a rich history of alternative therapies, including spa rejuvenation, holistic medicine, and Ayurveda—a practice that incorporates herbs, massage, and Yoga.

When travelers come to India, they can be assured that their surgery will be performed by some of the best-trained physicians in the world. That wasn't necessarily true decades ago, when it was common for doctors to leave India and travel to the West for medical school, where they often remained (more than one in six practicing surgeons in the United States are of Indian descent) (Woodman 2008). Today, thanks to a heavy investment by the Indian government in medical education and infrastructure, students train in India and stay there to take advantage of its excellent hospitals and low cost of living.

The biggest and best private hospitals are centered in India's big cities—Bangalore, Delhi, Chennai, and Mumbai. One of the largest health care providers in the country is Apollo Hospitals, which grew from a single hospital in 1983 to 46 hospitals with more than 8,000 beds today (Apollo Hospitals 2010). The hospital group is headquartered in Chennai, India's fourth largest city. Wockhardt Hospitals, which has 39 hospitals and performs some 48,000 surgical procedures annually, is another force in India's medical system (Wockhardt Hospitals 2010).

India's benefits as a medical tourism destination are plentiful. Its hospitals provide not only modern, high-tech equipment, but also highly personalized care and easily packaged services for the medical tourist.

Thailand

The Thai medical system has its roots in Western medicine. In 1928, Prince Mahidol of Sonkgla received his medical degree from Harvard University (his third child, the current King Bhumibol Adulyadej was born in Cambridge, Mass., in 1927). When the prince returned home, he helped set up a foundation (with the help of the Rockefeller Foundation) to provide Thai students with a Western-style medical education. Prince Mahidol not only helped to train a generation of doctors and nurses, but he was instrumental in building modern medical training facilities in Thailand. For his work, the prince was honored with the title, Father of Modern Medicine and Public Health of Thailand.

Today, Prince Mahidol's legacy lives on. Many Thai doctors are U.S.-certified, and a number of the country's hospitals have strong relationships with American hospitals. Thailand's medical infrastructure is modern, safe, and clean. Yet the prices (although higher than in India) are still about one-fifth of what they are in the United States, and the thriving tourism industry has kept rates on accommodations and food reasonable (*PR Newswire* 2009).

As a result of these benefits, in 2008 alone, Thailand attracted 1.4 million medical tourists and gained about $1 billion in revenue (Theparat 2010). Many of those tourists are from other Asian countries, as well as from the Middle East and Europe, although Americans also take advantage of Thailand's medical bargains. Among the most notable visitors have been the prime minister of Nepal, Girija Prasad Koirala, and Hawaiian entertainer Don Ho (who traveled there for a cardiac stem cell treatment).

The Thai medical tourism industry is growing at a rate of about 14 percent each year. By 2013, the country is expected to welcome more medical tourists than any other Asian country (*PR Newswire* 2009; Renub Research 2009).

People travel to Thailand for a range of medical services, including check-ups, dental procedures, organ transplants, and eye surgery. In 1997, when the Asian financial crisis led to the collapse of Thailand's currency, the country's government decided to take advantage of its existing medical infrastructure to market itself internationally as *the* destination for cosmetic surgery. Although all types of cosmetic surgery are performed in Thailand, the country has perhaps become best known for its sex reassignment (sex change) surgery. For as little as $5,000, those wishing to change gender can discreetly undergo surgery, without many of the counseling requirements that are necessary in the United States.

The centerpiece of Thailand's medical system is the JCI-accredited Bumrungrad International Hospital in Bangkok. Originally built in 1980 to care for the country's wealthiest residents, today Bumrungrad welcomes more than 400,000 foreign visitors each year (Bumrungrad International Hospital 2010).

Malaysia

Next door to Thailand is Malaysia, which has also asserted itself as one of the premier medical tourism destinations in Asia, and the world. Like its neighbor, Malaysia also turned to tourism to help itself rise from the ashes of the Asian financial crisis. The Malaysian government launched several initiatives to encourage medical tourism, including extending its visas, and helping private hospitals attract and retain foreign patients. The Ministry of Health works with a private organization called the Association of Private Hospitals of Malaysia (APHM) to promote medical tourism.

As a result of these efforts, medical tourism today is booming in Malaysia. In 2008, the country hosted about 374,000 medical tourists, up from just 39,000 in 1998 (RNCOS 2009b). Many of those tourists come from other Asian countries, such as Indonesia, Vietnam, Singapore, and Cambodia. One of the big draws for Westerners is Malaysia's history as a British colony. English is widely spoken, and Western culture is firmly ingrained in Malaysian society.

Medical facilities and practitioners in Malaysia are on par with those in India and Thailand, but the costs are often lower, especially for cardiac and orthopedic procedures. Malaysian hospitals not only treat what currently ails foreign patients, but they also offer "well-man" and "well-woman" preventive screenings, which evaluate patients' risk of future medical conditions. These services range from typical check-up tests, such as blood pressure and cholesterol levels, to more sophisticated screenings that evaluate patients' future risk for diseases such as cancer, heart disease, and stroke.

Singapore

In Asia, no other country has more JCI-accredited hospitals than Singapore, which boasts 16 of them. The country has promoted itself as a leading destination for cutting-edge medical technology and research, as well as pharmaceutical production.

The country's medical tourism industry has been on the rise. Singapore attracted 646,000 medical tourists in 2008, up from 571,000 the previous year. The government's goal is to attract 1 million medical tourists annually by the year 2012 (*International Medical Travel Journal* 2010). Most patients come from neighboring countries such as Indonesia, as well as from China, the Middle East, and the United States.

In addition to performing orthopedic, cardiac, neurological, oncological (cancer), and organ transplant procedures, Singapore has become known for its complex, cutting-edge surgeries. In 2001, doctors at the Singapore General Hospital attracted international attention when they separated 10-month-old Nepalese conjoined twins Jamuna and Ganga Shrestha. During the 96-hour operation, surgeons had to delicately separate the twins' brains, which shared many of the same blood vessels. It was one of only a handful of such surgeries that have ever been performed.

Because it has such a high standard of living compared to its neighbors, Singapore's prices for medical care are typically more than those in India or Thailand. However, the country has one of the highest-quality health care systems in Asia. In 2000, the World Health Organization ranked Singapore's health care system as number one in Asia and sixth in the world, ahead of the United States (although some critics charge that the WHO's methodology in compiling the list was flawed) (Woodman 2008). Singapore is home to one of the largest hospital networks in Asia, Parkway Group Healthcare.

The Singaporean government has been actively promoting the country's medical tourism industry. In 2003, the Ministry of Health, in conjunction with the Economic Development and Tourism Boards, launched SingaporeMedicine, an initiative aimed at branding Singapore as a leading health care destination in Asia. In 2006, the country hosted the first International Medical Travel Conference (IMTC), which attracted people from nearly two dozen countries.

In its efforts to reach out to Western patients, Singapore has established research partnerships with American universities, including Johns Hopkins and Duke Medical Center, as well as with pharmaceutical giants GlaxoSmithKline and Novartis. It has established a $300 million, 2-million-square-foot biotechnology research center, called Biopolis, which is made up of seven buildings connected by sky bridges, and includes a stem cell bank (the country has a liberal approach to stem cell research). The country also features one of Asia's most reputable cancer hospitals (National Cancer Centre) and a leading neurological research center (the National Neuroscience Institute).

Taiwan

When it comes to medical care, "made in Taiwan" means inexpensive care, but it doesn't mean cheap quality. Taiwan is a modern nation with a high-quality medical system. The teardrop-shaped island has nine JCI-accredited hospitals, three of them in the capital city of Taipei.

The costs of health care in Taiwan are on par with those in Thailand and Singapore, and are 30 to 60 percent lower than in the United States (Woodman 2008). Today, Taiwan is using its advantages—preventive health care and excellent customer service—to attract medical tourists from Western nations. The country's official tourism website proclaims, "Taiwan cares for your health," and boasts that its hospitals can perform coronary artery bypass graft surgery for one-fifth the price of the United States

(Taiwan Task Force for Medical Travel 2010). Taiwan is particularly targeting medical tourists from mainland China and Hong Kong. The goal is to attract 100,000 medical tourists annually, but so far Taiwan only hosts a few hundred people from China and Hong Kong each year (*International Medical Travel Journal* 2009).

South Korea

Though it's just a short flight from Beijing, Shanghai, Hong Kong, and Tokyo, and its hospitals are both modern and technologically advanced, South Korea's medical tourism industry is still trying to catch up to that of neighbors in the region, like Thailand and Singapore.

That may be about to change. The Korean government has launched a major initiative to boost its medical tourism industry. It has joined forces with 28 private hospitals to create the Council for Korea Medicine Overseas Promotion, a collaborative effort aimed at marketing affordable health care packages to patients overseas. In particular, South Korea is focusing on its strongest areas in medicine, such as preventive care (check-ups), skin care, plastic surgery, herbal medicine, and dental care. The government is also helping hospitals by easing regulations and simplifying the visa process for foreign patients, particularly those from other Asian countries. The ultimate goal is to attract 1 million foreign patients a year by 2020 (*Bangkok Post* 2010).

Helping South Korea reach that goal is a major new development—a $600 million complex called Jeju Healthcare Town, slated to open in 2015. Located on Jeju Island, Healthcare Town will feature not only a high-tech medical complex, but also a Wellness Park (for medical relaxation), entertainment and cultural venues, and space for other leisure activities (*Korea IT Times* 2009; *Industry and Technology Times* 2011).

Philippines

When it comes to medical tourism, the Philippines seem to have everything—at least on the surface. Hospitals and clinics on the archipelago offer low-cost dental work, eye care, and cosmetic surgery. The country has three JCI-accredited hospitals. The Philippine government is an active participant in its medical tourism industry, launching the Philippine Medical Tourism Program in 2004, and hosting a medical tourism convention two years later.

So why aren't the Philippines keeping up with other southeastern Asian countries in attracting foreign health care dollars?

The Philippines have a number of obstacles to overcome before they can become a major player in the Asian medical tourism industry. The medical infrastructure is still a work in progress. Customer service isn't as well developed as it is in other Asian countries. Political unrest and coup attempts are still unfortunate realities. And the capital city, Manila, has been plagued by a high crime rate (although crime has been decreasing in recent years). The Philippine government has been working hard to change its image, and if it has its way, the country may start creeping up on some of its neighbors to capture a bigger piece of the medical tourism economy.

Latin America

Although Latin America still hasn't become as big of a force as Asia in medical tourism, the region does have the advantage of its close proximity to the United States, and its abundance of cosmetic surgery practitioners. Despite persistently high poverty levels and governmental instability in some Latin American countries, the region has other advantages that draw American medical tourists, including a lower-cost labor force, Western-educated and English-speaking health care professionals, cultural similarities, a warm climate, and beautiful resorts. Thanks to these attributes, experts say half of medical travel could eventually be to Latin America (Vequist, Valdez, and Morrison 2009). The following countries are some of the most popular medical tourism destinations in Latin America.

Mexico

America's neighbor to the south is best known for its abundance of low-cost drugs, which drives droves of U.S. residents and citizens across the border every year. Medical procedures are also cheaper than in the United States—up to 40 percent less expensive, by some reports (Herrick 2007). Dental and cosmetic procedures are the main medical attractions in Mexico, because their costs are about half of what they are in the United States (Vequist and Valdez 2008).

Much of the health care that attracts Americans in Mexico is located just on the other side of the border. Dallas-based International Hospital Corp. operates four Mexican hospitals, and three are close to the United States. The company even has a medical tourism division that helps Americans plan their trips.

People who live in California, Texas, and other states in close proximity to the Mexican border are perfectly positioned to take advantage of the lower-cost health care. Health insurers Blue Shield of California and Health Net reward patients who use health care providers in Mexico, in the form of lower premiums and co-payments. Some Arizona retirement communities take their residents on bus trips to purchase prescription drugs and to take advantage of dental care that costs a fraction of the same services at home. For thousands of seniors, Mexico has become home. Nursing care there runs about a quarter of the $60,000 a year it costs in the United States (Herrick 2007). Along with round-the-clock medical care, seniors who relocate to Mexico also get an apartment with cleaning and laundry services, as well as meals.

The downside to medical care in Mexico has always been quality, but that is improving. The country now has eight JCI-accredited facilities. The number of private hospital beds increased 28 percent and the number of private doctors more than doubled between 2000 and 2005 (Vequist and Valdez 2008). Overall, Mexico offers Americans the advantage of saving money on health care, without the hassle of a long plane flight.

However, violence from drug gangs remains an issue in border cities like Juarez. Although the Mexican government is working to address this issue, many medical tourists have been scared away by rising murder rates along the U.S.–Mexico border.

Argentina

It may be less than three-tenths the size of the United States, but Argentina rivals America when it comes to plastic surgery (CIA 2010). It is estimated that 1 in 30 people in this South American country has had at least one plastic surgery procedure (Kumar 2009).

Foreigners began taking notice of Argentina's proficiency in cosmetic surgery when procedures became a bargain. In 2002, a financial crisis led the Argentine government to devalue the country's currency (the peso) by almost 30 percent, immediately giving Americans a discount on any goods and services they purchased. As a result, Argentina's medical tourism numbers began increasing at a rate of about 10 percent a year (Balch 2006).

The country's own high demand for breast augmentation, tummy tucks, and other cosmetic surgery procedures created an abundance of plastic surgeons, who are considered to be among the best in the world. Patients flock there from the United States and Europe to take advantage of this surgical skill, as well as the personalized service and gorgeous scenery.

Brazil

Argentina's not-too-distant neighbor, Brazil, is also no slouch when it comes to offering plastic surgery. The country has more than 4,500 licensed plastic surgeons, the highest per capita in the world (Woodman 2008). Most of these doctors are centered in the country's biggest cities—São Paulo and Rio de Janeiro. Among them is the most famous plastic surgeon in the nation (and possibly the world)—Ivo Pitanguy. Celebrities, statesmen, and socialites from around the globe have all flocked to his clinic in Rio.

Brazil has 11 JCI-accredited treatment facilities. Yet despite the high quality and low cost of its services, overall the country has languished among Latin American medical tourism destinations. In part, this lack of interest is because the Brazilian government has been slow to promote itself as a medical destination. The country lacks the medical tourism infrastructure that exists in other countries, and which make it easy for tourists to bundle travel services and medical care in one easy package. The issue of a language barrier (many hospitals have only Portuguese-speaking staff) has also kept medical tourists away from Brazil.

Costa Rica

Attracting medical tourists hasn't been an issue for Costa Rica, which has reportedly doubled its health care-seeking travelers since 2003 (Cook 2007). Although many people think of Costa Rica as an eco-tourism destination, it has also become a popular locale for medical tourism. Considering that Costa Rica is just a two-and-a-half-hour plane flight from Miami, and its health care costs are 40 to 70 percent cheaper than in the United States, it's no wonder that the country is among Americans' top five destinations for medical care (Cook 2007; Woodman 2008).

Costa Rica's focus on cosmetic surgery has earned it the nickname, "Beverly Hills of Central America." The country is unique in offering recovery retreats—hotels that cater specifically to the needs of tourists postsurgery. These specialized resorts, which are staffed by nurses and interns, combine the amenities of a hotel with the medical care travelers need during their recovery.

Caribbean

Just a short plane flight from the southeastern U.S. coast is an area where many Americans already spend their vacations. The Caribbean has the advantages of its close proximity to the United States, and its warm weather and white sand beaches are strong draws, as well. With regard to medical tourism, this area has become well known for its addiction recovery centers.

Antigua

Located less than 300 miles south of Puerto Rico, this island in the West Indies is just a short flight from Miami. Antigua is best known for its fertility and addiction centers. The serene environment is an ideal refuge for anyone who is trying to conceive or to recover from an addiction. In 1998, singer Eric Clapton (himself a recovering addict) founded one of the best-known recovery centers on the island. His Crossroads Centre uses a twelve-step program combined with complementary therapies to help people recover from drug and alcohol addiction.

Barbados

This former British colony has long been a popular vacation spot for Europeans and Americans. Travel there for medical reasons is nothing recent. In 1751, a young George Washington brought his half-brother, Lawrence, there for two months to help him recover from a severe lung infection.

Barbados also specializes in fertility treatments and addiction recovery. The centerpiece of the island's medical care is Queen Elizabeth Hospital, opened in 1964 as a 464-bed facility and since expanded to 600 beds. In recent years, the hospital has undergone a multi-million dollar renovation, updating its equipment and facilities.

The only JCI-accredited medical facility on the island is the Barbados Fertility Centre. The centre offers "IVF holidays," which combine fertility treatments with a vacation. For $6,000, guests can receive their procedure, plus basic accommodations in a beachfront hotel. Packages go all the way up to the $30,000 "elite" plan, which includes a five-star hotel and mind/body program (Barbados Fertility Centre 2010).

Europe

Western European countries have a long-established history of providing quality health care. Yet long waits and high prices have meant that health care isn't always easily accessible to everyone. Today, Eastern Europe is emerging as a prime medical tourism destination for Western Europeans, as well as American travelers.

Czech Republic

This former Soviet state is now a haven for tourists seeking cosmetic and dental procedures. Its capital city, Prague, is home to many of the best private clinics in the country. The clean, modern facilities and English-speaking staff attract many patients from the United Kingdom and United States. Because of the country's liberal policies on assisted reproduction, the Czech Republic has also become a popular location for in vitro fertilization and other fertility treatments. Low wages help keep prices far lower for medical procedures than in Western Europe and the United States.

Hungary

For a country of just 10 million people, Hungary has a staggering number of dentists—more per capita than any other country in the world (Woodman 2008). That's why the country is sometimes referred to as the "dental capital of Europe."

The Hungarian government ensures a consistently high quality of dental care by requiring dentists to complete five years of dental training and to be registered with the Hungarian Medical Chamber. Several entities, including the State National Health Commission and Medical Service, oversee accreditation and standards.

In most countries, the highest quality medical care is centered in the capital or largest cities. Though Hungary's capital, Budapest is home to many medical offices, patients can also find high quality care—and much better bargains—in small, rural towns like Mosonmagyaróvár (which lies on the border with Austria) and Gyõr (a northwestern town halfway between Budapest and Vienna). Mosonmagyaróvár has only 30,000 residents, yet it is home to 160 dental offices (Woodman 2008). The town of Sopron, also on the Austrian border, has just 20,000 residents, yet it has 200 dentists and 200 optometrists (Reier 2004).

For Western Europeans, Hungary is a quick trip for check-ups and cleanings. Americans and Canadians, who have much further to travel, typically visit for more involved surgical procedures.

Turkey

The seventeenth most populous country in the world is home to more JCI-accredited facilities than any other country—37 of them in all. Turkey's appeals to medical tourists include its Western-trained, English-speaking medical personnel and high quality standards, which are rigorously upheld by the Turkish government.

The Turkish Cultural and Tourism Ministry has spent more than $100 million to improve medical care and spread the word about its country's medical offerings, and the effort seems to have paid off (*Business Wire* 2010). In 2008, the country welcomed about 200,000 medical tourists, an increase of 40 percent from the previous year (RNCOS 2009a). Medical tourism to Turkey is expected to continue to increase in the coming years, in part driven by rising health care costs in Western Europe.

Middle East

The Middle East is better known for sending its residents abroad for medical care than for welcoming medical tourists. In the past, around 20 percent of United Arab Emirates residents traveled to the United States for their medical care (Florian 2009). However, that changed with more stringent travel restrictions into the United States following the terrorist attacks of September 11, 2001. As health care quality standards rise in the region, the Middle East could challenge Asia and other parts of the world for a bigger segment of the medical tourism industry.

Israel

It may be a small country with only 7 million residents, but Israel has developed one of the most sophisticated medical programs in the world. The country's medical facilities have the highest standards, its doctors are exceptionally well trained, and its medical technology is state-of-the-art. Israel is a world leader in research and development. It holds more life science patents per capita than any other country (Steiner 2009), and is known for designing and manufacturing cutting-edge medical equipment.

The country has well-rounded capabilities in cardiovascular, cancer, and neurosurgery, among other procedures. However, Israel is particularly renowned for its fertility centers. Its IVF facilities are among the best in the world, yet the prices are low in relation to Western fertility clinics. A cycle of IVF in Israel costs just $3,000 to $3,500, compared to $16,000 to $20,000 in the United States (Steiner 2009).

Jordan
Unlike many of its oil-rich neighbors in the Middle East, Jordan relies on tourism dollars for its economic growth. Realizing the revenue-generating potential of medical tourism, the Jordanian government has been aggressively promoting itself as a premier health care destination. The World Bank has ranked Jordan the number one medical tourist destination in the Middle East, and fifth in the world (Associated Press 2009).

In 2009, more than 200,000 foreign patients received heart, kidney, neurological, orthopedic, or other procedures in Jordan, bringing in more than $1 billion in total revenues (Malkawi 2010). Most patients come to the kingdom from Iraq and other Middle Eastern nations, but Jordan's government is working hard to also attract tourists from the United States and Europe. Costs at the country's hospitals (five of which are JCI-accredited) are about 40 percent lower than in the United States or Europe, and 5 to 10 percent lower than those of other countries in the region (Malkawi 2010).

United Arab Emirates
Though slightly smaller in size than the state of Maine, this federation of seven states (Abu Dhabi, Dubai, Sharjah, Ajman, Umm al Quwain, Ras al-Khaimah, and Fujairah) has 35 JCI-accredited medical facilities. Although Abu Dhabi is the capital, Dubai has been the UAE's leading promoter of medical tourism. Its tourism authority has optimistically predicted that Dubai will host more than 11 million medical tourists by 2010, mainly attracted by Dubai Healthcare City (DHCC) (Bladd 2008). This $500 million, 435-acre collaboration with Harvard Medical School is designed to provide state-of-the-art medical care and wellness services to both locals and tourists.

For now, however, the UAE is still struggling not just to attract medical tourists, but also to keep its own patients. An estimated 62,000 UAE nationals traveled to Thailand for medical care in 2006 alone (Florian 2008). It's still hard for the UAE to compete with Asian countries for medical tourists. Though its prices for medical procedures are about a third of those in the United States, they are still more than double the costs in

Singapore and Thailand (Bladd 2008). A heart bypass operation that runs about $44,000 in the UAE costs just $11,000 in Thailand (Florian 2008).

Africa

Africa lags behind much of the world when it comes to providing quality health care, and most of its countries do not have the medical infrastructure needed to attract patients on a global scale. Only South Africa has been highly successful in the medical tourism industry, thanks in large part to its high-quality medical facilities and surgeons, as well as its self-promoted "medical safaris." South Africa has been able to attract medical tourists not only from the United States and England, but also from other countries throughout Africa.

South Africa

There is likely nowhere else in the world where tourists can have a facelift one day, and drive around a game preserve snapping pictures of lions a couple of days later. Medical tourism facilitators make it easy for tourists to explore South Africa's considerable natural resources by offering packages that combine health care and luxury hotel stays with safaris. Sightseeing is one of the biggest draws to the country's medical services, and a big draw is a necessity because the logistics of getting to South Africa can be daunting. Johannesburg is about a 15-hour flight from New York, and flights are only available a few times a week. Although the South African Tourism Association does its best to guarantee quality standards and promote relationships between medical tourists and treatment centers, the country currently doesn't have any JCI-accredited facilities.

How Medical Tourism Markets Itself

Medical tourism destinations want their share of the $100 billion industry that medical tourism is anticipated to become. To that end, they are spending millions of dollars to improve their medical infrastructure, and advertise their services to potential patients around the globe. These are just a few of the ways in which the medical tourism industry markets itself.

International Outreach

Many countries have offices abroad, or organize seminars in other countries to promote their medical tourism industries. At the annual World Medical Tourism & Global Healthcare Congress in Los Angeles, international health care providers touted their services with videos and glossy brochures highlighting the cost-savings and luxury benefits patients can enjoy when they travel to countries like Thailand and Costa Rica for treatment. Indian hospitals promote themselves by sending representatives on global road shows, and by developing relationships with foreign medical associations.

Other countries bring their potential market to them, hosting trade shows or exhibitions at home. For example, Thailand holds an annual Tourism Festival and Travel Mart to promote its tourist industry, which includes medical tourism.

Internet Presence

Realizing that today's consumers are technology savvy, international governments, hospitals, and travel facilitators have all set up websites to tout their health care offerings. Companies such as MedRetreats, Healthbase, and Planet Hospital allow patients to bundle their health care and travel services into packages online.

Traditional Advertising

Medical tourism companies appeal to the people who are most likely to use their services—those who are already travelers. Airline magazines are one popular place to find medical tourism ads. Advertising is also targeted to immigrant communities in the United States via native language newspapers and radio stations.

Word of Mouth

Personal endorsements are powerful marketing tools. No message is as convincing as one that comes from a satisfied customer, and almost nothing will kill business faster than an unhappy, and vocal, ex-customer. To keep medical tourists raving to their friends, foreign hospitals do everything they can to make the patient experience as enjoyable as possible. They offer luxury accommodations, English-speaking staff, highly personalized care, and all the comforts of home. Hospitals also go above and beyond medical care, offering everything from travel and visa assistance, to helping with accommodations, transfers, and sightseeing tours.

Medical Tourism Facilitators

When a patient lives in the United States and is trying to arrange a surgery in Singapore, it helps to have someone knowledgeable to handle all of the arrangements. An entire business has sprung up to meet the needs of medical tourists. For a fee, medical tourism facilitators help travelers connect with the care they need, ensure that the medical care they receive meets the highest quality standards, and arrange everything medical tourists need during their stay—from accommodations to transportation. As many as 1,000 facilitators are in the market, charging commissions that may be as much as 20 percent of the medical bill (Reisman 2010). Because they work closely with hospitals and tourism industries, tourism facilitators can usually offer a much lower rate than what travelers would have to pay if they set up their medical treatment and travel arrangements themselves.

Different types of medical facilitators exist:

Medical tourism agencies such as MedRetreat, WorldMed Assist and Planet Hospital help travelers find the right medical facility for the procedure they need, and then plan out every aspect of their trip. These specialized travel agents have developed relationships with hospitals to ensure that medical tourists are getting the best possible care based on their individual needs.

Medical providers like Bumrungrad Hospital in Thailand and Apollo in India have representatives whose job it is to handle all travel arrangements for visitors. They will take care of everything from securing visas to making hotel reservations.

Travel agencies handle the travel portion of the vacation, arranging accommodations, transportation, and sightseeing tours for medical tourists.

Medical tourism facilitators may provide some or all of the following services:

- Match prospective medical tourists with the hospitals and doctors who perform the procedure they seek. They should be able to provide information about the hospital's accreditation, as well as details about the specific doctor's credentials, board affiliations, number of surgeries performed, and success rates of those surgeries.
- Set and confirm all appointments.
- Set up a phone consultation with the doctor before the patient leaves home, so that the doctor can review the patient's medical history and test results, and discuss the procedure that is going to be performed.
- Transfer the patient's medical records, including X-rays and lab test results, to the foreign hospital before the procedure.
- Book air travel and hotel accommodations, negotiating the best prices.
- Get answers to the patient's medical and travel questions.
- Help the patient obtain visas, passports, and other necessary travel documents.
- Arrange for transportation from the airport to the hospital or other accommodations, and back.
- Arrange for a representative to accompany the patient to medical appointments (and translate, if the hospital does not have English-speaking staff).
- Set up accommodations for recovery.
- Plan sightseeing trips and other excursions.
- Ensure that the patient has all of the necessary paperwork (prescriptions, posttreatment instructions, medical records) before returning home.
- Follow-up once the patient has returned home to make sure the procedure went smoothly and there aren't any complications or remaining issues.

Many of these services are bundled together into one convenient package. One price may include: surgery and other related medical expenses (including a hospital stay), hotel accommodations, meals, transportation, and personal assistance throughout the stay.

References

Apollo Hospitals. "Apollo Hospitals Overview." www.apollohospitals. com/about-us/apollo-hospitals-overview.html (accessed February 27, 2010).

Associated Press. "Jordan Launches Medical Tourism Advertising Campaign in U.S." July 13, 2009. www.haaretz.com/hasen/spages/ 1099866.html (accessed March 7, 2010).

Association of Americans Resident Overseas. "5.26 Million Americans Abroad Map." http://aaro.org/ (accessed March 7, 2010).

Balch, Oliver. "Buenos Aires or Bust." *Guardian.co.uk,* October 24, 2006. www.guardian.co.uk/business/2006/oct/24/argentina.travelnews/ print (accessed November 20, 2009).

Bangkok Post. "S. Korea Aims to Boost Medical Tourism Market." January 17, 2010. www.bangkokpost.com/news/health/165604/s-korea-aims-to-boost-medical-tourism-market (accessed March 3, 2010).

Barbados Fertility Centre. "Finance." www.barbadosivf.org/finance. htm (accessed March 7, 2010).

Bladd, Joanne. "Medical Tourism: A Hit and Myth Affair." *Arabian Business.com.* November 4, 2008. www.arabianbusiness.com/536827-medical-tourism-a-hit-and-myth-affair (accessed March 7, 2010).

Bookman, Milica Z., and Karla R. Bookman. *Medical Tourism in Developing Countries.* New York, NY: Palgrave Macmillan, 2007.

Bumrungrad International Hospital. "Overview." www.bumrungrad.com/ overseas-medical-care/about-us/overview.aspx (accessed March 2, 2010).

Business Wire. "Research and Markets: International Tourists Arrivals in Turkey Has Increased by 2.7% in 2009 Over 2008 As Compared to Negative Growth Faced by World Tourism Industry, Says New Report." January 25, 2010.

Chew, Geraldine, and Norzilawati M. T. "The Lure of Medical Tourism in Asia." *Medical Tourism Magazine.* October 17, 2007. www. medicaltourismmag.com/issue-detail.php?item = 8&issue = 1 (accessed February 27, 2010).

CIA. *The World Factbook.* www.cia.gov/library/publications/the-world-factbook/geos/in.html (accessed February 27, 2010).

Connell, John. *Medical Tourism.* Cambridge, MA: CABI, 2011.

Cook, William. "Costa Rica: From Ecotourism Leader to World Class Healthcare Provider." *Medical Tourism Magazine,* September 9, 2007. www.medicaltourismmag.com/issue-detail.php?item = 18&issue = 1 (accessed March 1, 2010).

Davis, Bronwyn. "The Borderless Bypass." *Intheblack* 78, no. 10 (2008): 38–42.

Deloitte Center for Health Solutions. "Medical Tourism: Consumers in Search of Value." October 2, 2008. www.deloitte.com/view/en_HR/hr/industries/lifescienceshealthcare/article/964710a8b410e110VgnVCM10 0000ba42f00aRCRD.htm (accessed November 20, 2009).

Deloitte Center for Health Solutions. "Medical Tourism: Update and Implications—2009 Report." www.deloitte.com/assets/Dcom-UnitedStates/Local%20Assets/Documents/us_chs_MedicalTourism_111209_web.pdf (accessed February 27, 2010).

Florian, Jeff. "Medical Tourism Poised for Growth in Middle East." AMEinfo.com. October 27, 2009. www.ameinfo.com/213847.html (accessed March 9, 2010).

Florian, Jeff. "UAI Sets Sights on Medical Tourism Industry." August 31, 2008. www.ameinfo.com/167433.html (accessed March 7, 2010).

Friedman, Thomas L. *The World is Flat: A Brief History of the Twenty-First Century.* Farrar, Straus and Giroux, 2005.

Herrick, Devon M. *Medical Tourism: Global Competition in Health Care.* National Center for Policy Analysis. NCPA Policy Report No. 304, November 2007.

Industry and Technology Times. "Jeju Healthcare Town, a Medical Tourism Hub in Northeast Asia." September 23, 2011. www.koreaittimes.com/story/16797/jeju-healthcare-town-medical-tourism-hub-northeast-asia (accessed October 3, 2011).

Interlandi, Jeneen. "Not Just Urban Legend." *Newsweek,* January 10, 2009. www.newsweek.com/id/178873 (accessed February 25, 2010).

International Medical Travel Journal. "Singapore's Medical Tourism Business Is Recovering." www.imtj.com/news/?EntryId82 = 174348 (accessed March 2, 2010).

International Medical Tourism Journal. "Taiwan: Limitations on Taiwanese Medical Tourism." July 7, 2009. www.imtjonline.com/news/?EntryId82 = 141960 (accessed March 3, 2010).

Joint Commission International. *Joint Commission International (JCI) Accredited Organizations.* www.jointcommissioninternational.org/JCI-Accredited-Organizations/ (accessed March 15, 2010).

Kaiser Family Foundation. "Trends in Health Care Costs and Spending." March 2009. www.kff.org/insurance/upload/7692_02.pdf (accessed March 15, 2010).

Korea IT Times. "Korea's Local Governments Build Health Care Clusters to Attract Foreign Patients." September 18, 2009. www.koreaittimes.com/story/5068/south-korea-boosting-medical-tourism (accessed March 3, 2010).

Kumar, Rajesh. *Global Trends in Health and Medical Tourism.* New Delhi: SBS Publishers & Distributors Pvt. Ltd., 2009.

Madhok, Diksha. "Medicine: The Cutting Edge; State of the Art Hospitals, Groundbreaking Research and Major Government Reforms Are All Changing the Face of Healthcare Industry in India." *India Today,* October 12, 2009.

Malkawi, Khetam. "Medical Tourism Sector Weathered Economic Crisis." *McClatchy-Tribune Business News,* January 14, 2010.

Medical News Today. "Organ Transplant Waiting List Reaches High in U.S." April 11, 2008. www.medicalnewstoday.com/articles/103727.php (accessed February 25, 2010).

Medical News Today. "VA Regularly Understates Wait Times for Veterans in Need of Medical Care, VA Inspector General Report Finds." 2007. http://www.medicalnewstoday.com/articles/82174.php (accessed February 19, 2010).

Pickert, Kate. "Medical Tourism." *Time.* November 25, 2008. www.time.com/time/printout/0,8816,1861919,00.html (accessed October 21, 2009).

PR Newswire. "Thailand's Medical Tourism Growth Rate Continues to Increase." November 6, 2009.

Reier, Sharon. "Medical Tourism: Border Hopping for Cheaper and Faster Care Gains Converts." *The New York Times,* April 24, 2004. www.nytimes.com/2004/04/24/news/24iht-rhealth_ed3_.html?pagewanted = 1 (accessed March 6, 2010).

Reisman, David. *Health Tourism: Social Welfare Through International Trade.* Cheltenham, UK, Edward Elgar, 2010.

Renub Research. "Asia Medical Tourism Analysis (2008–2013)." September 2009. www.researchandmarkets.com/research/5b1fd2/asia_medical_touri (accessed December 7, 2009).

Riczo, Steve, and Sarah Riczo. "Globalizing Health Care Through Medical Tourism." *USA Today* 138, no. 2772(2009): 26–28.

RNCOS. "Emerging Medical Tourism in Turkey." April 2009a. www.rncos.com/Report/IM040.htm (accessed March 7, 2010).

RNCOS. "Malaysia Expects to Earn RM330 Million from Medical Tourism This Year." November 10, 2009b. www.rncos.com/Blog/2009/11/

Malaysia-Expects-to-Earn-RM330-Million-from-Medical-Tourism-This-Year.html (accessed March 2, 2010).

Steiner, Nathalie. "Israel's Pioneer in Medical Tourism." December 18, 2009. www.medicaltourismmag.com/detail.php?Req = 316&issue = 14 (accessed March 8, 2010).

Taiwan Task Force for Medical Travel. "Genesis." www.medicaltravel. org.tw/en/about.aspx?id = P_00000020 (accessed March 3, 2010).

Theparat, Chatrudee. "Medical Tourism Set for Rebound." *McClatchy-Tribune Business News,* May 11, 2010.

United Nations. "World Population Will Increase by 2.5 Billion by 2050; People Over 60 To Increase by More Than 1 Billion." March 13, 2007. www.un.org/News/Press/docs//2007/pop952.doc.htm (accessed February 24, 2010).

USA Today. "Report: Health Care Costs to Rise 9% in 2010." June 19, 2009. www.usatoday.com/money/industries/health/2009-06-18-health-care-costs_N.htm (accessed February 27, 2010).

U.S. Census Bureau, Current Population Reports, P60–233, *Income, Poverty, and Health Insurance Coverage in the United States: 2006.* U.S. Government Printing Office, Washington, DC, 2007.

U.S. Department of Health and Human Services (HHS), Health Resources and Services Administration (HRSA). "Organ Procurement and Transplantation Network. National Data." 2010. http://optn. transplant.hrsa.gov/latestData/step2.asp (accessed February 18, 2010).

Vequist, David G., and Erika Valdez. "Economic Report: Inbound Medical Tourism in the United States." *Medical Tourism Magazine,* August 4, 2009. www.medicaltourismmag.com/detail.php?Req = 234&issue = 11 (accessed February 24, 2010).

Vequist, David G., and Erika Valdez. "Medical Tourism Economic Report—Monterrey, Mexico." *Medical Tourism Magazine,* April 1, 2008. www.medicaltourismmag.com/issue-detail.php?item = 77&issue = 4 (accessed March 1, 2010).

Vequist, David G., Erika Valdez, and Billy Morrison. "Medical Tourism Economic Report: Latin America vs. Asia." *Medical Tourism Magazine,* June 1, 2009. www.medicaltourismmag.com/detail.php?Req = 214&issue = 10 (accessed December 16, 2009).

Wockhardt Hospitals. "About Wockhardt Hospitals." www.wockhard thospitals.net/about-wockhardt-hospitals.html (accessed February 27, 2010).

Woodman, Josef. *Patients Beyond Borders: Everybody's Guide to Affordable, World-Class Medical Travel.* Chapel Hill, NC: Healthy Travel Media, 2008.

2

Problems, Controversies, and Solutions

Although travel for the purpose of receiving medical care is becoming increasingly popular, medical tourism is not without controversies. Several of those debated areas are highlighted here, and discussed in concert with future directions and potential solutions. One theme that runs throughout these concerns relates to the speed at which medical tourism has grown, which has outpaced oversight ability. Another theme concerns access—access to accurate information, ethical procedures, and affordability. A third theme surrounds health care delivery systems, not only from patient-level quality and access perspectives, but also from the impact on both the destination countries to which medical tourists travel and the travelers' home countries.

Gathering Accurate Data and Conducting Research

By all accounts, medical tourism is a booming industry. But just how much is it booming and what are the implications of that boom? What do we really know about it? These basic questions lie at the heart of the issues surrounding medical tourism. On their face, these questions may seem deceptively simple. However, they actually encompass complex and often controversial issues. As Bookman and Bookman (2007) point out, writing from their backgrounds in economics and law, "because of [medical tourism's] rapid expansion, writing about it is akin to shooting a moving target" (7–8). The industry is rapidly evolving. Attention from

35

academics and research scholars, even those in the fields of both tourism and medicine, has yet to catch up. Information sources have largely been governments, media, international organizations, and consulting firms (Bookman and Bookman 2007).

Because of the problems with gathering and determining accurate data, the answer to even the most basic question remains unsettled. How many medical tourists are there? One report that tries to pin down an actual number, to quantify how many people cross borders for health care, finds that estimates on the numbers of American medical tourists range from 150,000 to upwards of 1 million American medical tourists annually. As these wildly divergent estimates might suggest, in the absence of accurate, verifiable numbers, those with various interests in medical tourism can choose the estimate that best serves their purposes (Youngman 2009a), for example, choosing suspiciously high estimates if they have interests in selling services or touting the popularity of the practice. Quite simply put, although there is widespread agreement that the practice is growing, no one knows exactly how many medical tourists there are.

Definitional and Related Problems

One of the most basic problems in gathering accurate data and conducting research on medical tourism derives from defining what medical tourism actually encompasses. In other words, it is not always easy to determine what medical tourism is and what it is not.

Researchers and others interested in medical-related travel have used terminology loosely and unclearly. While the term "medical tourism" is perhaps the most widely used, other commonly used terms include "health tourism," "medical travel," "health travel," "healthcare travel," "value medical travel," "medical outsourcing," "global healthcare" (Pollard 2010), and "cross-border healthcare."

Exactly what these terms encompass is also diverse. These and other terms may be used interchangeably, or to differentiate between specific services. For example, "wellness tourism" may be used in reference to travelers seeking to preserve or promote healthy lifestyles, such as visiting a spa, while "medical tourism" may refer to those seeking interventions, such as surgery. "Medical wellness" may be used to encompass those seeking services, such as rehabilitation. Even more broadly, while "global health" is used to focus on medical tourists, as discussed in this book, the term is also commonly used in a wider context to refer to health systems worldwide, or more specifically to focus in on inequalities between health care systems worldwide.

The facilities at which services (which may be encompassed within these varying definitions) are offered also vary markedly. In addition to those who receive services at hospitals and clinics, medical tourists may include visitors to spas, retreats, resorts, festivals, and even cruises (Smith and Puczko 2009).

Research Approaches

In addition to having no agreed on and standard definition for medical tourism, there is also no agreed on methodology for data collection. Medical tourism initially evolved with little emphasis on data collection for descriptive, evaluative, or even marketing purposes. Thus, the medical and tourism processes have not been designed to facilitate purposeful and meaningful data collection processes. This makes collecting accurate and comparable data, or even seemingly basic information such as counting numbers of patients, a challenge.

No one is actually counting, with any good degree of accuracy, the number of medical tourists leaving (outbound travelers) or entering (inbound travelers) the United States or other countries to obtain care. When attempts are made to count medical tourists, exactly who should be counted is up for debate and varies from attempt to attempt. For example, one estimate of how many Americans travel abroad for medical care is based on numbers of outbound travelers, but excludes all those traveling to Cuba, Mexico, Canada, or to other places bordering the United States (Youngman 2009a).

In an effort to quantify medical tourism, some countries attempt to count the number of hospital visits medical tourists make in their country, while other countries attempt to count the actual number of patients entering into the country. Estimates based on the number of inbound travelers to a country sometimes include expatriates returning home for routine medical care. However, expatriates are not included in counts of medical tourists everywhere. In fact, information on patients' home countries may not even be collected.

The practice of patients returning to their home country to receive medical care has been dubbed "disapora tourism." For some of these travelers, the main purpose of their travel is medical, and seeing friends and relatives is a side benefit of the trip. For others, the main purpose of their travel may be the visit itself, with medical attention being secondary (Connell 2011). Many people return to their home country to obtain care near family and familiar surroundings, to use home insurance benefits, or simply because they find it convenient and cost effective to bundle visits with friends and loved ones into their travel plans. These tourists may also stay with friends and family to reduce the costs of the trip. Research on these diaspora tourists is almost nonexistent, as is research on medical tourists from poor countries in general (Connell 2011). Researchers and data collection entities may not even be clear on exactly what or who is included in their data (Menvielle 2010).

Another challenge in conducting research on medical tourism is the cross-disciplinarity of the topic. Medical tourism encompasses a range of disciplines—medical, recreation and leisure studies, bioethics, business, sociological perspectives, and political interests, among others. Each discipline tends to use its own perspectives and professional jargon when examining medical tourism. This makes cross-disciplinary dialogue and the understanding of unfamiliar views especially important. Researchers need to understand varying approaches and perspectives to communicate effectively among themselves. Medical tourism also has implications across various levels of abstraction and analysis. It variously impacts individuals, communities, and nations. (Researchers might refer to these as micro, meso, and macro levels.) Each of these levels must be addressed to get a full picture of the situation (Snyder, Crooks, and Turner 2011). This means research needs are complex. Demographics are intertwined with the interests of individuals and systems, including families, communities, national health care systems, and even international systems of commerce and medical service delivery.

Some Basic Unanswered Questions

What is the quality of care patients are actually receiving abroad? Although some patients have clearly received substandard care while abroad, patients sometimes receive poor care at home, as well. There is no systematic reporting of clinical outcome data, especially for hospitals that serve medical tourists in developing countries. Crucial data on treatment received, how it was paid for, and the outcomes of the treatment are also often not collected.

The Organization for Economic Cooperation and Development (OECD) and the World Health Organization (WHO) are working together to devise and standardize data collection on these statistics (Helble 2011). Carefully designed research must be done to better compare these quality of care issues (Crooks and Snyder 2011; MacReady 2007; Snyder, Crooks, and Turner 2011).

Patients and providers alike are also interested in patient satisfaction. How do patients feel about their medical tourism experience overall? From a marketing perspective, word-of-mouth advertising is vital to the medical tourism industry. Satisfied patients make recommendations to their friends, post good reviews on social media websites, and provide positive public relations for the destination in particular, and medical tourism in general. Dissatisfied customers might harm these business interests, but they might also provide feedback needed for improvement.

Research on a sample of patients who received care in India shows that both medical (curative vs. preventive services) and tourism factors are at play in impacting satisfaction, illustrating the need for more research attention to the complexities of these interlinkages (George, Henthorne, and Williams 2010). Most available information on patient experience, however, is not based on empirical data. Rather, it is most often based on speculation, media reports, or anecdotal data. A comprehensive review of 216 publications, including academic articles and media sources, revealed that only five publications were based on original data gathered directly from patients to get their take on the experience (Crooks et al. 2010).

As medical facilities compete to attract medical tourists, some have turned to more hotel-like processes and operations. Hospitals may also accommodate a patient's travel partners. Scenic views from hospital rooms may be part of the facility design. Bumrungrad International Hospital in Thailand offers a range of services, including transportation packages and even concierge services. Dubai Healthcare City was designed with a luxury resort adjacent to it. Some United States hospitals, including the famous Mayo Clinic and Yale-New Haven Medical Facility, have even incorporated luxury amenities. Thus, it is important that research also address the hospitality aspect of medical tourism to ascertain its impact on patient satisfaction and medical care (Cormany 2010).

A small selection of printed guidebooks on medical tourism have appeared. Aside from news items that tend to focus on the problematic aspects or outcomes of medical tourism, and occasional items in tourist-targeted brochures and publications in destination countries, in-flight magazines are one of the few sources of print advertising for medical tourism. The vast majority of advertising and available information on medical tourism is located on the Internet (Connell 2011). This makes the Internet a primary source of information about medical tourism for potential travelers.

Importantly, of course, researchers must be able to answer the question, "What outcomes do patients experience?" Posts by travelers or testimonials on online forums and websites are a major source of outcome data. This anecdotal information is interesting and useful for marketing and networking between patients and prospective travelers, but it is problematic as a data source. It cannot provide the solid medical data that researchers need to properly assess clinical outcomes. For veracity, necessary data includes the types of follow-up care medical tourists require, where they receive that care (at home or in the destination country), the costs of any such care, and how that care is paid for. Do financial savings offset other costs, such as the costs of complications (Carruth and Carruth 2010)?

These online sources are also important for better understanding the "front end" of medical tourism, as well as the outcomes. Patients get much of their information about medical tourism from these sorts of online resources, yet little is known about how patients use these tools in their decision-making processes. Indeed, little is known about patients' decision-making processes overall. What sources of information do these travelers consult and how do they derive their decision to travel? Do they differentiate between research conducted and published by professional researchers or scientists and articles written by journalists, travel facilitators, or marketing sources who are not experts in conducting or interpreting research? Do they accept marketing materials at face value, or dig further? Much of the research that does exist has been focused on the marketing and business aspects of medical tourism, rather than on the medical aspects (Hall 2011).

Travel patterns must also be better understood. How many people in each travel party receive medical care? Is there generally only one person in a group of travelers receiving medical care, and are the other members of the party only traveling companions? Is the travel a couples' trip during which both partners undergo some procedure? Or is medical tourism a family affair, with multiple members, perhaps even children, undergoing a procedure? What time of year do people travel, or prefer to travel? How long do they stay? What recreational activities do they engage in while at their destination (Gahlinger 2008; Lee, Groves, and Lengfelder 2010)? Are travelers influenced to undergo unplanned procedures, or to add on additional procedures by in-country ads in local media or on signs? How often do travelers change their plans and decide not to undergo some planned procedure?

Because medical tourism has evolved so quickly and without comprehensive regulatory oversight, solid information on the operations of the businesses so central to the practice is lacking. Even much basic empirical data is lacking that examines the business practices of medical tourism destination countries. How do they market their "product"? What information do they provide to prospective patients (Snyder, Crooks, and Turner 2011)? It is also unknown how carefully medical tourism companies guard patient confidentiality, how conscientious they are in regard to privacy issues, or how they manage patients' medical records and transmit confidential information (Turner 2011).

There is no mechanism in place for independent monitoring and verification of data produced by many entities. Safety records are a good example of why this is a problem. While some organizations, such as Britain's National Health Service, are transparent in how they generate their data so that the data bear up under scrutiny, not all organizations are so straightforward. At the individual level, misleading and potentially dangerous information can be problematic when potential patients rely and act on it (Lunt 2009). At the systems level, little is known about the wider impacts that medical tourism has had, or will have, on public health systems, general access to health care, health care finance issues, and the health workforce (Helble 2011). Vastly improved data collection, measures, and research studies are all needed to adequately understand the magnitude and impact of medical tourism (Hopkins et al. 2010).

Meeting Research Needs

In the face of this dearth of empirical research about medical tourism, experts call for better data collection, measures, and studies of medical tourism overall (e.g., Carrera and Lunt 2010; Hopkins et al. 2010; Lunt and Carerra 2010), as well as research-based global monitoring of medical tourism (Crooks et al. 2010; Crooks and Snyder

2011). This research should address the patient's experience, among other areas (Crooks et al. 2010). We even need to better understand the role of facilitators (Snyder et al. 2011), health care providers, and the other players in the medical tourism arena, as well as systemic impacts on health care and other social institutions.

Research attention to medical tourism is increasing. At the international level, for example, the OECD and the WHO are working together to improve international systems that will help lead to more standardized and complete data sets (Helble 2011).

Dedicated research centers are also being established specifically to address medical tourism. In 2008, the Center for Medical Tourism Research was established in the H-E-B School of Business and Administration at the University of the Incarnate Word in San Antonio, Texas. Current research is wide ranging and includes the marketing aspects of medical tourism, quality and continuity of care, attitudes toward medical tourism, the socio–cultural aspects of medical tourism, the economic aspects of medical tourism, and legal issues surrounding the topic. Simon Fraser University near Vancouver, Canada, has established a Medical Tourism Research Group, with international collaborations in Barbados and Southern India. However, the reality remains that solid empirical data are sorely needed. We need these data to gain a better picture of the magnitude of the situation, assess the implications, and look to the future health, economic, and legal implications of medical tourism.

Safety Concerns

Americans have grown accustomed to one of the highest standards of medical care in the world. The suggestion of traveling to a developing nation to have surgery invariably brings to mind a single, important question: Is it safe?

It's no wonder that people are nervous about getting their medical care overseas, when they're bombarded with ideas and images suggesting how dangerous a proposition seeking medical care in a foreign country can be. First there are the post-9/11 travel worries, fueled by incessant media coverage of not only the event itself, but also a steady and seemingly endless parade of hijackings, kidnappings, and military coups on foreign shores. Generally, however, medical tourism has been safe. Most of the time, medical tourists are under the supervision of a hotel, travel broker, or tour agency while in the destination country, and travel straight from the airport to their hotel to their medical facility (Woodman 2008).

Then there are the manufactured fears, triggered by fictionalized portrayals like the Robin Cook medical thriller, *Foreign Body*, in which a medical student travels to India to investigate after her grandmother mysteriously dies following a hip replacement procedure. Finally, and probably most pervasive, is the fear of traveling to a less-developed nation and discovering untrained doctors and unclean facilities. Many of the countries where surgery is being performed—for example, Thailand, Costa Rica, and India—are considered far less advanced than the United States and Europe. Yet, developing countries like these have surprisingly high-tech medical care. "Doctors and consumers alike have a built-in bias that they're going to get surgery in a mud hut with a rusty scalpel and untrained physicians; nothing could be further from the truth," says Josef Woodman, author of *Patients Without Borders*. "We're talking about a very select group of hospitals that are built and maintained to cater to affluent international patients" (Law 2008).

Ensuring Patients Are Getting High-Quality Care Abroad

The biggest safety issue medical tourists worry about is the quality of the medical care they are receiving, particularly because many medical tourism destinations are in the developing world. Decades ago, few developing nations could afford to provide the same standard of medical care that is available in the West. Today, however, many international clinics have standards that meet—or even exceed—those in the United States.

Traveling abroad for medical care can be just as safe as seeking care at home, provided that tourists carefully research their options before they go. Information is the single biggest resource people have when they're investigating medical services in a foreign country.

Information on the Internet

The Internet is a vast source of information on medical tourism. Many prospective medical tourists begin their search for information with online sources, and a website is frequently their first contact with potential service providers.

However, consumers are advised to use caution when researching medical tourism on the Internet. There is no way to police the quality and accuracy of the information posted on most websites. Therefore, the Internet is awash in information, but much of it is of dubious quality. In his book *The Medical Tourism Travel Guide*, physician and medical tourism expert Paul Gahlinger calls much of this information "junk," and labels a good deal of the online health care advice "nonsense."

Although excellent websites do exist, many sites intermingle advertising with objective information, making it difficult to sort out what's what. Information may be out of date and pricing and contact information may be lacking. Data may consist primarily of anecdotal testimonials from former patients. Additionally, the bulk of medical tourism information is provided on facilitation service sites, where selling a product (the trip) is the main interest. Some sites might advertise facilities that pay referral fees, and some are outright scams (Gahlinger 2008; Youngman 2009b).

Many of these websites contain errors in basic grammar and wording because non-native English speakers often write them. The medical tourism online guide *Treatment Abroad* offers to edit and correct English language versions of destination websites for a fee through its "Perfect English" service. The purpose of this service is to professionalize the look of travel websites to better attract English-speaking patients ("The Perfect English Service" n.d.). The lesson to prospective patients is to take online information with the proverbial grain of salt and do extensive homework when considering medical tourism as an option.

Accreditation and Medical Standards

Before patients will travel to another country, they need some assurance that the hospitals they'll be visiting are safe. Ensuring quality requires some level of standardization and oversight. Standardization requirements involve both products and processes—procedures and equipment that will be used on patients are tested, regularly monitored, and kept clean and sterile, and medical staff are well-trained, certified, and licensed. Insurance companies want similar assurance before they will pay for their customers to travel abroad for a procedure. Insurance companies hold a vested interest in standardization and oversight, even if they do not pay for medical care obtained internationally, because a patient who returns home after receiving poor care may become a cost to them (Bookman and Bookman 2007, 146). Treating the complications of a botched surgery can be more expensive than the original operation (Reier 2004).

The International Organization for Standardization (ISO) develops standards of health care technology and health protection for its 161 member countries. It is a nongovernmental organization made up of a network of its members' national standards institutes.

The first consideration medical tourists need to make is whether the hospital they're evaluating is accredited. Accreditation covers everything from the training of medical personnel, to the type of equipment used, as well as hospital ethics and patient-to-staff ratios. Virtually every medical tourism destination has at least one—and usually several—hospitals accredited by the same U.S. organization (the Joint Commission) that accredits American hospitals. The Joint Commission International (JCI) provides accreditation for hospitals, laboratories, and other health care facilities that meet its patient safety standards. In 2005, the number of JCI-accredited foreign medical sites worldwide was 76; in 2008, that number had more than tripled to 220 sites (Shetty 2010). Approximately 450 health care organizations in 50 countries had been JCI accredited or certified in early 2012 (JCI, n.d.). JCI accreditation standards are published in its *Joint Commission International Accreditation Standards for Hospitals*. The fourth edition of the manual became effective January 1, 2011, and it extends the focus on safety issues from previous versions.

Accreditation by organizations such as the JCI and the ISO assures patients that the facility meets standards comparable to those in the United States. However, although JCI standards are intended to ensure uniformly high quality, some U.S. physicians and other health care professionals question whether such accreditation always means a comparable quality of care to American health care facilities (Rodriguez-Williams and Williams 2011).

Most international hospitals are not accredited with organizations such as the JCI, so it's important to check for this approval. Some hospitals will, however, be accredited through other organizations and may still be good. Many countries also have their own accrediting, which can be rigorous. The Australian Council of Healthcare Standards, the Canadian Council on Health Services Accreditation, the Council for Health Services Accreditation of Southern Africa, the Egyptian Health Care Accreditation

Organization, the Irish Health Services Accreditation Board, and the Japan Council for Quality in Health Care are all national accrediting agencies (among other organizations) (Woodman 2008). Patients are cautioned to do especially thorough research on any hospitals that are not JCI accredited. Travelers should also keep in mind that, even if facilities are part of a chain, they are accredited individually. Travelers should check the duration of a hospital's accreditation, and validate that the information is current by consulting the accrediting agency's website.

Many of the doctors who perform surgery at accredited hospitals were trained at medical schools in Great Britain, Canada, and the United States. The medical schools at Cornell and Duke Universities both have programs in which they train doctors in countries other than the United States. International partnerships provide further assurance that a foreign hospital meets American medical standards. The success rates at some of these facilities rivals, or even exceeds, those in the West. For example, the success of cardiac bypass operations in India is 98.7 per cent, compared to 97.5 percent in the United States (Kapil 2007). Escorts Heart Institute and Research Centre in Delhi and Faridabad in India performs nearly 15,000 heart operations every year. The postsurgery mortality rate is 0.8 percent, less than half the rate of most major hospitals in the United States. (Kumar 2009).

For even greater peace of mind, travelers can choose a hospital that is owned, managed, or affiliated with a medical center in the United States. Dubai Healthcare City in the United Arab Emirates and Wockhardt Hospitals, Ltd., in Mumbai, India, for example, worked with Partners Harvard Medical International (PHMI). Johns Hopkins University also has associations with hospitals in India (Apollo) and in Panama. The Cleveland Clinic, Columbia University, Memorial Sloan Kettering, and the University of Pittsburgh are just a few of the other U.S. facilities that have partnered with medical centers abroad.

Some hospitals in India have International Patients Departments (IPDs) dedicated to patient service. Case managers negotiate, process, and facilitate communication between medical tourists, service providers, and the hospital. The case managers are accessible 24 hours a day, every day of the week (Pawar 2011).

As patients are navigating their options for medical care abroad, they should be equipped with a list of questions to ask their prospective hospital and practitioner, including:

- Is the hospital accredited? How often is the accreditation renewed?
- What safety and hygiene practices does the hospital follow?
- Are staff members fluent in English?
- What are the procedures for care after the surgery has been completed? Will the hospital coordinate care for patients on their return home?
- Will the doctor be reachable in case the patient has complications after they have returned home?
- How do the doctor, hospital, and country handle malpractice claims? Who is accountable, and what recourse do patients have if medical mistakes occur? How are malpractice claims regulated in the country's legal system?
- Does the medical facility accept insurance from the patient's home country? If so, are all costs for service out-of-pocket?

Medical Personnel/Licensing

Patients should be choosy about the doctors they select. Many health care providers in developing nations completed their medical degrees in the United States, Canada, or Europe. They received the same training as Western doctors.

Assessing licensing quality is a bit trickier than finding accredited organizations, however. As of today, no international licensing or certification organization exists. Licenses are issued by individual countries (in the United States, licensing is done on the state level), and standards can vary from country to country.

Even credentials that appear valid can be fake. Studies in both India and Saudi Arabia, for example, uncovered thousands of fraudulent medical certifications among various practitioners. Although JCI does not accredit individual practitioners (only organizations), it does require that these institutions be vigilant and have processes in place to help ensure that only qualified doctors are allowed to practice there (Timmons 2008).

Prospective medical tourists should thoroughly investigate the doctor they are considering. However, they probably won't have access to as much information on foreign doctors as they would be able to find on U.S. doctors through state medical boards, insurance plans, and the National Practitioner Data Bank (NPDB).

In the United States, patients can find out what complaints (if any) have been filed against doctors, learn their malpractice history, and assess their patient outcome data.

It is still possible to check out foreign doctors. To do so, patients should get the doctor's resume and check his or her references. Recommendations from former patients and referrals from friends are informative. Other considerations are the doctor's education, certification, professional history (including publications and honors), affiliations, and continuing education (Woodman 2008).

The best-selling medical tourism guide *Patients Without Borders* suggests that medical tourists ask the following series of questions to their prospective doctors:

- What are the physician's credentials? Where did she or he receive his or her medical degree? Where did she or he complete his or her internship? What types of continuing education has she or he completed recently?
- How many patients does the physician see each month? For this question, more than 50 but less than 500 is considered a good number.
- To what associations does the physician belong? Physicians should belong to at least one medical association. Ideally, they should also belong to at least one American medical association.
- How many patients with the condition for which treatment is sought has the physician treated? For this question, the patient wants to find a doctor who is experienced in treating their condition. Numbers will vary, but a general rule of thumb is that "five cases is not good. Fifty or 200 are much better" (Woodman 2008, 59).
- What are the fees for the physician's initial consultations? Some initial consultations may be free or the cost may be deducted from the final bill.
- Will the physician be available by e-mail or cell phone before, during, and after treatment?
- What medical records does the physician need? Doctors who do not request any medical records should be approached with caution, and the patients should probably go elsewhere.
- Where and with whom does the physician practice? Physicians who practice with a group of professionals are recommended.

- Who actually "holds the knife" and performs the surgery, the doctor or an assistant?
- Will the physician oversee the patient's entire treatment, from presurgical evaluation to postoperative care? (Woodman 2008, 58–60)

Standards for Medical Tourism Facilitators

There has been a call for stringent regulation and oversight of medical tourism companies, as well as of individuals acting in facilitator roles, which would require adherence to strict standards of practice. Additionally, it has been suggested that medical tourism companies be required, as a condition of accreditation or licensure, to contribute to a compensation fund that will reimburse clients when promised services are not delivered (Turner 2011).

In 2007, Healthcare Tourism International (HTI) became the first accreditation service for health travel safety. The nonprofit HTI focuses on the nonclinical aspects of medical tourism, and is designed to be a complementary system to JCI clinical accreditation. Organizations apply for the HTI compliance program through the organization's HealthCare Trip website (Merrill 2007).

The Medical Tourism Association (MTA), an international nonprofit trade association, has established five medical tourism certification programs. The certifications offered are for Medical Tourism Facilitators, International Patient Departments, Hotel and Hospitality Organizations, Travel and Tour Operators, and Global Spas. Each program is aimed at improving business processes for MTA members. Creating "best practices" and increasing patient safety are the anticipated outcomes (MTA 2010).

In the fall semester of 2012, the University of Richmond in Richmond, VA, and the MTA will partner to offer a Certificate in Medical Tourism Studies. The certification will be offered through the School of Professional and Continuing Studies. Six courses are required and students earn continuing education units (CEUs) for their coursework. Students can complete courses online, while they attend the annual World Medical Tourism and Global Healthcare Congress, or through a combination of online and conference courses (University of Richmond n.d.).

Continuity of Care

After treatment, and before leaving for home, patients should get all the information they and their medical providers at home will potentially need (Gahlinger 2008; Woodman 2008). They should get copies of their all test results and X-rays. They should be certain that their postoperative instructions are clear, and do the same for physical therapy instructions or other follow-up guidance. Patients should have their prescribed medications and know the comparable drug in their home country. Having all paperwork in order—exit papers, insurance claim forms, receipt for payments—before departing for home is also important.

Once patients do return home, another question arises: who will treat any complications that potentially occur? Doctors in the patient's home country are often reluctant to intervene in procedures performed by doctors abroad. They may worry about the legal implications of attempting to fix a botched surgery, or be concerned if the procedure used devices or medication that is not approved in the United States. In a call for more accreditation and better regulatory oversight of the medical tourism industry, medical tourism expert Leigh G. Turner says: "Continuity of care needs to be recognized as a key feature of arranging international health care" for which medical tourism companies should be held accountable (2011, 4).

Some botched procedures can be not only dangerous physically and stressful psychologically, but extremely expensive financially, as well. In countries that offer public health insurance, covering the cost of poor care received elsewhere potentially drains money from public coffers that could be spent elsewhere in the system (Snyder and Crooks 2010). Research on the complications of bariatric surgeries (surgical procedures that treat obesity) obtained abroad have shown the associated costs to be potentially quite high. In one especially egregious case of botched gastric bypass surgery, an American patient who had her procedure performed in Mexico needed a half million dollars worth of emergency follow-up care after she was rushed back to the United States with severe complications. Whether she, her insurer, or the hospital will ultimately have to bear those costs is unclear (Kraus 2010). Bariatric surgery is considered risky anyway, but based on a review of bariatric medical tourists' records, one team of Canadian physicians concluded that a "medical tourism approach to the surgical management of obesity—a chronic disease—is inappropriate" (Birch et al. 2010).

Liability

No matter how rigorous its standards, no country can entirely guarantee a patient's safety. There have been reports of medical tourists experiencing complications or dying in foreign hospitals. In 2006, Jude Jarvis, a 35-year-old mother from Rhode Island, died from a pulmonary embolism after undergoing a tummy tuck operation at Wockhardt Hospital in Mumbai. The reason for her death was unclear (Wolff, Bianchi, and Kearl 2007). Yet even in the United States, where the standards of medical care are high, major medical mistakes have cost people their health, and even their lives.

It's difficult to tell with any certainty whether patients who travel to a reputable hospital abroad face any greater risk than they would in the United States, because so little research has been done comparing procedures and hospitals between countries. Researchers at UCLA found that medical tourists had higher rates of rejection, and reduced survival at one year (89% for tourists vs. 98% for UCLA patients) after kidney transplant surgery (Gill 2008), but this was just one small study.

One significant patient concern is that other countries don't have the same level of medical oversight as exists in the United States. Without a Food and Drug Administration (FDA) to evaluate and approve medical devices and medications before they are put to use, patients may be subjected to insufficiently tested or even untested therapies. Other countries might not put their blood supply through the same rigorous testing for infectious diseases, such as HIV and hepatitis. This means that if patients need to undergo a transfusion while having surgery, the safety of the blood they receive could be questionable.

Even under the most skilled surgeon's care, accidents can happen. A scalpel can slip. The wrong medicine can be administered. As a result of these mistakes, patients can be injured, or even killed. In the United States, patients who have been injured during a medical procedure have rights under the law. They can file a medical malpractice claim. In 2008 alone, more than 11,000 medical malpractice claims were filed in this country (Kaiser State Health Facts 2008). American doctors carry expensive malpractice insurance so that they can cover the costs of these claims.

Other countries have their own systems for dealing with malpractice, and they are often not as generous as the United

States. In many countries, such as India, doctors carry only limited malpractice insurance, and damages to plaintiffs are limited.

Just trying to navigate the legal system in a foreign country can be tricky, and patients may be left with little or no recourse if something goes wrong during the procedure. Patients may look to their health insurance plan, employer, or medical tourism facilitator, only to find little or no help. The problem may be compounded by cultural differences. "Foreign cultures may have a different interpretation of anxiety, pain, or inconvenience," as noted by author David Reisman (2010, 61).

Insurance may offer a means for some compensation when malpractice does occur. Patients may take out individual insurance riders against malpractice by a foreign doctor. Or, if they are insured through an employer or group plan, the policy may have such a rider. Polices vary in their coverage, but they might include the costs related to legal action, repairing botched surgeries, follow-up care, complications, lost wages, mishandling of confidential information, disfigurement, and death (Reisman 2010).

The facilitators who book the trip may also have coverage that assists in reparations. Liability in this case is yet unclear, as the facilitator is acting only as an intermediary. One Swedish-based laser eye specialty facilitator that sends medical tourists to Istanbul offers guarantees on quality of service. The company reduces its risks by dealing only with a well-experienced physician who has a proven track record of thousands of successful procedures (Reisman 2010: 64).

Traveling across Borders

Travel (particularly travel abroad) encompasses its own set of risks, even for the healthiest medical tourist. Likewise, all medical procedures carry some level of risk. In recent decades, a field of medicine has evolved that is devoted to the health of international travelers. "Travel medicine" focuses on helping travelers prevent infectious diseases, increase personal safety, and avoid environmental risks (Hill et al. 2006). These risks may be exacerbated for medical tourists who are still recovering from their procedures, or who have lowered immunity.

Health Risks of International Travel

Even healthy travelers can face a number of health risks. Part of the safety concern is not with the hospitals or procedures, but with the rigors involved in traveling to a foreign nation. Many countries have endemic diseases that are no longer seen in the United States. With no natural immunity, travelers run the risk of contracting malaria, hepatitis A, or another deadly disease while they are trying to get well.

Commonly documented complaints are gastrointestinal problems or diarrhea when tourists venture to locations where water sanitation is lacking. Tourists to tropical areas such as Central and South America have arrived back home to discover they have acquired a botfly after being bitten by an insect carrying botfly eggs. Mosquito bites may spread malaria or dengue fever to travelers in areas of the world where those diseases are widespread. Tourists are also widely warned to take precautions against transmitting HIV if they engage in behaviors that could potentially transmit that virus.

Hospitals carry their own risks for medical tourists. Medical tourists from several countries who underwent surgery in India were infected with a "superbug" dubbed NDM-1 (which stands for New Delhi metallobeta-lactamase 1) (Moellering 2010). Superbugs are bacteria that are particularly difficult to treat because they have developed a resistance or immunity to many antibiotics. A kidney transplant patient from the United Kingdom was infected with hepatitis B during the procedure in India. A New York hospital discovered mycobacterium infections among a handful of patients who had undergone cosmetic surgery in the Dominican Republic. Possible sources of infection could have been contaminated water, surgical instruments, medications, and antiseptic solutions. Hospitals in any country, including the United States, also must guard against spreading infections to and between patients. However, while the risk of nosocomial infections (those resulting from medical treatment) in intensive care is estimated to be 25 percent in developed countries, it is estimated to be as high as 40 percent in developing countries (Reed 2008).

Travelers sometimes inadvertently spread diseases by the act of physically moving from one place to another. In historical perspective, this is the way the plagues that decimated much of the European population during the Middle Ages moved so quickly, and the way that yellow fever moved so readily around some port regions of the United States until the early 1900s. In recent years, severe acute respiratory syndrome (SARS) and the avian flu have spread internationally, carried by travelers. It is also conceivable that medical tourists could carry disease into their destination countries (Johnston et al. 2011).

The return home after surgery poses its own health concerns. Sitting on a long flight, especially after major surgery, increases the risk of deep vein thrombosis, a condition in which a blood clot forms in the deep veins (usually in the leg). The clot can break off and travel to the lung, where it creates a life-threatening condition called a pulmonary embolism (Carabello 2008). In 2003, NBC reporter David Bloom died of a pulmonary embolism while covering combat operations in Iraq.

Entry Requirements

Foreign countries don't necessarily welcome everyone to their shores. For security reasons, they need to see documentation. At the very minimum, a passport is required to travel internationally. Some countries also require a visa, which allows tourists to remain in the country for a designated period of time, and for a specific reason.

India, one of the leading medical tourism destinations, requires visitors to obtain a visa at an Indian embassy or consulate prior to traveling. Anyone who attempts to enter India without a valid visa and passport risks immediate deportation (U.S. Department of State 2010). Americans who travel to Israel face extensive background checks, as well as exhaustive questioning by immigration authorities.

The more stringent a country's requirements for entry, the less attractive that country becomes to medical tourists. Long flights and having to make numerous connections also restrict tourism. To make travel for medical tourists more convenient and, thus, more attractive, some countries have developed simplified visa requirements and are also looking to establish direct flights from major world airports (Bookman and Bookman 2007; Helble 2011).

Avoiding Travel-related Problems for Medical Tourists

It is imperative for medical tourists to pay attention to routine travel details, as well as to details specific to their medical concerns before traveling (including making checklists and backup plans). *The Medical Tourism Travel Guide* authored by physician and medical tourism expert Dr. Paul Gahlinger urges medical tourists to organize their preparations into three categories—things at home, medical, and travel.

Details at Home

This category includes the sorts of things travelers should think about for any trip—not just trips related to medical tourism. For example, how will the mail be handled while the traveler is away? Who will care for the pets? And who will handle job coverage while the traveler is absent?

Medical Details

Before traveling, prospective medical tourists should get a thorough medical workup from a licensed physician in their home country to make sure they're healthy enough to travel. The U.S. Centers for Disease Control and Prevention (CDC) recommends that all travelers with health problems (as well as those travelers who have complex itineraries) see doctors who specialize in travel medicine before taking their trip. They should do so at least four to six weeks, if possible, before their trip. Travelers can also contact the International Society of Travel Medicine (ISTM) or the American Society of Tropical Medicine and Hygiene (ASTMH). Both of those professional organizations maintain directories of private travel medicine clinics (CDC 2011). State and local health departments are often able to provide pretravel assistance.

At least one survey of physicians (Hitt 2010) has shown that doctors who see the most travelers are better versed in relevant literature, treatment, and vaccines than their counterparts who see fewer than 50 travelers per year. Doctors who see fewer than 50 travelers annually were less likely to be aware of international travel recommendations, and even less likely to prescribe appropriate treatments, such as the best anti-malarial drug for patients who are preparing to travel to areas where malaria is found. Medical professionals can take an exam offered by the International Society for Travel Medicine to increase their expertise, or they can refer travelers to travel medicine specialists (Hitt 2010).

The discussion between the patient and physician should include such things as the risks and benefits of the anticipated medical procedure, plans for communicating during the trip, and post-trip care plans. The planned stay in the destination country should be long enough to have follow-up care done by the same surgeon who performed the operation. This approach establishes the continuity of care that is vital for many medical procedures to have a successful and safe outcome (Gahlinger 2008; Woodman 2008). All travelers should get any needed immunizations in advance of the trip and have written prescriptions in hand for any medications they will need.

Medical records should be transmitted to the hospital and doctor abroad before the patient leaves home. Because there are not adequate systems and oversight in place to oversee the international transfer of medical records, ensuring both the continuity of those records and patient privacy are major concerns (Crooks and Snyder 2011). For American medical tourists, their patient medical records should be transferred to and from facilities outside the United States in accordance with the strict guidelines of the U.S. federal Health Insurance Portability and Accountability Act of 1996 (HIPAA) Privacy and Security Rules. These HIPAA guidelines protect the privacy of personal health information and ensure the electronic security of that information. HIPAA does not apply in most foreign countries (except for limited privacy protection in Europe), so patients should ascertain how their medical records will be handled outside of the United States.

Patients should learn the risks of surgery and plan for postsurgical care in the United States before leaving for their trip. They should talk to the surgeon who will perform the procedure themselves; their home physician should also communicate with the surgeon, to arrange follow-up care ahead of time. Travelers should think through how they will keep up with receipts for medical care, aftercare instructions, and the like. Financing arrangements should be in place to pay for the procedure and to provide continuity of care. Recommendations also include getting a written quote from the hospital, which covers their payment terms (Gahlinger 2008; Woodman 2008).

Travel Details
Pretrip checklists should include other travel practicalities, including ensuring that passports and all other travel documents

are in order. Travelers should also check on cell phone coverage, finding out whether their own phone will work at their destination, or whether they will need an international plan or a different cell phone if they want to rely on that method of communication during their trip. International cell phone rates can be quite expensive, so patients should investigate the rates for various options (e.g., calling cards, Skype, or other Voiceover Internet Protocols [VoIP]) in advance. Another practicality involves checking whether any medical equipment (or personal items like blow dryers, for that matter) require an electric plug that is compatible with the outlets and voltage in the destination countries. If not, travelers may need to purchase inexpensive converters to safely use those items abroad (Gahlinger 2008; Woodman 2008).

It is also widely recommended that medical tourists take out short-term health insurance policies (sometimes referred to as "holiday insurance") that offer travel medical insurance, as well as medical complications and errors insurance for their trip. This insurance will not cover the cost of their planned medical procedure; however, it will cover any medical emergencies that arise during the course of travel (Reisman 2010).

Medical tourists should also take out general travel insurance to cover unforeseen mishaps that might occur, including lost luggage, missed flights, or transportation delays that might mean missing prepaid appointments or scheduled procedures. There may still be gray areas in coverage if patients need to make a claim. For example, will a policy cover the repatriation of a body if a person dies during an elective, preplanned medical procedure? Will it pay to evacuate a patient to another country for further care if the procedure goes awry? And will it cover additional expenses when complications arise that delay scheduled departures (Reisman 2010, 34)?

Disabled patients, or those who will have a disabled person in their travel party, should realize that accessibility standards and anti-discrimination laws vary by country. This situation requires additional advance research to ensure that all needed services (e.g., local transportation, etc.) will be available. Restrictions on service dogs, required veterinary immunizations, documentation, and quarantine vary by country and also need to be well researched in advance of any international travel (U.S. Department of State 2011).

The Internet, Distance Care, and Telemedicine

Can a person be a medical tourist without ever leaving home? Modern medical care increasingly involves varieties of distance care. In other words, the patient and the health care provider do not have to have any physical contact; the treatment or service is provided in a physically separate location from the patient.

Medical practice has a long history of providing various forms of distance care (e.g., diagnosing through postal mail exchanges), dating at least from ancient Greece. Today, the Internet and other information and communications technologies have provided and popularized new and cost-effective options for distance care. Distance care is also a lucrative business. The industry is expected to reach $6.28 billion annually by 2020 (Terry 2011).

Telemedicine, defined as "the use of medical information exchanged from one site to another via electronic communications to improve patients' health status," is an interactive modern form of distance care ("Telemedicine Defined" n.d.). The technologies used can be either synchronous (meaning real-time interactions between the parties involved in the communication) or asynchronous (meaning information can be shared by parties who access it at different times). A "live" online chat room and instant messaging are widely familiar examples of synchronous communication. E-mail, posting information on listservers or bulletin boards, or status postings and responses on Facebook are familiar examples of asynchronous communications.

Telemedicine covers a range of services (ATA n.d.). Specialists in an increasing variety of areas diagnose or consult with patients via live online interactions, and by viewing diagnostic test results, images, and videos that are transmitted electronically. Specialists in the United States might consult over the Internet with physicians on another continent about a difficult case. Real-time video applications allow doctors to consult during surgery. Remote-control surgery is on the horizon (Simon 2008). The field of radiology relies heavily on telemedicine, with thousands of images being read by distant providers annually. Through outsourcing, for example, an American patient's X-rays may be interpreted by a radiologist in India. Remote patient monitoring allows a patient's vital signs to be transmitted (sometimes even from the patient's home) to health care providers who can monitor and assess the patient's condition. Patients can log on to websites and confer with other patients and support groups, and even receive a diagnosis or treatment plan from a health care provider they never meet in person.

Telemedicine offers both benefits and challenges (Simon 2008). On the one hand, it allows remote areas to receive new levels of care. Providers in those areas have increased opportunities to learn and improve their own knowledge and skill sets via increased interaction with specialists. Care can be provided more quickly and costs can be decreased by lessening travel. Online seminars and programs offer opportunities for medical education in remote areas.

On the other hand, for telemedicine to continue to grow in outlying or poor communities, costs will need to be controlled so that it is affordable. Confidentiality can also be a challenge. Adequate security must be in place to safeguard medical records and other private information that is electronically transmitted, and to guard against other cybercrimes, such as financial fraud. This also results in electronic waste that will require disposal (e.g., discarded, obsolete electronic equipment). Additionally, laws overseeing telemedicine vary by country, resulting in the challenge of meeting laws in both (or all) countries involved in the interaction.

Finally, medical tourism is not marketed by standard travel agencies. Most, if not all, medical tourism companies are online only entities. They have no bricks-and-mortar travel agency storefront. This makes marketing and promoting medical tourism particularly challenging to monitor and police (Connell 2011).

Ethical Issues

Much attention to medical tourism has come from the field of bioethics. Bioethicists study a range of ethical, moral, and social issues related to biological research, medicine, and health care. Medical tourism is rife with ethical issues.

Medical ethicists are particularly concerned about the growing emphasis on high technology in a market-driven context. When patients, including those desperate for any shred of hope, can purchase tests, procedures, or treatments in a largely unregulated and competitive profit-oriented marketplace, great potential exists for exploitation and manipulation. Patient reliance on unregulated marketing claims may even change public perception. Bypassing less technologically intensive, invasive, expensive, or even experimental options in favor of high-tech approaches (often aside from expert medical consultation) may become defined as "normal" approaches to medical issues, rather than choices within a larger menu of options (Connell 2011).

Shortcutting Cost and Quality

Some ethical issues in medical tourism involve undercutting cost and safety regulations. Sometimes, providers allow patients to bundle too many procedures—for example, several cosmetic surgical procedures—into a compacted time frame that is easier on the wallet, but is much shorter than the timeline that would generally be recommended. Unethical providers may disregard other aspects of healing. Any medical tourism brochure that proclaims, "Enjoy horseback riding excursions while recuperating from your tummy tuck" is a sure sign that a prospective patient is in for trouble.

Illegal Procedures

Some patients travel to undergo procedures that are illegal in their own country. Women who live in countries with restrictive abortion policies might travel abroad to obtain an abortion (e.g., Muslim women obtaining abortions in India [Gahlinger 2008]); travelers might seek out particular countries for assisted suicide, or for solutions to infertility problems. An emerging term for this type of travel is "circumvention tourism" because the point of the travel is to bypass (i.e., circumvent) the laws or restrictions in place in their home country.

Legal scholars point out that these circumvention tourists, as well as medical tourism facilitators, must be aware of the legal ramifications of these situations. According to Glenn Cohen, Assistant Professor at Harvard Law School, "It is a matter of international law that you can make criminal the activities of citizens abroad." Cohen illustrates this point by offering the example of Turkey, where the use of certain fertility treatments is banned. Turkish citizens who undergo banned treatments elsewhere can be imprisoned for up to five years when they return home. Cross-border surrogacy arrangements can also raise citizenship problems for the child

(Ratner 2011). When patients return home, physicians in their home country may have a hard time providing follow-up care for procedures they are unfamiliar with treating (Crooks and Snyder 2011).

Marketing can also involve practices that are not only misleading, but are patently illegal. The Australian Society of Plastic Surgeons criticized one Australian tour provider for misleading potential patients by giving the impression that it was qualified to administer medical advice. To counteract bad publicity, the company violated the local law by flying in Asian physicians to recruit Australian women to travel overseas for cosmetic procedures (Duff and Hall 2007).

Suicide Tourism

An extreme example of travel to obtain illegal procedures is when travelers are seeking euthanasia. Euthanasia is intentionally ending life or allowing a body to die, usually to alleviate the pain and suffering of an incurable or terminal condition. The term "suicide tourists" is sometimes applied to these travelers, although the word "tourism" seems particularly inappropriate here.

Only a few countries allow any form of euthanasia, and then only under certain circumstances. Currently, the Netherlands, Belgium, Luxembourg, Colombia, Albania, and Switzerland are on that list. In the United States, the states of Oregon and Washington allow euthanasia under certain circumstances. Debates about euthanasia are ongoing in several other countries and states.

All countries other than Switzerland, however, forbid foreigners from seeking suicide within their boarders (*Final Exit* 2010), and even in Switzerland that option is controversial. A May 2011 vote in Zurich defeated a proposal to restrict access for foreigners ("Zurich voters" 2011). The Swiss association Dignitas (founded in 1998), widely known for arranging euthanasia, argues that "[b]ecause a person's wish to end his or her life is a human right recognised by the Federal Supreme Court of Switzerland and protected by Article 8 of the European Human Rights Convention, no one should be discriminated against in any way, not even on the basis of where they live" (Dignitas 2010).

Dignitas acts as a neutral party for its members. It provides counseling, which may involve suicide and suicide-attempt prevention. Patients get an appointment with a Swiss doctor who will prescribe lethal medication (usually barbiturates), if the decision is made that the patient is serious and rational. Dignitas also provides assistance with legal issues and accompanies dying patients who request it. Dignitas has also experimented with oxygen deprivation, using helium and a common face mask and reservoir bag. This method bypasses the prescribing role of physicians, and potentially provides a quick and painless death. However, in practice, appropriate mask fit has proven problematic (Ogden et al. 2010). In 2011 Dignitas's cost for euthanasia was US$12,600 if it made funeral and administrative arrangements, and US$8,400 if it did not provide these services (Dignitas 2010).

Sometimes, people will travel to their "home" country or culture for a familiar context, not to end their lives, but to live out their remaining time in familiar or comforting surroundings. They may be seeking support or may have nostalgia for the past (Connell 2011). Although right-to-die organizations supporting euthanasia exist around the world, the moral, ethical, and religious aspects are hotly debated. For many commentators, suicide tourism epitomizes these debates.

Unproven Treatments

Treatments are sometimes unavailable domestically because their safety, effectiveness, or value has not been demonstrated to the satisfaction of oversight bodies. Medical tourists have long traveled to obtain these unproven treatments. People who are desperate for hope often fall into this category. For example, in 1980 before medical tourism was regularly making headlines, the popular American actor Steve McQueen made big news when the media discovered that he had traveled to Mexico for unapproved cancer treatments (Lerner 2005). More recently, another Hollywood star, Farrah Fawcett, traveled to Germany to undergo cancer treatment that was not available in the United States (Hitti 2009). For years, Canadians with multiple sclerosis traveled to the United States and elsewhere for chronic cerebrospinal venous insufficiency (CCSVI) surgery, more popularly known as "liberation therapy." Their travel and pressure from advocates were instrumental in convincing Canada to begin research on the treatment (liberationtreatmentccsvi.com n.d.). Rather than undergoing hip replacement, many Americans traveled abroad for a hip-resurfacing procedure before it was available at home. In September 2011, a Mexican-based provider announced weekly lottery drawings through Facebook, offering regenerative cellular therapy cancer treatments as the prize for two winners each week for five weeks. Travel costs to the treatment site remained the winner's responsibility. Americans and others outside the country were eligible to participate, although the treatments being offered were unavailable in the United States ("Cancer Cure" 2011).

Stem cell therapies, many of which are unproven, are a fast growing segment of medical tourism that raises many ethical concerns (Barclay 2009). Stem cells are cells that are able to "self-renew;" in other words, to divide and produce more stem cells. They are also said to be able to "differentiate" into various types of specialized cells with specific functions in the body, such as blood or muscle cells. Stem cells have the ability to serve as an "internal repair system," repairing or replenishing worn out cells. Because of stem cells' unique properties, researchers are increasingly looking at whether they can be used to treat a variety of ailments.

Researchers have found specific properties and uses of stem cells, based on the source of those cells. Stem cells may come from adult cells, early embryos, fetuses, and umbilical cord blood. Embryonic stem cells appear to have especially promising properties. In 2006, in another promising approach, researchers learned how to genetically "re-program" adult stem cells to make them behave more like stem cells that come from embryos. Researchers call these induced pluripotent stem cells (iPSCs), and foresee potentials in drug development and a wide range of treatments (National Institutes of Health 2009).

Although embryonic stem cells are derived from embryos grown in a laboratory rather than from inside a woman's body, they have raised moral and religious objections among some groups, leading to significant restrictions on their research and use. Different countries address this controversy through regulations that vary widely. In many places, there are fewer restrictions on embryonic stem cell use and research than in the United States. Critics argue that the resulting controversy has put stem cell research in the United States behind research occurring in other parts of the world. (In "science tourism," stem cell researchers themselves may travel to countries where they are able to conduct research with fewer restrictions [Bookman and Bookman 2007].) United States restrictions on stem cell use also have the unintended consequence of making medical tourism the only option for some patients who are interested in, or perhaps even desperate to try, stem cell therapies.

Proven stem cell therapies based on clinical research are used for blood disorders, in bone marrow transplants, and to treat some immune deficiencies. Studies are investigating the use of stem cells in a wide number of conditions, including heart disease, spinal cord injury, and cancer. Other stem cells therapies are still experimental. Stem cell therapies with unsubstantiated claims are being widely advertised to attract medical tourists. This practice has caught the attention of some critics, who have called for legislation and standards that would prohibit advertising these unapproved treatments (Turner 2011).

In reality, however, medical tourists do seek stem cell research for many unproven therapies. Some of these therapies have harmed patients. In one case, an Israeli boy with a rare brain disease was taken by his parents for treatment in Russia, against the advice of his home physicians. The boy's stem cell therapy may have led to the growth of a brain tumor. In another case, spinal injury patients contracted meningitis from stem cell treatments they received in China. Other patients have wasted money on worthless treatments or undergone unproven treatments rather than participate in legitimate research (Barclay 2009).

The International Society for Stem Cell Research (ISSCR) recommends that people who are considering stem cell therapy do their homework. They should use caution and ask numerous questions. They need to be sure that scientific evidence shows the safety and effectiveness of the treatment, that qualified providers have been involved throughout the research process, and that their rights to fully understand the procedure (known as "informed consent") and all of its benefits and risks are respected (ISSCR 2008).

Informed Consent

Informed consent is a legal procedure required in the United States and by many other medical systems. It means that before undergoing any medical procedures or participating in any medical research, a patient who is considered competent (e.g., who is not a young child or mentally impaired) receives an explanation of the procedures, their potential benefits and risks, and alternative courses of action. The patient must be able to understand and agree, or not agree, to participate. Patients who have gone through this process are considered to have all the information they need (they are "informed") about the procedure and are able to legally agree ("consent") to undergoing that procedure.

Informed consent is a concern in medical tourism, because there is no mechanism in place to ensure that the information prospective patients have in advance of their travel and treatment is accurate, or applicable to the specifics of their individual case. It is also unknown how well patients understand the risks and benefits of the procedures they are contracting (Snyder, Crooks, and Turner 2011). While some medical tourists are well armed with accurate medical information from medical professionals who are well versed in their case, it is likely that others commit to and undergo procedures without this process. Informed consent should be in place before medical tourists sign contracts or pay for any services (Turner 2011). The facilitator's role in this process is still a matter of debate.

Selling Organs

Purchasing organs for transplant is another serious ethical problem in medical tourism. The term "transplant commercialism" is used to describe situations in which organs are bought and sold as other commodities. As identified in Chapter 1, transplant tourism occurs when travelers obtain organs through illicit means or transplant commercialism, or when transplant resources benefit travelers at the expense of the local population ("Organ Trafficking" 2008). Evidence from Pakistan, for example, showed a disproportionate percentage of kidney transplants going to foreigners (Naqvi et al. 2007). Many of the living kidney donors were poor and unhealthy themselves, so donating a kidney put their own health at significant additional risk (Naqvi et al. 2008). Additionally, recipients can be put at undue risk because of inadequate donor screening, and poor tissue matching and testing.

Transplant tourism flourishes because the demand for donated transplant organs far outstrips the supply. People travel to get organs for which they would have had to wait a long time in their home country. In the United States alone, more than 100,000 individuals need lifesaving transplants. The wait time to receive a compatible organ ranges from days to years. Eighteen Americans die each day, on average, while waiting on an available organ (UNOS 2009).

In the United States, where selling organs for transplant is illegal, transplants are coordinated by the United Network for

Organ Sharing (UNOS). UNOS applies medical and scientific criteria in matching organ donors and transplant recipients. While UNOS does not oversee transplants elsewhere in the world, the organization does provide a contact list for those seeking information on transplants in other countries. UNOS opposes transplant tourism.

Patients from other countries can travel to the United States to undergo transplants. International patients must be accepted by one of the more than 250 accredited transplant centers in the United States. The same policies apply to international patients as to Americans seeking transplants. However, the number of such transplants is limited (UNOS 2009).

Globally, the poor and vulnerable are subject to exploitation for transplant tourists to obtain organs. According to WHO estimates, approximately 10 percent of all transplants around the world involve exploitation. The percentage is much higher in some locations ("Organ Trafficking" 2008). Organ traffickers in developing countries prey on the poor and uneducated, paying them as little as $1,000 for an organ that is then sold for as much as one hundred times that price in the West (World Health Organization 2004).

Among the plethora of transplant tourism practices that have raised ethical concerns, a Colombian-based company promised healthy kidneys or livers within the suspiciously short waiting time of 90 days (Fabregas 2007). More recently, Prime Minister Hashim Thaci of Kosovo was even being investigated at the time of this writing because of a Council of Europe report alleging that he was involved in organ trafficking at secret detention centers in the aftermath of the Balkan wars. Thaci has denied the allegations and threatened a libel lawsuit ("Kosovo" 2011). Some transplant tourists have gone to China, potentially receiving organs from executed prisoners who never agreed to the organ donation (Macartney 2005). Faced with stiff international criticism, China is attempting to address illegal transplants. Some of its efforts have generated controversy, both outside and inside the country ("Chinese Organ" 2011). Chinese researchers are now attempting to become leaders in the field of xenotransplantation (i.e., transplantation between species) with genetically modified pigs being bred specifically to supply organs to humans ("China to Host" 2011).

In 2008, more than 150 scientists, government officials, ethicists, and other representatives met in Istanbul, Turkey, to address many of the increasing and serious problems surrounding transplant tourism. The result was *The Declaration of Istanbul on Organ Trafficking and Transplant Tourism,* which condemns exploitative practices and encourages countries to develop "self-sufficiency" in the area of organ donation and transplantation. The Steering Committee of the Istanbul Summit observed that unethical practices involved in transplant tourism were harmful to the "legacy of transplantation" and the "nobility of organ donation" overall, and that the "success of transplantation as a lifesaving treatment does not require—or justify—victimizing the world's poor as the source of organs for the rich" (*The Declaration* 2011). It also called attention to the need to care for the health of living donors, reaffirming concerns expressed in the 2004 International Forum on the Care of the Live Kidney Donor (known as the Amsterdam Forum on Donors because the meeting was held in Amsterdam, Netherlands). The WHO is trying to control exploitative organ trade practices (WHO 2010). Although laws are being enacted, and transplants to travelers are increasingly being scrutinized or officially disallowed, enforcement remains a challenge.

The Economics of Medical Tourism

The U.S. health care system is very expensive. Compared to all other members of the 194 member states of the WHO, the United States spends the highest percentage of its gross domestic product (GDP) on health care (WHO 2000). Projections are that U.S. health care spending will be $4 trillion in 2015, equating to 20 percent of the national GDP (Nath 2007). Yet for all the money spent, the American health care system is not the top-ranked system in the world. In rankings that were contested by critics for the methodology, the WHO ranked the overall performance of the U.S. health care system as 37th in the world (WHO 2000).

Affordability

Traveling to another country for medical care can save consumers, by some reports and depending on the procedure, up to 80–90 percent off their medical bills. Yet procedures can still cost in the thousands of dollars. Add the costs of airfare, food, and accommodations, and medical tourism is still an expensive proposition—one that is not generally covered by insurance. Most U.S. private health insurers, as well as Medicare and Medicaid, won't cover health care abroad. Some insurers will cover emergency treatment overseas, but this coverage is designed for travelers, not the specific needs of medical tourists, and coverage expires within a month or two of the patient's arrival. (Medical evacuation to the United States, according to the U.S. Department of State, can cost upwards of $50,000.) The lack of insurance coverage for procedures performed in other countries may be one of the biggest barriers to the expansion of medical tourism.

Ironically, that means that the procedures that could save consumers considerable amounts of money are often out of reach to the people who need them most. Patients must pay their own expenses out-of-pocket. When the economy is strong, these costs are generally easier to bear. But during a recession, medical procedures—especially elective procedures such as cosmetic surgery—become luxuries. From 2007 to 2009, at the height of the U.S. recession, the number of Americans traveling abroad for elective procedures dropped by nearly 14 percent (Riczo and Riczo 2009). The combination of rising transportation costs and decreased incomes made it harder for many Americans to afford foreign health care.

Health Insurance

Many Americans rely on health insurance to help them pay for their health care needs. However, health insurance is expensive. In 2011 the average annual premiums for employer-sponsored health insurance were $5,429 for single coverage and $15,073 for family coverage. Insurance costs have increased disproportionately to workers' wages. Between 2001 and 2011, the average health insurance premiums for Americans covered under family plans increased by 113 percent (Kaiser 2011). In 2006, almost 47 million Americans, accounting for more than 15 percent of the entire U.S. population, did not have health insurance at all. Only 50 percent of all Americans had dental insurance. These statistics are even higher for foreign-born Americans (Kaiser Commission on Medicaid and the Uninsured 2007; Reed 2008).

Having insurance is no guarantee that medical bills can be paid. Twenty-five million Americans are underinsured, meaning that they do not have adequate health care insurance to cover their needs (Riczo and Riczo 2009). Many Americans are also precariously insured. Being precariously insured means living with the reality that they may lose their insurance at any time if circumstances change. Most insured Americans have health insurance that is provided through their employer's insurance plan. As overall health care costs go up, employers might drop or reduce benefits, or divorced spouses might lose coverage if their insurance was through their spouse's employer (Weitz 2010). Medical expenses are the main reason cited for personal bankruptcies in the United States. A sizeable portion of these bankruptcies are people who had health insurance, just not enough coverage to actually take care of their needs (Riczo and Riczo 2009; Sered and Fernandopulle 2005).

About half of all small businesses don't offer health insurance to their employees because of the cost. Even large businesses have begun to eye insurance costs more critically and reduce benefits accordingly. In 2006, employer health premiums increased by twice the rate of inflation. Insurers argue that they must increase premiums because of the rising costs of medical services (Nath 2007).

Employers and insurers in the United States and elsewhere have begun to investigate foreign medical care. Some insurers are starting to recognize how much money they can save by sending their customers abroad. Because insurers project that costs will be less for treatment abroad, these plans may also be offered at a lower cost to the insured. They may also offer to share cost savings with the insured and reimburse travel costs.

Industry analysts say that the availability of health insurance coverage for procedures performed in India, Thailand, or other countries could potentially expand the market, making medical tourism more accessible to the middle class. It also could relieve the strain on overburdened public health care systems (such as in Canada and Great Britain), while potentially saving health insurance companies—and the health care system as a whole—a great deal of money. By one estimate, if just 1 in 10 patients traveled abroad for treatment, the United States could save $1.4 billion a year (World Trade Organization 2009).

Several insurance models already in place incorporate medical tourism as an option. California legislation passed in 1999 allowed insurers operating in that state to reimburse authorized providers in Mexico. Access Baja, through BlueShield of California, offers a health network for people who travel to Mexico for their health care, with premiums that cost less than two-thirds of the other BlueShield of California plans. By 2005, 40,000 people had signed on for this less expensive coverage provided by Mexican health care providers (Herrick 2007).

David Boucher, with Blue Cross and Blue Shield of South Carolina, vacationed with his wife in 2006 to Thailand's Bumrungrad Hospital, staying in the hospital's hospitality suites and touring the medical facilities. His impression was so positive that he was quoted as saying, "If I or anyone in my family needs an operation, we're coming here." After returning home, he began Companion Global Healthcare, which assists members in seeking care in Bumrungrad and other destinations (Lindsay 2008). Companion Global Healthcare now provides discounts on services, including allergy control, hair restoration, cosmetic surgery, hearing aids, LASIK eye surgery, and prescription drugs.

In 2007, U.S. health insurer Aetna acquired Goodhealth Worldwide, an overseas private insurer. CEO Ronald Williams saw medical tourism as "an important emerging trend" (Lindsay 2008). Aetna then launched a pilot plan, partnering with Singaporean hospitals for expensive procedures (Anonymous 2008). Through Aetna, the New England-based grocery chain Hannaford began offering its insured employees the option of traveling to Singapore for knee and hip replacement (McQueen 2008).

Other companies are also adding, or seriously considering adding, travel abroad options. Among them, Florida's United Group Programs (UGP) began promoting special plans for medical tourism and surgeries in a Thai hospital in 2006. WellPoint introduced a pilot program in 2008 to let its members opt to have procedures in India. Corporate Synergies Group, Inc., which advises companies on worker benefits, says that at least a dozen of its clients with 250 to 2,000 employees are considering adding medical tourism programs in the next few years (McQueen 2008). By 2010 more than 200 employers across the country covered treatment abroad, and some included airfare for a travel companion in their benefits (Martin 2010).

Health insurers outside of the United States are also taking advantage of medical tourism to cut costs, decrease wait times, and alleviate overburdened systems. British insurer BUPA contracted with Ruby Hospital in India (McQueen 2008). Some Japanese companies send their employees to Thailand and Singapore, even for routine care (Connell 2011). In the European Union (EU), agreements between member nations allow cross-border health care, and require insurers to reimburse some medical care obtained in member countries other than the patient's home country. EU travelers can be covered by their home insurance in any EU or European Economic Area (EEA) country, as long as they have their proper paperwork or their European health insurance card (EHIC)—formerly the E111 form (Helble 2011). Early estimates suggest that approximately 4 percent of EU citizens have crossed borders for health care (Gallup Organization 2007).

Satori World Medical offers an innovative "Health and Shared Wealth Program." The program ties to employer-funded Health Reimbursement Accounts (HRA) that reimburse employees for qualified medical expenses. The program also works with Health Savings Accounts (HSA) and other models. Through Satori's shared savings model, some of the cost-saving is deposited (tax-free) into the employee's HRA, allowing the employee to use the funds for future health care. The deposits are also tax-deductible for the employer. Participants receive a package deal, including the medical procedure, travel, and accommodations in Satori facilities located in several countries. Satori claims several corporate partners. In June 2011, Hartford, CT, became the first major U.S. city to sign on with Satori services. The contract was to provide discounted surgical services in Puerto Rico. However, amid concerns that came to light about a previous unrelated fraud conviction of Satori CEO Steven Lash, the city of Hartford cancelled the contract before any patients actually took advantage of the agreement ("USA: Satori World" 2011).

Opposition to Insurance Coverage

Not all U.S. insurers are sold on the benefits of medical tourism, and others are approaching the issue tentatively. Insurers are concerned about whether the benefits will actually outweigh the risks. A botched procedure abroad can be very expensive when the patient returns home. As a result, some insurers only offer incentives to employees who are willing to travel within the United States to get discounted care (domestic medical tourism). Or, they offer reduced copayments or no out-of-pocket costs, in order to entice employees to stay in the United States.

Although the assumption might be that labor unions would support benefit changes that reduce insurance costs, some labor unions have actually opposed medical tourism benefits. The unions have expressed fears that allowing employees to seek care abroad reflects, and even extends, the practice of outsourcing. One blog on the AFL-CIO website was headlined, "First Employers Send Your Job Overseas. Guess What? You're Next" (Lindsay 2008).

Faced with fast growing health costs, Blue Ridge Paper Products (a North Carolina company that makes milk cartons) offered its employees the option of medical travel. Arguing that this constituted a unilateral change in the "terms and conditions" of employment, unions put an end to the plan before the first patient could travel to India for his procedure. "You create a slippery slope where medical tourism starts out as an option, maybe even an attractive option, but over a short period of time I believe will become mandated," said Stan Johnson, a union director in Nashville, TN (McQueen 2008).

Johnson also voiced concerns that medical tourism could become mandatory. "Do you end up sending your 80-year-old mother to India when she has never been sent outside of a 50-mile radius from home? You're going to put her on a plane and ship her to a hospital where they don't understand her language or her culture and where conditions may be suspect?" (Lindsay 2008). Supporters of medical tourism dismiss these concerns as misplaced and overblown.

References

Adlung, Rudolf. "Trade in Healthcare and Health Insurance Services: The GATS as a Supporting Actor (?)" World Trade Organization, December 15, 2009. www.wto.org/english/res_e/reser_e/ersd200915_e.pdf (accessed May 26, 2010).

American Telemedicine Association (ATA). "Telemedicine Defined." No date. www.americantelemed.org/i4a/pages/index.cfm?pageid = 3333 (accessed July 18, 2011).

Anderson, Lindsey. "Ailing U.S. Economy Delivers a Blow to 'Medical Tourism'; Fewer Americans Travel Abroad for Procedures." *USA Today,* November 30, 2009, D11.

Anonymous. "Operating Profit; Globalisation and Health Care." *The Economist* 388, no. 8593(2008).

Bajaj, Kapil. "Come, Heal Thyself." *Business Today,* March 11, 2007.

Barclay, Eliza. "Stem-Cell Experts Raise Concerns About Medical Tourism." *The Lancet* 373 (2009): 883–884.

Bezruchka, Stephen. "Medical Tourism as Medical Harm to the Third World: Why? For Whom?" *Wilderness and Environmental Medicine* 11 (2000): 77–78.

Birch, Daniel W., Lan Vu, Shahzeer Karmali, Carlene Johnson Stoklossa, and Arya M. Sharma. "Medical Tourism in Bariatric Surgery." *American Journal of Surgery* 199, no. 5 (2010): 604–608.

Bookman, Milica Z., and Karla R. Bookman. *Medical Tourism in Developing Countries.* New York, NY: Palgrave Macmillan, 2007.

"Cancer Cure Lottery: 10 Vaccine Treatments to Be Given Away Over 5-Week Period." *Yahoo! News.* September 13, 2011. http://finance.yahoo.com/news/Cancer-Cure-Lottery-10-prnews-502609295.html?x = 0 (accessed October 1, 2011).

Carabello, L. "A Medical Tourism Primer for U.S. Physicians." *Journal of Medical Practice Management* 23, no. 5 (2008): 291–294.

Carrera, P., and N. Lunt. "A European Perspective on Medical Tourism: The Need for a Knowledge Base." *International Journal of Health Services* 40, no. 3 (2010): 469–84.

Carruth, P. J., and A. K. Carruth. "The Financial and Cost Accounting Implications of Medical Tourism." *International Business and Economics Research Journal* 9, no. 8 (2010): 135–140.

Centers for Disease Control and Prevention (CDC). "Traveler's Health." July 25, 2011. wwwnc.cdc.gov/travel/ (accessed July 28, 2011).

"China to Host First Pigs for Animal-to-Human Organ Transplants." *People's Daily Online.* March 25, 2011. http://english.peopledaily.com.cn/90001/98649/7331430.html (accessed September 5, 2011).

"Chinese Organ Donation Plans Slammed." *HuffPost World.* September 5, 2011. http://www.huffingtonpost.com/2011/04/26/china-organ-donor-incentives_n_853794.html (accessed September 5, 2011).

Connell, John. *Medical Tourism.* Cambridge, MA: CABI, 2011.

Cormany, Dan. "Hospitality and Destination Marketing's Role in Medical Tourism: A Call for Research." *International Journal of Behavioural and Healthcare Research* 2, no. 1 (2010): 38–58.

Crooks, Valorie A., Paul Kingsbury, Jeremy Snyder, and Rory Johnston. "What Is Known About the Patient's Experience of Medical Tourism? A Scoping Review." *BMC Health Services Research* 10 (2010): 266–278. www.biomedcentral.com/1472–6963/10/266 (accessed July 3, 2011).

Crooks, Valorie A., and Jeremy Snyder. "Medical Tourism: What Canadian Family Physicians Need to Know." *Canadian Family Physician* 57 (2011):527–529.

"The Declaration of Istanbul on Organ Trafficking and Transplant Tourism." *Clinical Journal of the American Society of Nephrology* 3 (2008): 1227–1231. http://www.asn-online.org/press/pdf/2008-Media/

Declaration%20of%20Istanbul%20Study.pdf (accessed September 28, 2011).

Dignitas. "How DIGNITAS Works." June 2010. www.dignitas.ch/images/stories/pdf/so-funktioniert-dignitas-e.pdf (accessed July 30, 2011).

Duff, Eamonn, and Louise Hall. "The Ugly Facts Behind Beauty Tourism." The Age/Theage.com.au. September 30, 2007. www.theage.com.au/news/beauty/the-ugly-facts-behind-beauty-tourism/2007/09/29/1191090984137.html (accessed July 5, 2011).

Fabregas, Luis. "Transplant 'Tourism' Questioned at Medical Centers in Colombia." *Tribune Review*. February 18, 2007. www.pittsburghlive.com/x/pittsburghtrib/news/cityregion/s_493727.html (accesses July 1, 2011).

Final Exit. "World Laws on Assisted Suicide." August 28 2010. www.finalexit.org/assisted_suicide_world_laws_page2.html (accessed July 30, 2011).

Frenk, Julio, Lincoln Chen, Zulfi qar A Bhutta, Jordan Cohen, Nigel Crisp, Timothy Evans, Harvey Fineberg, Patricia Garcia, Yang Ke, Patrick Kelley, Barry Kistnasamy, Afaf Meleis, David Naylor, Ariel Pablos-Mendez, Srinath Reddy, Susan Scrimshaw, Jaime Sepulveda, David Serwadda, and Huda Zurayk. "Health Professionals for a New Century: Transforming Education to Strengthen Health Systems in an Interdependent World." *The Lancet* 36 (2010): 1923–1958.

Gahlinger, Paul. *The Medical Tourism Travel Guide: Your Complete Reference to Top-Quality, Low-Cost Dental, Cosmetic, Medical Care & Surgery Overseas*. North Branch, MN: Sunrise River, 2008.

Gallup Organization. Cross-Border Health Services in the EU: Analytical Report. *Flash Eurobarometer 210*. June 2007. http://ec.europa.eu/public_opinion/flash/fl_210_en.pdf (accessed January 22, 2012).

George, Babu P., Tony L. Henthorne, and Alvin J. Williams. "Determinants of Satisfaction and Dissatisfaction among Preventive and Curative Medical Tourists: A Comparative Analysis." *International Journal of Behavioural and Healthcare Research* 2, no. 1 (2010): 5–19.

Gill, J., B. Madhira, D. Gjertson, G. Lipshutz, J. M. Cecka, P. Pham, et al. "Transplant Tourism in the United States: A Single-Center Experience." *Clinical Journal of the American Society of Nephrology* 3, no. 6 (2008):1820–1828.

Hall, C. Michael. "Health and Medical Tourism: A Kill or Cure for Global Public Health?" *Tourism Review*. 66, no. 1/2 (2011): 4–15.

Helble, Matthias. "The Movement of Patients Across Borders: Challenges and Opportunities for Public Health." *Bulletin of the World Health Organization* 89 (2011): 68–72.

Herrick, Devon M. "Medical Tourism: Global Competition in Health Care." National Center for Policy Analysis. NCPA Policy Report No. 304, November 2007.

Hill, David R., Charles D. Ericsson, Richard D. Pearson, Jay S. Keystone, David O. Freedman, Phyllis E. Kozarsky, Herbert L. DuPont, Frank J. Bia, Philip R. Fischer, and Edward T. Ryan. "The Practice of Travel Medicine: Guidelines by the Infectious Diseases Society of America." *Clinical Infectious Diseases* 43, no. 12 (2006): 1499–1539.

Hitt, Emma. "Training Needed for U.S. Doctors Providing International Travel Advice." MedScape Medical News. November 11, 2010. www.medscape.com/viewarticle/732105_print (accessed July 10, 2011).

Hitti, Miranda. "Farrah Fawcett's German Cancer Care." WebMD. May 15, 2009. www.webmd.com/cancer/news/20090515/farrah-fawcetts-german-cancer-care (accessed July 5, 2011).

Hopkins L, R. Labonté, V. Runnels, and C. Packer. "Medical Tourism Today: What Is the State of Existing Knowledge?" *Public Health Policy* 31, no. 2 (2010): 185–198.

International Society for Stem Cell Research (ISSCR). *Patient Handbook on Stem Cell Therapies.* December 3, 2008. www.isscr.org/PatientHandbook.htm (accessed July 22, 2011).

Johnston, Rory, Valorie A. Crooks, Jeremy Snyder, and Paul Kingsbury. "What Is Known About the Effects of Medical Tourism in Destination and Departure Countries? A Scoping Review." *International Journal for Equity in Health* 9 (2010): 24–37.

Joint Commission International (JCI). "About Joint Commission International." No date. http://www.jointcommissioninternational.org/About-JCI/ (accessed February 21, 2012).

Kaiser Commission on Medicaid and the Uninsured. *The Uninsured and Their Access to Health Care: Fact Sheet 1420–09.* Washington, DC: Kaiser Family Foundation, 2007.

Kaiser Family Foundation and The Health and Research and Educational Trust. *Employer Health Benefits: 2011 Summary of Findings* (2011). http://ehbs.kff.org/pdf/8226.pdf (accessed September 28, 2011).

Kaiser State Health Facts. "Number of Paid Medical Malpractice Claims, 2008." www.statehealthfacts.org/comparemaptable.jsp?ind=436&cat=8 (accessed August 4, 2010).

Kraus, Jennifer. "Common Operation Across Border Goes Horribly Wrong." May 17, 2010. Available at: http://www.newschannel5.com/Global/story.asp?S=12487185 (accessed February 21, 2012).

"Kosovo Promises to Co-operate with EU Organ-Trafficking Probe." *Gulf Times.* June 14, 2011. www.gulf-times.com/site/topics/article.asp?cu_no=2&item_no=440841&version=1&template_id=39&parent_id=21 (accessed July 5, 2011).

Kumar, Rajesh. *Global Trends in Health and Medical Tourism.* New Delhi: SBS Publishers & Distributors Pvt. Ltd., 2009.

Law, Jacklyn. "Medical Tourism: Sun, Sand, and Stitches." *Canadian Business Online,* May 2008. www.canadianbusiness.com/entrepreneur/personal_development/article.jsp?content=20080501_198719_198719 (accessed May 24, 2010).

Lee, Bob, David Groves, and Julie Lengfelder. "The Changing Landscape of Health Care in the United States and Its Potential Influence Upon Medical Tourism." *International Medical Travel Journal* (2010). www.imtj.com/articles/2010/health-care-in-the-united-states-30600/ (accessed September 1, 2011).

Lerner, Barron H. "McQueen's Legacy of Laetrile." *The New York Times.* November 15, 2005. www.nytimes.com/2005/11/15/health/15essa.html (accessed July 5, 2011).

Lindsay, Greg. "Medical Leave." *Fast Company* 125 (May 2008): 109–120.

Lunt, Neil. "An Academic's View of Medical Tourism." *International Medical Travel Journal* (2009). www.imtj.com/articles/2009/an-academics-view-of-medical-tourism-30025/ (accessed July 10, 2011).

Lunt, N., and P. Carrera. "Medical Tourism: Assessing the Evidence on Treatment Abroad." *Maturitas* 66, no. 1 (2010): 27–32. Epub 2010 Feb 24.

Macartney, Jane. "China to 'Tidy Up' Trade in Executed Prisoners' Organs." *The Times.* December 3, 2005. www.timesonline.co.uk/tol/news/world/asia/article745119.ece (accessed September 1, 2011).

MacReady, N. "Developing Countries Court Medical Tourists." *The Lancet* 369, no. 9576 (2007): 1849–1850.

Madhok, Diksha. "Medicine: The Cutting Edge; State of the Art Hospitals, Groundbreaking Research and Major Government Reforms Are All Changing the Face of Healthcare Industry in India." *India Today,* October 12, 2009.

Martin, Richard. "Medical Tourism Draws More U.S. Patients to Travel for Care." Tampa Bay Times. March 15, 2010. http://www.tampabay.com/news/health/article1079824.ece (accessed February 21, 2012).

McQueen, MP. "Paying Workers to Go Abroad for Health Care." *The Wall Street Journal,* September 30, 2008, B9.

"Medical Tourism: Opportunity or Problem." No date. http:// liberationtreatmentccsvi.com/2011/05/medical-tourism-opportunity-or-problem/ (accessed July 5, 2011).

Medical Tourism Association (MTA). "Certification Programs." 2010. www.medicaltourismassociation.com/en/certification.html (assessed August 25, 2011).

Menvielle, Loick. "Medical Tourism: Paradoxes of Globalisation and Ethical Issues." *The Paradoxes of Globalisation.* Edited by Eric Millinot and Nadine Tournois. New York: Palgrave/MacMillan, 2010, 145–165.

Merrill, Molly. "First Nonprofit Medical Tourism Accreditation Service Launched." *Healthcare Finance News.* September 18, 2007. www. healthcarefinancenews.com/news/first-nonprofit-medical-tourism-accreditation-service-launched (accessed July 4, 2011).

Milstein, Arnold, and Mark Smith. "America's New Refugees—Seeking Affordable Surgery Offshore." *New England Journal of Medicine* 355 (2006): 1637–1640.

Moellering, Robert C., Jr. "NDM-1—A Cause for Worldwide Concern." *The New England Journal of Medicine* 363, no. 25 (2010): 2377–2379.

Naqvi, S.A.A., B. Ali, F. Mazhar, M. N. Zafar, and S.A.H. Rizvi. "A Socioeconomic Survey of Kidney Vendors in Pakistan." *Transplant International* 20 (2007): 934–939.

Naqvia, S.A.A., S.A.H. Rizvi, M. N. Zafar, E. Ahmed, B. Ali, K. Mehmood, M. J. Awan, B. Mubarak, and F. Mazhar. "Health Status and Renal Function Evaluation of Kidney Vendors: A Report from Pakistan." *American Journal of Transplantation* 8 (2008): 1444–1450.

Nath, Shyam Varan. "Global Medical Tourism: Dawn of a New Era." *Journal of Information Technology Case and Application Research* 9, no. 3 (2007): 1–5.

National Institutes of Health. "Stem Cell Basics." 2009. http://stemcells. nih.gov/info/basics/ (accessed September 5, 2011).

Ogden, Russel D., William K. Hamilton, and Charles Whitcher. "Assisted Suicide by Oxygen Deprivation with Helium at a Swiss Right-to-Die Organisation." *Journal of Medical Ethics* 36, no. 3 (2010): 174–179.

Patients Without Borders. "Ten 'Must-Ask' Questions for Your Physician Candidate." No date. www.patientsbeyondborders.com/ten-must-ask-questions-your-physician-candidate (accessed September 10, 2011).

Pawar, Sumit. "How Hospitals can Benefit by International Patients Service." June 9, 2011. www.medicaltourismcity.com/profiles/blogs/how-hospitals-can-benifit-by (accessed July 10, 2011).

"The Perfect English Service." Treatment Abroad Website. No date. www.treatmentabroad.com/about/client-services/perfect-english/ (accessed January 22, 2012).

Pollard, Keith. "Let's Abandon Medical Tourism!" *International Medical Travel Journal* (2010). www.imtj.com/articles/2010/lets-abandon-medical-tourism-30074/ (accessed July 23, 2011).

Ratner, Caroline. "A Legal Perspective on Medical Tourism in the USA." *International Medical Travel Journal* (February 18, 2011). www.imtjonline.com/articles/2011/a-legal-perspective-on-medical-tourism-in-the-usa-30094/ (accessed July 23, 2011).

Reed, Christie M. "Medical Tourism." *Medical Clinics of North America* 92 (2008): 1433–1446.

Reier, Sharon. "Medical Tourism: Border Hopping for Cheaper and Faster Care Gains Converts." *The New York Times,* April 24, 2004. www.nytimes.com/2004/04/24/news/24iht-rhealth_ed3_.html?pagewanted = all (accessed November 30, 2009).

Reisman, David. *Health Tourism: Social Welfare Through International Trade.* Cheltenham, UK: Edward Elgar, 2010.

Riczo, Steve, and Sarah Riczo. "Globalizing Health Care Through Medical Tourism." *USA Today* 138, no. 2772 (2009): 26–28.

Rodriguez-Williams, Yarissa, and Shawn Williams. "Medical Tourism: A Continuing Public Health Concern?" *International Medical Travel Journal* (2011). www.imtj.com/articles/2011/medical-tourism-a-continuing-public-health-concern-30108/ (accessed September 30, 2011).

Sered, Susan Starr, and Rushika Fernandopulle. *Uninsured in America: Life and Death in the Land of Opportunity.* Berkeley, CA: University of California Press, 2005.

Shetty, Priya. "Medical Tourism Booms in India, But at What Cost?" *The Lancet* 376 (2010): 671–672.

Simon, Tobby. "Symposium on Telecommunications." *Synergia.* www.wto.org/english/tratop_e/serv_e/telecom_e/sym_feb08_e/simon_e.pdf (accessed September 5, 2011).

Smith, Melanie, and Laszlo Puczko. *Health and Wellness Tourism.* Oxford: Butterworth-Heinemann, 2009.

Snyder, Jeremy, and Valorie A. Crooks. "Medical Tourism and Bariatric Surgery: More Moral Challenges." *The American Journal of Bioethics* 10, no. 12 (2010): 28–30.

Snyder, Jeremy, Valorie A. Crooks, Krystyna Adams, Paul Kingsbury, and Rory Johnston. "The 'Patient's Physician One-Step Removed': The Evolving Roles of Medical Tourism Facilitators." *Journal of Medical Ethics*. 2011. Published Online First: 8 April 2011 doi:10.1136/jme.2011.042374. http://jme.bmj.com/content/early/2011/04/06/jme.2011.042374.full.pdf (accessed July 3, 2011).

Snyder, Jeremy, Valorie Crooks, and Leigh Turner. "Issues and Challenges in Research on the Ethics of Medical Tourism: Reflections from a Conference." *Bioethical Inquiry* 8 (2011): 3–6.

Terry, Ken. "Telehealth Market To Hit $6.28 Billion By 2020." *InformationWeek*. September 20, 2011. www.informationweek.com/news/healthcare/mobile-wireless/231601670 (accessed October 10, 2011).

Timmons, Karen. "JCI Standards Address Physician Competencies." *Medical Tourism*. March 25, 2008. www.medicaltourismmag.com/article/jci-standards-address-physician-competencies.html (accessed July 7, 2011).

Turner, Leigh G. "Quality in Health Care and Globalization of Health Services: Accreditation and Regulatory Oversight of Medical Tourism Companies." *International Journal for Quality in Health Care* 23, no. 1 (2011): 1–7.

United Network for Organ Sharing. "What Every Patient Needs to Know." *UNOS* (2009). www.unos.org/docs/WEPNTK.pdf (accessed July 5, 2011).

University of Richmond, School of Professional & Continuing Studies. Certificate in Medical Tourism Studies. http://spcs.richmond.edu/professional/medical-tourism.html (accessed October 10, 2011)

"USA: Satori World Medical CEO's Chequered Past Brings End to Hartford Medical Tourism Deal." *International Medical Travel Journal*. 16 September 2011. www.imtj.com/news/?EntryId82 = 307508 (accessed September 25, 2011).

U.S. Department of State. "Health Issues." http://travel.state.gov/travel/tips/health/health_4971.html (accessed July 4, 2011).

U.S. Department of State. "India." http://travel.state.gov/travel/cis_pa_tw/cis/cis_1139.html (accessed August 5, 2010).

Weitz, Rose. *The Sociology of Health, Illness, and Health Care: A Critical Approach*, 5th ed. Boston: Wadsworth Cengage, 2010.

Wolff, Jennifer, Jane Bianchi, and Mary Kearl. "Passport to Cheaper Health Care?" *Good Housekeeping* 245, no. 4 (2007): 190–281. www. goodhousekeeping.com/health/cheaper-health-care-1007-5 (accessed January 22, 2012).

Woodman, Josef. *Patients Beyond Borders: Everybody's Guide to Affordable, World-Class Medical Travel.* Chapel Hill, NC: Healthy Travel Media, 2008.

World Health Organization. "Country Health System Profile: India." Last updated August 6, 2007. http://searo.who.int/EN/Section313/Section1519_10855.htm (accessed May 25, 2010).

World Health Organization. "Organ Trafficking and Transplantation Pose New Challenges." September 1, 2004. www.who.int/bulletin/volumes/82/9/feature0904/en/index.html (accessed May 25, 2010).

World Health Organization. *WHO Guiding Principles On Human Cell, Tissue And Organ Transplantation.* Resolution WHA63.22. May 2010. www.who.int/transplantation/Guiding_PrinciplesTransplantation_WHA63.22en.pdf (accessed July 6, 2011).

World Health Organization. The World Health Report 2000. *Health Systems: Improving Performance.* Geneva, Switzerland: WHO, 2000. www.who.int/whr/2000/en/index.html (accessed March 5, 2011).

Youngman, Ian. "How Many American Medical Tourists Are There?" *International Medical Travel Journal* (2009a). www.imtjonline.com/articles/2009/how-many-americans-go-abroad-for-treatment-30016/ (accessed July 20, 2011).

Youngman, Ian. "The Importance of Social Media and the Web in Medical Tourism." *International Medical Travel Journal* (2009b). www.imtj.com/articles/2009/medical-tourism-social-media-30023/ (accessed July 21, 2011).

"Zurich Voters Reject Ban on 'Suicide Tourism.'" May 15, 2011. www.swissinfo.ch/eng/politics/Zurich_voters_reject_ban_on_suicide_tourism.html?cid = 30236234 (accessed July 30, 2011).

3

Worldwide Perspective or Special U.S. Issues

The evolving picture of medical tourism is increasingly complex. It intertwines business and economic interests with health and wellness, leisure, politics, culture, and divergent value systems in an increasingly globalized world. It reflects patterns of power and privilege. Although cross-national regulation exists, this evolution in medical tourism is taking place with, some would argue, only minimal oversight.

Global Tourism

Tourism has become a major sector in international commerce, outpacing oil exports, food, and automobiles in volume. It is a motor for economic and social development and has become a major income source in many developing countries, with destinations competing for a share of the tourism market. Tourism provides economic growth in the form of demand for construction, food, and technologies ("Why Tourism?" n.d.).

The World Tourism Organization (UNWTO), a UN agency, focuses on tourism policy and practices. It promotes the development of responsible, sustainable, and universally accessible tourism practices, with an emphasis on reducing poverty in developing nations. At this writing, the UNWTO has 154 member countries and seven territories. Another 400 affiliate members are from the private sector, education, or tourism associations or authorities in various countries ("About UNWTO" n.d.).

In 1999, the UNWTO adopted the Global Code of Ethics for Tourism (GCET). The code consists of 10 articles (see chapter 6).

These principles promote responsible and sustainable tourism, and cover economic, social, cultural and environmental aspects of travel and tourism (UNWTO "Global Code" n.d.).

On the one hand, tourism can have detrimental impacts on the local economy. Tourism requires public resources to be spent on infrastructures rather than on education or health assets for the local population. Prices can increase with an infusion of tourists with money to spend, meaning locals also must pay more for basic necessities. In tourism, a high percentage of travelers' expenditures is not direct income supporting local businesses or workers. Labeled "leakage" in the travel industry, as much as 80 percent of these expenditures from "all-inclusive travel packages" go to entities such as airlines, hotels, or travel agencies in the traveler's home country (Kumar 2009, 179). Over reliance on tourism at the expense of other development puts economies at the mercy of wider economic problems and natural disasters, and if the tourism jobs are seasonal, workers experience insecurity from season to season.

On the other hand, tourism can contribute to economic growth. For example, tourists may spend locally and generate tax revenue. Tourism may stimulate local investment, create jobs, and encourage investment in infrastructure (Kumar, 181–185). While the impacts are a matter of debate, what is clear is that the tourism market itself globally has been booming, including "old favorites," but especially in developing countries (Menvielle 2010).

How medical tourism fits into this picture is still evolving. However, medical tourism clearly is a huge and increasing part of the picture. Emphasizing the medical rather than leisure aspect of medical tourism, medical tourism has become the fastest growing segment of the tourist market in many countries, including Thailand, Malaysia, and India (Bookman and Bookman 2007). Even the cruise industry is an emerging part of the medical tourism boom (Moran 2010; Ratner 2010).

Globalization and Medical Tourism

The importance of tourism generally, and medical tourism more specifically, to the world economy are facets of the phenomenon of globalization. Anthony Giddens, a sociologist and Director of the London School of Economics and Political Science who is well-known from his work on globalization, identifies globalization as "the intensification of worldwide social relations which link distant localities in such a way that local happenings are shaped by events occurring many miles away and vice versa" (1990, 64). Ongoing debates about the impact of tourism (including medical tourism) on destination locations certainly fit into that definition.

Although the specific definition of "globalization" varies somewhat among commentators, the term is commonly used to describe the increasing economic, social, and cultural connectedness of the world. Themes identified as occurring regularly in definitions of globalization and in literature on the topic include delocalization and supraterritoriality. (In delocalization, "[m]any of the activities that previously involved face-to-face interaction, or that were local, are now conducted across great distances" [Smith and Doyle 2002]. Supraterritoriality means that social and economic exchanges occur across borders or are even controlled elsewhere in the world). Other regularly occurring themes in discussions of globalization are impacts of the rapid spread of technological innovation, the rise of multinational corporations, the potential for economic instability and competition (Smith and Doyle 2002) and a diffusion of cultures around the world.

Globalization has facilitated the rapid expansion of medical tourism. It has lowered transportation costs and reduced language barriers. New developments in information technology have allowed easy access to information about foreign health providers. Globalization involves trade liberalization in services, another driving force in enhancing medical travel (Helble 2011). Globalization as applied to health care includes not only medical tourism, but also medical education, outsourcing and the movement of medical workers (Jenner 2008).

Medical tourism, in turn, is only one facet of the globalization of health care and biotechnology more generally (Connell 2011). This larger context, intertwining inseparably with medical tourism, includes:

- Organizational issues: transnational hospital groups and medical conglomerates, and the establishment of global standards (for example, through JCI) as discussed in chapter 2;
- The Internet, distance care, and telemedicine issues (also in chapter 2);
- Outsourcing (including a range of services such as laboratory diagnostics, call centers, medical transcription,

and insurance processing), telemedicine (including a range of delivery from reading X-rays to robotic surgery), social media that allows patient-to-patient networking, and the Internet as a major source of information on health care in general, and providers and options more specifically (see chapter 2);

- The cross-border mobility of skilled heath care workers (discussed further in this chapter);
- International pharmaceutical development and trade (discussed further in this chapter);
- The role of global nongovernmental organizations (e.g., *Medecins sans Frontiers*, known in English as Doctors Without Borders), and global programs targeting specific diseases such as HIV/AIDS.

These final bullet topics intersect with medical tourism in perhaps less obvious and often complicated ways that exceed the scope of this text's discussion.

How Does Medical Tourism Fit into a World Economy?

Increasingly, health care is treated as a commodity on the world marketplace, and a lucrative commodity at that. Developing countries see the potential for great economic benefits from medical tourism. Before the medical tourism boom, an Organisation for Economic Cooperation and Development (OECD) report noted that building their health care market provides developing countries with a competitive opportunity in the world economy (Bookman and Bookman 2007). More recently, Narsinha Reddy, marketing manager for Bombay Hospital, has said that "medical tourism would do for India's economic growth in the 2000s ten to twenty times what information technology did for it in the 1990s" (Bookman and Bookman 2007, 3). According to Renee-Marie Stephano, co-founder of the Medical Tourism Association (MTA), plans for promoting medical tourism have been established by 87 countries around the globe (Fiore 2011).

The privatization of health care in former socialist countries has also fueled the international health care market (Jenner 2008). Cuba was an early, major player in the medical tourism arena, targeting Latin American and Caribbean patients who would have otherwise traveled to the United States for medical care. Unlike most medical tourism destinations, the Cuban government maintains a monopoly on medical tourism in that country. Cuba has become a regional medical tourism destination, as well as being recognized for medical research and development and technology (Bookman and Bookman 2007). Filmmaker Michael Moore highlighted the Cuban health care system in his documentary *Sicko* (2007), which criticized the expensive, for-profit U.S. health care system.

In response to the opportunity to create an economic windfall, a number of governmental and business entities in developing countries are positioning themselves as destination countries. Many are investing in state-of-the-art medical capabilities and devoting other key resources to capture a share of the lucrative medical tourism market. In the summer of 2011, for example, Malaysia Airlines (MAS) announced an ambitious goal of flying 200,000 medical tourists (primarily from Indonesia, Bangladesh, and Cambodia) to Malaysia within a two-year timeframe to be treated in Malaysia's 35-plus hospitals targeting medical tourists ("MASholidays" 2011). Other countries planning or actively promoting medical tourism include Costa Rica, Cuba, Guatemala, India, Mexico, Thailand, and Lithuania (Fiore 2011; Jenner 2008).

Developed countries are also actively pursing the potential benefits of medical tourism both outside, and internal to, their own borders. These countries are responding to medical tourists' demands for high technology and high levels of customer service. The Munich Airport, for example, has established a clinic for medical tourists who never even have to leave the airport (Bookman and Bookman 2007). The U.S. Commercial Service (an entity within the U.S. Department of Commerce that is responsible for helping American companies establish new international markets) has recognized opportunities for medical equipment and instrument sales in the Philippines (Jenner 2008).

Some critics, however, see medical tourism as one facet of a troubling emerging global pattern of privatizing and commercializing health care. Allegedly encouraged by major financial institutions, medicine and health care are being treated as any other consumer good in a capitalist market. A direct consequence of such commodification according to this perspective is the exacerbation of systemic inequalities (O'Neill 2011).

Medical Tourism and Systemic Inequalities

Clearly, medical tourism is having an impact on health care systems in both sending and destination countries. What is much less clear, however, is exactly what those impacts are. Unfortunately, empirical data is sorely lacking. As author John Connell observes, "Detailed analysis of the national impacts of medical tourism is yet to occur and evaluations of its local, social, and economic effects are scarcely even fragmentary" (147).

What is clear is that medical tourism has forced attention to global inequalities. On the one hand, some commentators argue that developing countries are clearly strained for resources and medical tourism may exacerbate existing problems, or even create new ones. On the other hand, the argument is forwarded that medical tourism may result in changes that prove beneficial in the developing country.

Heath Care Inequities

Previous patterns of medical tourism generally involved rich travelers seeking expensive care at private facilities in developed countries. Increasingly, however, less-developed countries have sought to position themselves as leaders in the medical tourism market and to shed stereotypes of "Third World" facilities and poor quality care (Johnston, Crooks, Snyder, and Kingsbury 2010). As David Boucher, a Blue Cross and Blue Shield of South Carolina representative, said after visiting Thailand's Bumrungrad Hospital, "This is not a straw-village clinic with rusty scalpels!" and Curtis Schroeder of Bumrungrad said, "we're selling Cadillacs at Chevy prices" ("Operating Profit" 2008).

What happens to the local population when health care systems turn their focus to pampering medical tourists? Commentators on medical tourism look to the developing nations that are leading, or attempting to position themselves as major players, in the medical tourism market, and ask whether quality health care is available for all, or just for some? Often in developing nations, the state-of-the-art medical care that helps save tourists' lives is entirely unavailable for much of the country's population. Less-developed countries struggle with unsanitary conditions, diseases such as tuberculosis (TB) and malaria, high infant and maternal mortality, and a pervasive lack of health care. When a poor country's health care system focuses on high-tech and specialized medicine, the health care priorities are potentially distorted and drawn away from these more basic and pervasive issues (O'Neill 2011). This creates a two-tiered health care system—one for travelers and another for residents.

In India, for example, where medical tourists find outstanding hospitals equipped with the most modern technology, rural Indians lack basic medical services. Preventable diseases such as malaria and TB are still endemic, and the poor, in particular, struggle with diarrhea and measles. Life expectancy in some states is just 55 to 60 years, two decades less than in the developed world (World Health Organization 2007). Malnutrition deaths of Indian children top those in sub-Saharan Africa, and HIV/AIDS is a growing concern. Only a few of the country's 299 medical colleges produce quality doctors. Yet, the 1 percent of its GDP that India spends on public health ranks below the expenditures of most low-income countries (Madhok 2009). Similarly, in Thailand's Phuket International Hospital, the posh wing catering to medical tourists is far removed from the non-air-conditioned section that serves locals (Connell 2011).

The lower costs of medical services in developing countries are due to the lower cost of living, lower wages paid to physicians and health care workers, lower administrative costs, and cheaper medical devices. Concerns are raised that resources are being diverted from government-run health services. For example, the Indian government has offered financial incentives for medical tourism by giving it special tax status. Yet, while medical tourists experience first-class accommodations, the situation is vastly different for much of the local population. Author Christine Reed notes that in India fewer than half of the primary health centers have a labor room or laboratory, less than a third stock essential drugs, and only 20 percent have a telephone connection (Reed 2008). If medical tourism is to be ethical and sustainable, attention must be given to widening access and preventing exploitation of local citizens.

Medical tourists spend more than other tourists, pumping more dollars into local communities (Connell 2011; Johnston, Crooks, Snyder, and Kingsbury 2010). While this may be argued as a benefit, some critics also raise the issue of dependency, arguing that the economies of medical tourism destinations risk become dependent on foreign dollars, rather than on building sustainable local economies. Medical tourism also raises the standard of care to equal those of American hospitals. However, concerns have been raised that this may happen at the expense of local customs and that Western-style hospitals may replace local aesthetics (Johnston, Crooks, Snyder, and Kingsbury 2010).

Public Health

Unlike clinical care that focuses on individual patients, public health is concerned with the health of entire communities. Public health incorporates many different disciplines. Medical care providers such as doctors and nurses, social workers, social scientists (e.g., sociologists and psychologists), environmental scientists, and health educators work together to "fulfill society's interest in assuring conditions in which people can be healthy" (MedicineNet.com n.d.). Public health systems work to monitor community health, identify emerging concerns, and intervene when problems arise. They evaluate the effectiveness of health care interventions and programs. Public health systems also work to ensure access to quality, cost-effective health care for the entire population (Definition of Public Health n.d.). Major public health achievements of the 20th century include vaccinations, sanitation programs, and infectious disease control therapies that have reduced the spread of infectious diseases such as typhoid, cholera, and TB, and increased access to safe, effective family planning, among other notable achievements (CDC 1999).

The World Health Organization (WHO) is the authority within the United Nations system that is responsible for providing leadership on global public health. By the early 1990s, the WHO was already exploring medical tourism. At that time, Social Sector Development Strategies, Inc. (SSDS) was commissioned to assess the potential for selected Caribbean countries to attract medical tourists. Several of these islands have since become thriving medical tourism draws, even though the assessment concluded that they would be unlikely to do so (Gahlinger 2008). While Cuba (which has developed a specialization in skin diseases and eye treatments) has been the most successful of the Caribbean locations in attracting medical tourists, Antigua has become recognized as a destination for dental work and addiction recovery, and Barbados has focused on fertility tourists with in vitro fertilization clinics (Connell 2011).

Some proponents of medical tourism say that it is just what developing nations need to solve the enormous health disparities that currently exist and shore up public health systems. They argue that taxing health care on wealthy tourists could fund a broader public health system and improve access to care for poor residents. For example, after the breakup of the Soviet Union, the Cuban economy stayed afloat, buoyed by medical tourist dollars that supplied much of the country's hard currency revenues (Bookman and Bookman 2007). Trickle-down economic theories suggest that medical tourist dollars will benefit not only hospitals and hotels but also the wider local economy overall (Connell 2011).

But does public health benefit from medical tourism? In India, hospitals targeting medical tourists have benefitted from lobbying the government. Their efforts have resulted in inexpensive land, financing, and tax breaks. Yet, a 2005 report by the Indian government's own public accounts committee found that most subsidized private hospitals had not offered the free care for the local poor (meaning 25% of inpatients and 40% of outpatients) they were asked to provide. Because of the lack of accurate data other than "speculations and assumptions," it is impossible to get a clear picture of medical tourism's impact on Indian inequality (Shetty 2010). And what about other public sector resources in India and elsewhere? For example, when state resources are diverted from other uses to promote medical tourism, do other local needs on which the funds might otherwise be spent suffer (Connell 2011)?

And what about public health care systems in medical tourists' home countries? Medical tourists may have more nursing staff while traveling. Will they bring high expectations home with them and demand the same staffing, for example, after their return? This type of scenario could potentially tax publicly funded systems. Similarly, in the case of patients who require care through publicly funded health care systems after their return home, is medical tourism diverting public resources? Or do cost-savings even offset these potential expenses (Johnston, Crooks, Snyder, and Kingsbury 2010)? Like many aspects of medical tourism, the myriad questions raised in this area are in need of solid empirical data to provide answers that are based on fact rather than informed speculation.

Global Health Workforce

A complete picture of medical tourism requires considerations of the global health care workforce (Frenk et al. 2010). Like patients, medical workers also travel across borders. Their migration around the globe reflects larger patterns of globalization, trade in health services and products, increasing interdependence in health issues, and even intensified competition within and between medical entities (Frenk et al. 2010).

Migration of Skilled Medical Professionals out of Poorer Countries

The flow of providers has traditionally been out of poorer countries and into wealthier countries. Doctors and other skilled medical professionals from less-developed countries have often migrated to more-developed countries to take advantage of job availability, higher pay and standards of living, and the technology widely available in those countries. One-third or more of all doctors in the United Kingdom, Ireland, and New Zealand are foreign-trained. In the United States, one-quarter of all doctors are graduates of foreign medical schools (OECD 2010). The percentage of foreign-trained nurses in developed countries tends to be lower than the percentage of doctors, but in many countries this percentage has been increasing significantly (OECD 2010).

The large-scale movement of these health professionals can be problematic, resulting in a so-called brain drain, as medical expertise leaves less-developed countries, resulting in a shortage of skilled providers. According to the WHO, the worldwide shortage of health professionals topped four million in 2006. This shortage was especially critical in low-income countries, partially due to this "brain drain" factor (OECD 2010).

In 2006, a group of physicians in the Philippines ardently opposed a Philippine government initiative to promote medical tourism, arguing that it would further commercialize the country's health care system and exacerbate inequalities. Faced with a lack of jobs, Filipino doctors actually sought nursing credentialing to come to the United States. This "brain drain" in the Philippines resulted from systemic problems in paying physicians, not from too few physicians.

In general, the migration of health care workers from poorer to more-developed countries reflects such systemic problems; in other words, the migration is a symptom of problems rather than the cause. The loss of skilled health care providers then further exacerbates these problems and places additional stress on already over-stressed systems. However, in many countries, there would not be enough skilled health professionals being trained or available to meet the population's needs, even if all outward migration were stopped (OECD 2010). Proposed solutions lie not only in increasing retention, but also in improved educational opportunities and systemic efficiencies.

The role of medical tourism in this situation remains a matter of debate. On the one hand, concerns are raised that even if health professionals remain in their home countries, an internal "brain drain" will still pull them to the well-appointed facilities that cater to medical tourists. The concern is that even if physicians do stay or return to less developed countries, that these physicians may opt to treat wealthier international patients in well-equipped, private hospitals rather than practicing in poor areas, public institutions, or even teaching in medical schools (Kanchanachitra et al. 2011).

On the other hand, medical tourists bring money that can attract medical professionals, and can have the additional effect of improving health care for local impoverished populations. Some hospitals that serve tourists in developing countries must depend on locals for most of their business, and patients who have the means to travel potentially elect to get treated locally when there are quality facilities available (Johnston, Crooks, Snyder, and Kingsbury 2010). While new high-tech facilities do attract medical professionals, their presence, combined with competitive wages, may also encourage skilled medical professionals from the area to stay close to home, and the demand for their skills may result in training opportunities for locals (Gahlinger 2008; Johnston, Crooks, Snyder, and Kingsbury 2010). Training basic health care workers from the local area or region can be of significant benefit to the local population (Frenk et al. 2010).

Migration of Skilled Medical Professionals into Poorer Countries

The health workforce migration flow may also be in the other direction, with health care providers from wealthier countries traveling to poorer countries to provide care. (Physicians from poorer countries who return home after receiving their medical education in a wealthier country also fall into this category.) Increasingly, medical professionals from developed countries travel abroad to volunteer their expertise in a wide range of settings. Their destination has often been clinics or other locations where they could provide care to impoverished populations who lack other access to care.

Will medical tourism impact the practices and destinations of these traveling medical professionals? The growth of medical tourism may attract physicians to the same hospitals that also attract patients as medical tourists. Some physicians are attracted by the modern technology and state-of-the-art equipment that such facilities often offer. Some are attracted by the opportunity to live in a particular location. Some are attracted by the ability to pursue research agendas (for example, certain stem cell research) that are prohibited in their home country. These professionals are urged to learn and respect the local culture, and to find ways to teach and build using local resources, rather than creating a local reliance on outsiders or replacing local culture and resources (Bezruchka 2000).

Impacts of Migration on Medical Education and Ethics

Medical education can also be impacted by workforce migration and medical tourism. Currently, no global standard exists for health education and there is no systematic assessment of accreditation practices around the world. An unknown number of medical practitioners around the world have not even graduated from an accredited school. Migrating medical professionals also need cultural and global health competencies. Practitioners in the home countries of large numbers of medical tourists will increasingly need to manage patient cases of medical tourists (Frenk et al. 2010).

In response to these types of problems, medical education is being re-shaped. International bodies, including the WHO; the United Nations Educational, Scientific and Cultural Organization; the UNWTO; the International Institute of Medical Education (IIME); the World Federation for Medical Education (WFME); and regional organizations are working to establish standards for professional education, competency assessments, and collaborations.

The U.S. Institute of Medicine is also involved in this process (Frenk et al. 2010).

In May 2010, the 63rd World Health Assembly approved a voluntary code of conduct for the international migration of professionals. The "WHO Global Code of Practice on the International Recruitment of Health Personnel" aims to establish principles and practices for ethical health care recruitment and discourages active recruitment of health care workers from countries already facing personnel shortages. The intent is to strengthen the struggling health care systems in these countries (WHO 2010).

Regulatory Guidelines Impacting Medical Tourism

Regulatory guidelines are important in ensuring that medical tourism regulations in both destination and source countries are integrated rather than being piecemeal efforts. Otherwise, the guidelines may be less effective than desired, or enforcement may be lax if fears arise that less-regulated countries will develop pricing advantages (Crooks and Snyder 2010).

Oversight, however, has not kept pace with practice. Economics professor Davis Reisman (2010, 137–138) summarizes the complexities and interconnectivities of medical tourism, the larger public health picture, and globalization:

> The provision of public goods, the prevention of public bads, have long been regarded as a core duty of the State...Globalisation, however, alters the nature of the debate...SARS, AIDS, TB, H1N1, H5N1, Ebola, the Nipah virus are global bads that, like the fish in the ocean, cross the borders without a permit. Laboratory research, medical education, the Salk-Sabin vaccine are global goods that, like the eradication of smallpox or the containment of a pandemic, gift good health even on countries that have not made the investment...Globalisation is in the water and in the air. It is not just the health tourists who are crossing the borders. It is public health and public illness as well...however...There is no supra-national sovereignty. There is no international regulator. There is no effective courtroom. There is no cosmopolitan police

> force. There is no world authority with the power to tax,
> to compel or to quarantine. There is no border-free Minis-
> try of Finance that can compensate the victims...There is
> no border-free Ministry of Health that can guarantee the
> neighbourhood clinics that can deliver the incremental
> injections that can eradicate polio worldwide...Politics
> has lagged behind economics. Communicable diseases,
> environmental pollution, systemic inequities are no one's
> business precisely because they are everyone's business.
> It is a serious shortcoming.

Cross-national regulation, support, and private philanthropies
and cross-national charities have been instrumental in tackling
various aspects of medical tourism and related issues. What is
needed, however, is a "joint public venture" interested in the good
of all (Reisman 2010). The regulatory items discussed in this chapter represent some of the major international efforts in medical
tourism oversight.

International Health Regulations

Recognizing that germs know no political boundaries and can be
readily spread by international trade and travel in an increasingly
globalized world, the International Health Regulations (IHR) aim
to support public health measures, with minimal interference
to international traffic and trade. The IHR are legally binding in
194 countries.

The initial IHR of 1969 (preceded by the post–World War II
International Sanitary Regulations) focused on six "quarantinable
diseases": cholera, plague, yellow fever, smallpox, relapsing fever,
and typhus. Prompted by resurgences in the early 1990s of cholera
in South America, Ebola hemorrhagic fever in Africa, and severe
acute respiratory syndrome (a sometimes deadly viral respiratory
illness known widely as SARS that moved internationally with
travelers), the IHR was revised. The current version was adopted
in 2005 and became effective in 2007.

The 2005 IHR expands the scope of the regulations to any applicable health risk. These updated regulations also incorporate:
disease surveillance and response; transportation nodes such as
ports for ships, airports, and border crossings; and health documentation for such things as ship sanitation, vaccinations, and
prophylaxis (disease prevention or protection) for travelers. For

individual travelers, that means countries may require health information, basic examinations, and vaccination documentation. In turn, countries are required to respect travelers' dignity, human rights, fundamental freedoms, and confidential personal information (WHO 2008).

General Agreement on Trade in Services

The World Trade Organization (WTO) was established in 1995 with a mission "to open trade for the benefit of all." It promotes barrier-free, international trade by providing a negotiating forum for its members to work out agreements, legal and institutional frameworks for putting these agreements into practice and monitoring them, and settling disputes that arise involving these agreements.

The WTO's predecessor, the General Agreement on Tariffs and Trade (GATT), had been in place since the 1940s, but it covered only trade in merchandise, not services. Services have traditionally been viewed as domestic activities or governmental responsibilities. However, as the trade in world services outpaced trade in merchandise in the 1980s, the need for international rules regarding trade in services became apparent. The response to this need became the General Agreement on Trade in Services (GATS). Also put in place in 1995, the GATS became the first, and remains as the only, such set of widely agreed on rules governing international trade in services. All 153 members of the WTO have signed the GATS, and are expected to abide by its provisions.

The GATS covers all internationally traded services, including tourism in general, getting or receiving health care, telemedicine, and medical education. Questions have been raised as to whether the bureaucratic dispute process provided under the GATS is sufficient to balance commercial interests against medical interests that protect health and safety. Additionally, how can decision-making occur such that all interests are protected with the least conflict among members? Such questions are still in need of an answer (Lee, Sridhar, and Patel 2009). The WHO has some input into discussions on health-related matters, but not as much as some critics feel should exist (Lee, Sridhar, and Patel 2009).

Two additional WTO agreements (the Sanitary and Phytosanitary Measures Agreement [the SPS], and the Technical Barriers to Trade Agreement [the TBT]) are also in place, and specifically address food safety as well as the health and safety of animals and plants, and other general product standards. When a country abides by international standards on these types of matters, their practices are less likely to be challenged or disputed by the WTO than when a country uses only their own standards for oversight. (WTO "Standards" n.d.) The SPS Agreement and the TBT Agreement set the basic WTO rules in response to important questions surrounding food safety and trade.

Agreement on Sanitary and Phytosanitary Measures

"Sanitary" measures deal with human and animal health. "Phytosanitary" measures deal with plant health. The Agreement on Sanitary and Phytosanitary Measures (SPS) applies to both domestic and imported products. These measures incorporate a variety of safeguard approaches, including product processing, inspection, and treatment, and allowable pesticides and food additives.

The first question the SPS seeks to address is how to ensure that a country's consumers are supplied food that is safe to eat, as determined by appropriate standards. The second question under its purview is how to ensure that strict health and safety regulations are not used as an excuse for protecting the business interests of domestic producers. Thus, the challenge becomes ensuring a safe food supply for everyone, but doing so without impeding trade.

Under the SPS, countries can set their own standards for basic food safety, and to prevent the spread of pests or diseases among animals and plants, as long as these standards are based on science. Unjustified sanitary and phytosanitary measures cannot be established for trade protection. In fact, the SPS allows countries to prioritize food safety, and animal and plant health over trade (WTO 1998).

Technical Barriers to Trade Agreement

The Technical Barriers to Trade Agreement (TBT) is important in international trade to ensure the demand for high-quality consumer products are met, and that the costs of doing business internationally are manageable. Additionally, the agreement addresses growing global interest in environmentally friendly products, as concerns about water, air, and soil pollution mount.

Under the TBT, consumer products are dealt with through an assortment of technical regulations, standards, and conformity assessments. The technical regulations and standards address product characteristics such as size, how the product works, and presale labeling and packaging. Conformity assessment involves procedures such as testing, verification, inspection, and certification, which confirm that required regulations and standards are indeed being met.

The majority of technical regulations deal with protecting human health and safety. Requirements that motor vehicles have seat belts and that cigarette packages have labels warning of the health risks of smoking are two examples. Deceptive labeling practices also fall under the TBT. Importantly for medical tourists, pharmaceuticals and other health care products are incorporated under the quality standards it puts in place (WTO "Technical" n.d.).

Trade-related Aspects of Intellectual Property Rights

As part of the very structured and formalized governance of the WTO are various committees and councils for the Trade-related Aspects of Intellectual Property Rights (TRIPS). Because the TRIPS Agreement deals with patent law, including patents on medicines, it has important ramifications for medical tourism regarding pharmaceuticals and drug imports. The availability and quality of pharmaceuticals is an obvious concern as patients move across borders and trade zones.

The manufacture and import of generic versions of patented pharmaceuticals before the patent expires is an issue under TRIPS. This has proven to be an especially contentious issue with powerful interests, such as the pharmaceutical companies and U.S. government, attempting to protect their trade interests (Lee, Sridhar, and Patel 2009; Smith, Correa, and Oh 2009). Patents provide decades-long product protections that are potentially very lucrative financially. To maximize profits by holding off competition from generic versions of their drugs that can be legally manufactured and marketed after the patent on the original drug expires, pharmaceutical manufacturers have a financial interest in pressing for patent law enforcement. One result is that the cost of some pharmaceuticals remains high (critics argue excessively so), due to the lack of competition from less-expensive generic versions. Conflicts over access and affordability of HIV drugs in

Africa and elsewhere brought this issue to the world's attention (Ferreira 2002; Raja 2011).

In 2001, the WTO's Ministerial Conference (its highest-level decision-making body) met in Doha, Qatar. Among the business conducted at that conference was approval of the Declaration on the TRIPS Agreement and Public Health, commonly called the Doha Declaration (WTO 2011). The Doha Declaration affirms the importance of public health, promotes access to medicines for all, and takes the position that flexibilities in the TRIPS Agreement give governments the ability to deal with pressing health problems. In 2011, the Joint United Nations Programme on HIV/AIDS (UN-AIDS), the United Nations Development Programme (UNDP), and the WHO issued a joint policy brief, recommending that the flexibilities in the TRIPS Agreement and the Doha Declaration on the TRIPS Agreement and Public Health should be more widely used to ensure the affordability of HIV and other drugs vital to public health (UNAIDS, WHO, and UNDP 2011). However, numerous bilateral and regional agreements have also been negotiated separately by nations with regulations (TRIPS-plus provisions) that are even more stringent than the TRIPS Agreement. Critics argue that these provisions make flexibility more difficult in providing public health measures (Lee, Sridhar, and Patel 2009).

Why are international regulations addressing intellectual property rights important in medical tourism? One reason is because these rights are important to investors. "If a new endoscope or a wonder drug is easily pirated, the danger is real that First World innovations will not be taken abroad nor intellectual property developed" (Reisman 2010, 121). These regulations also impact the availability of medications and pricing. Drugs may be priced much higher in some nations than others. Americans travel to Canada or Mexico and elsewhere as pharmaceutical tourists for lower-priced drugs, which would cost them much more money if purchased in the United States. Pricing and other regulations can also mean that medicines are not available at all (Reisman 2010).

European Union (EU) Directive on Cross-border Health Care

The European Union, at this writing, is comprised of 27 member states: Austria, Belgium, Bulgaria, Cyprus, Czech Republic, Denmark, Estonia, Finland, France, Germany, Greece, Hungary,

Ireland, Italy, Latvia, Lithuania, Luxembourg, Malta, Netherlands, Poland, Portugal, Romania, Slovakia, Slovenia, Spain, Sweden, and the United Kingdom. Legal cases decided in the European Court of Justice have established that EU citizens have the right to travel to other EU member nations for health care that may be paid for by their home nation. The EU Directive on Cross-Border Healthcare has written these decisions into legislation.

The directive clarifies that patients may cross national borders to receive health care in EU member states other than their home country, with their home country paying as much of the patient's bill as would have been paid had the patient received care at home. Nations may require preauthorization in certain cases (e.g., especially for expensive or potentially risky procedures) and are expected to adopt measures to ensure access to treatment. They must also provide a range of information to their residents, informing them of their rights, entitlements, and the practicalities of receiving cross-border health care. Improved cooperation on aspects of telemedicine, diagnosis, and the treatment of rare diseases, and access to prescribed pharmaceuticals are all expected to be positive outcomes of the directive. Internet sales of medicinal products and medical devices, long-term care services provided in residential homes, and transplant organ allocation are, however, excluded from the directive, which was passed in 2011. Member states were given 30 months to enact the directive into national legislation, meaning that all state enactment should be completed in 2013 (Council of the European Union 2011).

Dr. Uew Klein, chair of the European Medical Travel Conference 2011, called the directive, "the most interesting experiment in global healthcare we ever have had" (Verrasto 2011). While Klein optimistically sees the directive as "the starter point for future integration of the European health care systems, involving all their standards and financial aspects," others feel that there may be little change in medical travel (Verrasto 2011).

Why Do Medical Tourists Pick One Country Over Another?

As these cross-border regulations reflect, a medical tourism industry can't exist in a vacuum. Not every country is equipped to handle medical tourists. Several criteria must be met in order for a nation to establish a successful industry and attract medical tourists. There must be infrastructure, trained personnel, money, economic and political stability, a supportive government, public administration, regulatory oversights, and operative legal systems. The geographic proximity of home and destination countries, medical specializations, and reputation also influence travelers' choices (Bookman and Bookman 2007). Additionally, countries need tourist appeal to be an attractive medical tourism destination. They must also look at factors such as costs, hospital accreditation, quality of care, and doctor training (see chapter 2).

Distance

Medical tourists are obviously willing to travel. However, proximity still plays a significant role in the destinations they select. Many medical tourists choose destinations that are closer, rather than farther, from their home. For example, India draws regional medical tourists from Bangladesh, Mauritius, and Nepal. China is a destination for tourists from Taiwan, Hong Kong, and Macau, as well as the far-eastern sections of Russia. Pacific Islanders often choose medical care in Australia or New Zealand. Medical tourists venture to Chile from its South American neighbor countries, while those from sub-Saharan Africa often head south for care in South Africa. Destinations for northern Africa and the Arab world often include Jordan and Dubai. Europeans move around the continent in search of medical care. Miami, Florida, hospitals attract patients from Latin America and the Caribbean. Mexico is a major source of services for Americans, especially those living near the border. Americans also seek care in Costa Rica and Canada (Bookman and Bookman 2007; Connell 2011; Gahlinger 2008); Reisman 2010 ; Woodman 2008). Conversely, Mexicans may seek emergency care in U.S. hospitals, or even citizenship by giving birth to a child on American soil and Canadians travel to U.S. destinations to avoid long wait times in the Canadian health care system ("USA: US Hospitals" 2011).

Geography also impacts health care systems and where care centers are established to attract medical tourists. Some Mexican hospitals that are destinations for medical tourists are owned by American-based hospital chains (Reisman 2010). India's Narayana Hrudayalaya hospital chain has identified northern Mexico as a favorable location for expansion due to its proximity to the United States (Reisman 2010). Similarly, Naresh Trehan (a cardiac physician and founder of India's Escorts Heart Institute) saw the possibility of a large health care complex in the Bahamas as a means to "deliver better medical care than America at half the price and half an hour away" (Bookman and Bookman 2007, 58).

Specialization and Reputation

Distance, while important to many, is often not the determining factor in choice of destination. New hospitals targeting American tourists often woo them by offering state-of-the-art medical equipment, streamlined paperwork and billing, and no waiting time for service (Gahlinger 2008). Hospitals in various locations have cultivated reputations and specializations that attract medical tourists. For example, medical tourists travel to Michigan hospitals for robotic procedures, high-beam radiation for cancer, spinal cord rehabilitation, and treatments for epilepsy. Babies with blinding eye conditions become medical tourists when taken to Michigan for specialized treatment ("USA: US Hospitals" 2011). Thailand is well known for sex reassignment surgery. King Hussein Cancer Center in Jordan attracts medical tourists seeking state-of-the-art cancer treatments. Escorts Heart Institute and Research Centre in Delhi and Faridabad are destinations for heart patients (Bookman and Bookman 2007). (Chapter 1 provides more specifics on the medical specializations for which various areas are known.)

The Medical Travel Quality Alliance (MTQUA) lists the world's 10 best medical tourism destinations. The rankings are based on aspects of quality, outcomes, patient management and marketing, value, safety and security, transparency, and service. The top-ranked hospitals in their assessment are:

- Fortis Hospital in Bangalore, India (formerly Wockhardt Hospitals)
- Gleneagles Hospital in Singapore
- Prince Court Medical Centre in Kuala Lumpur, Malaysia
- Shouldice Hospital in Toronto, Canada
- Shoen-Kliniken in Munich, Germany
- Bumrungrad International in Bangkok, Thailand
- Bangkok Hospital Medical Center in Bangkok, Thailand
- Wooridul Spine Hospital in Seoul, Korea
- Clemenceau Medical Center in Beirut, Lebanon
- Christus Muguerza Super Specialty Hospital in Monterrey, Mexico ("Top 10" 2010)

Infrastructure

For a country to attract medical tourists and for its medical tourism industry to thrive, it must have adequate infrastructure in place to support travelers' demands and expectations (Bookman and Bookman 2007). This means investing in transportation, communication, electricity, water, and sanitation. Travelers will go elsewhere if poorly maintained roads make transiting between locations uncomfortable or dangerous, and if taxis, buses, or rental vehicles are unavailable, dirty, or unsafe. Medical tourists expect to have clean water, clean and sanitary facilities, and reliable electricity. They will want to be able to communicate with friends and family "back home" and some will need to have reliable Internet connections for business reasons. Many will want to use the Internet wirelessly, or pay through e-commerce (Reisman 2010).

Political Stability

Political stability is essential for a medical tourism industry. Without a stable government in place, tourists will find it far too risky to travel to the country. Political unrest in the form of terrorism or riotous protestors is ongoing throughout parts of the developing world. The 2011 rioting of the "Arab Spring" that encompassed several Middle Eastern countries reversed the growth in medical tourism that Jordan had worked hard to develop. Much of the Jordanian market had depended on medical tourists from Libya and Yemen. In reaction, the Jordanian Ministry of Health set up a medical tourism unit specifically to promote Jordan as a medical tourism destination ("Jordan: Regional Turmoil" 2011; "Middle East, North Africa" 2011).

Other forms of civil disturbance can also increase the danger and inconveniences of travel. Criminals (including kidnappers) sometimes target tourists. Curfews may impede travel plans. Escalating violence from drug wars in Mexico have frightened off tourists seeking both recreation and medical care.

Political instability is not always avoidable in some developing nations, but countries do realize the importance of keeping their medical tourists safe. As a result, travelers are kept under careful supervision from the airport, to their hotel, to the medical facility. Before embarking on any trip, international travelers should always check with the U.S. State Department to make sure the country is stable. The State Department's Office of American Citizens Services and Crisis Management (ACS) administers the Consular Information Program that provides country-specific information, travel alerts, and travel warnings worldwide (U.S. Department of State n.d.).

Cultural and Language Issues

Medical tourists also need to be aware that they are traveling to locations that often have different cultural expectations than in their home country. Medical issues are not immune to culture. If anything, they have the potential to exacerbate cultural difference and misunderstandings. Some cultures recognize diseases that other cultures view as nonexistent. Causes of the same malady may be variously attributed to biological, psychological, or even supernatural causes across different cultures. How pain is perceived, addressed, and treated varies by culture. Medical treatment also varies widely across cultures. What is considered proper treatment for conditions as common as high or low blood pressure or a headache are even sometimes artifacts of culture. What is considered mainstream or alternative treatment also varies (e.g., Payer 1996). In other words, medicine is a science, but it also is culture.

Sometimes religion is important (Bookman and Bookman 2007). Muslims from the Middle East travel to Jordan and Malaysia for care. Infertility treatment clinics in Israel are open to all, but target Jewish clients. Clinics in Lebanon and London offer "second virginity" thorough hymenoplasty (hymen reconstruction), capitalizing on the Arabic world's emphasis on virginity (Menveille 2010). People want to know that they can pray and have their dietary needs met when they travel. Other travelers may be deterred from destinations where they are concerned that a religious focus might be overly emphasized.

Additionally, gender-based cultural expectations are critical in some countries. For example, women traveling to Middle Eastern countries, and certain areas in India and Southeast Asia, must be prepared to wear a scarf or cover their body. Gender relations may also be reflected in the health care institutions. The patient–physician relationship may be more patriarchal than some tourists from Western countries are used to having at home. Male doctors in other countries may not be as willing to collaborate with female nurses as they are in the United States. In some cultures, female doctors must attend to female patients.

Having a shared language and culture makes people more likely to visit a country (Bookman and Bookman 2007). Language barriers are a basic concern. It is reassuring to patients and their families to be able to communicate with the medical staff. Patients should be comfortable that language will not be problematic in terms of care or travel. It can help for patients to go to a country where they don't need an interpreter. Hospitals that cater to medical tourists, including those in the United States, have recognized the need for interpreters and may hire multilingual locals or immigrants to fill that role. When an interpreter is needed, it is important to be aware that interpreters come with varying levels of skill and cultural understanding. An interpreter who is unfamiliar with medical terms or issues can make effective communication with the hospital staff challenging or even dangerous.

Tourists should also remember that communication involves more than just words. Styles of communication, nonverbal communication, gestures, mannerisms, even how closely people stand to one another when conversing and which member of a group they address varies from culture to culture. Familiarity with these cultural protocols beyond just the spoken word can also be crucial to effective communication.

Before traveling, it is a good idea to learn about the cultural aspects of the destination country. The *CIA World Factbook* (www.cia.gov/library/publications/the-world-factbook/index.html) and the U.S. Library of Congress Country Studies (http://lcweb2.loc.gov/frd/cs/cshome.html) are two resources that provide a wealth of information, including historical, cultural, political, economic, geographic, military, and transnational issues for countries around the globe. (See chapter 8 for these and other resources.) Preparing for the culture of the destination country is a crucial part of trip planning that should not be overlooked or treated as an afterthought.

Choosing a Destination

Obviously, not all medical tourist destinations are the appropriate choice for every patient. Potential medical tourists are encouraged to do their homework on medical as well as social and cultural factors when considering the destination that is the best fit for their preferences and situation. The Medical Travel Quality Alliance (MTQUA) suggests that prospective medical tourists consider the following questions (MTQUA n.d.) when choosing a medical tourism destination.

One set of questions takes into account personal profiles.

- What are the patient's needs? A highly specialized surgeon or physician? Sophisticated high-tech equipment? Being near the familiar - home, family, friends?
- How big a factor is cost?
- Will this be a one-time-only event for the patient?
- Does the patient care if others know about the trip?
- What about travel plans? Will the trip also be a holiday? Is the patient well-traveled or experienced in living abroad? Will the patient be traveling alone? Does the patient have a passport that is valid for at least six months?
- Regarding destination choice, is the patient concerned about language and communication? Social and cultural customs, or religious practices? Seeing poverty?
- What expectations does the patient have for their accommodations (both in the hospital and after discharge)? Will recovery time be required before returning home?

A second set of questions address the medical procedure or treatment needs.

- Is the procedure a major surgery? Is it elective? Is it being performed as a corrective or follow-up procedure?
- Does the patient have support for this travel from his or her local physician? What about access to all reports of investigations and recommendations of any doctor who has seen the patient?
- How long will each stage of the procedure, from presurgery to postdischarge care management, take?
- What, if any, special physical or medical needs, allergies, or conditions does the patient have?
- What additional concerns does that patient have?

The U.S. Health Care System and Medical Tourism

The United States is both a source of medical tourists and a medical tourism destination. While some Americans travel abroad to seek cost savings, specialty care, or adventure, medical tourists from around the globe travel to the United States seeking faster treatment or specialties that are unavailable in their own countries. Americans also move internally around the United States to meet their health care needs. Indeed, this domestic medical tourism involves larger numbers of American travelers than does international medical tourism.

The United States as a Medical Tourism Destination

The post–World War II era established the United States as a leader in medical innovations. Inbound medical tourists (often the wealthy) came to centers such as the Mayo Clinic, Stanford University, Johns Hopkins, and the Cleveland Clinic, each of which established programs in the late 1980s for travelers seeking care at their facilities (Jenner 2008). Philadelphia International Medicine (PIM), consisting of the University of Pennsylvania Medical Center, Temple University Hospital, Children's Hospital of Philadelphia, and other entities, formed as a medical consortium specifically to attract international medical tourists (Abramson 2006). Other American health care centers also sought international patients.

American health care centers continue to market their services to the international community. They generate listings in international medical directories, court foreign business interests, and look to the Internet and social networking to attract medical tourists to U.S. shores. Some institutions have cultivated international partnerships targeting medical tourists, and marketed their reputations in various specialties. Miami Children's Hospital (MCH), for example, treats Russian children who are brought to the United States through an agreement with the Moscow Center for Pediatric Craniofacial Surgery and Neurology in Moscow. The hospital's medical helicopter also transports children from Latin America and the Caribbean to Miami for critical care. To offset costs for families traveling to be with ill children, the hospital has negotiated special housing rates ("USA: Miami" 2011).

More than 400,000 foreign medical tourists came to the United States in 2008. Their expenditures for health services approached US$5 billion. Many of these patients came to the United States from Middle Eastern countries, South America, and Canada. (Due to visa delays in the aftermath of the 9/11 attacks, the number of inbound medical tourists to the United States from Middle Eastern countries has fallen.) Overall, this inbound medical tourism accounts for approximately 2 percent of U.S. hospital patients (Deloitte 2008).

Most of these inbound medical tourists to the United States pay cash. However, some may pay for their care through third parties. Middle Eastern embassies may arrange payments for their patients. Other patients use insurance. Foreign patients can pay as much as 100 percent more than domestic patients (Abramson 2006). U.S. health care centers find affluent medical tourists who pay full price, rather than the discounted rates insurance companies often negotiate with hospitals, an attractive market. Reportedly, some Chicago area hospitals treat medical tourists from abroad who pay $120,000 for heart surgery and $40,000 for prostate surgery. Because insurers often have negotiated special lower rates with care providers, the financial return on the surgeries for an insured American might be much less for the hospital ("USA: US Hospitals" 2011).

Domestic Medical Tourism

Within the United States, where some patients find they can save 20–40 percent by obtaining their health care in another state, the domestic medical tourism market is also growing (Appleby 2010). Just like many international medical tourists, many domestic medical tourists travel in search of specialized care they are unable to get closer to home. For example, 70 percent of all Cancer Treatment Centers of America (CTCA) patients have traveled to CTCA hospitals from another state ("USA: 70%" 2011). The CTCA patient-empowered care model targets advanced-stage and complex cancers with a mix of high technology and complementary approaches that patients may not be able to readily find elsewhere.

Corporations and insurers are starting to pay more attention to domestic medical tourism as a cost-cutting measure. Lowe's, a self-insured national home improvement chain, made a three-year deal with the prestigious Cleveland Clinic to send its employees there for specific kinds of cardiac care. Similarly, the coal-mining firm Alpha Coal West sends Wyoming employees to Montana, Minnesota, and Houston for treatment of difficult ailments. The employees of both companies have no, or reduced, out-of-pocket costs and the travel costs for the employee and his or her partner or spouse are covered expenses (Appleby 2010).

Some insurers are utilizing, or favorable toward utilizing, such a model and even see it as an inevitable future. According to data from the Aon Hewitt Company, one in four U.S. employers are currently using domestic medical tourism for managing costs associated with critical and specialist care. Almost 40 percent of employers are considering this as an option within the next five years ("USA: Domestic" 2011).

Not everyone sees the increasing use of domestic tourism as a positive trend. Some find the practice concerning. Fully one-third of the employers in the Aon Hewitt data reported no interest in using domestic medical tourism ("USA: Domestic" 2011). Peter Hayes, a consultant with Health Care Solutions in Scarborough, Maine, observes that some insurers do not get on board because "it really angers the (local) provider community" when patients are sent elsewhere for health care (quoted in Appleby 2010).

American Opinion on Medical Travel

But what do Americans actually think about traveling to obtain medical care? According to a 2011 Deloitte Center for Health Solutions survey, fully 40 percent would travel domestically out of their local area for care if their doctor recommended that they do so. One-quarter of Americans would consider traveling to another country for a necessary or elective procedure. (Three percent said they would definitely do so; 22 percent indicated they might travel across borders for their care.) The percentage of potentially willing travelers is higher for the uninsured (31%) and for the young adults responding to the survey than for senior citizens (31% to 17%, respectively). However, the actual number of travelers is much lower. Only 1 percent of those polled said that they had traveled outside the United States to consult with a doctor, undergo a medical test or procedure, or receive treatment in the 12 months preceding the survey (Deloitte 2011).

Superior quality of care was the most important criteria that people cited in any decision to seek hospital care in another country. Seventy-nine percent of those who said they would definitely travel for care gave that response, as did 77 percent of those indicating "maybe" they would travel. The availability of needed services followed in a close second, cited by 77 percent of "definite" travelers and 74 percent of the "maybe" group. Lower out-of-pocket costs and more up-to-date technology were also cited as important by more than 70 percent of respondents in each category. Costs to third-party payers and shorter wait times trailed these other criteria, but were still important to at least half of all potential medical travelers. "Other benefits including the opportunity to see another country" were the least influential criteria in considering medical tourism. Only one-quarter of the definite travelers considered this important, as did one-third of the possible travelers (Deloitte 2011).

U.S. Health Care Reform and Medical Tourism

Although the percentage of Americans who have engaged in medical tourism seems relatively small, the significant number who have expressed favorable attitudes—or at least an openness toward the possibility of traveling abroad for medical care—raises the question of how medical tourism might impact health care at home. What will the impact be on domestic health care systems if patients increasingly seek care abroad? If insurers increasingly encourage medical tourism? If outsourcing, telemedicine, and distance care continue to take larger shares of the industry? And how do the costs of American health care and looming federally mandated changes in the health care system figure into the answers to these types of questions?

Cost control has become crucial for American health care. The United States has the costliest health care system in the world. Yet, for all that money, Americans get a health care system that ranks well out of first place when compared to the overall performance of other health care systems around the world. Problems with cost and performance are exacerbated by the significant number of Americans who are uninsured or underinsured (see chapter 2 for a discussion of these issues). Additionally, just less than one-quarter (24%) of Americans think the U.S. health care system works better than other health care systems around the world, and only 16 percent are satisfied with how the U.S. health care system performs (Deloitte 2011).

In 2006, the West Virginia state legislature entertained a bill (HB 4359) to allow state employees to obtain surgery outside of the United States. That was the first such bill to ever be introduced in a U.S. state legislature. The following year, a similar bill was brought before the Colorado General Assembly. Neither bill passed ("Colorado" 2007; Unti 2009; "West Virginia" 2006). However, the message is clear that medical tourism is increasingly being seen as a cost-control option. In 2006, the U.S. Senate Special Committee on Aging held special hearings on the subject of medical tourism and health care cost control. The hearing raised concerns, including lack of affordable insurance and quality, but also recognized the growth of medical tourism and its potential role in cost control (Jenner 2008; U.S. Senate 2006).

Some observers argue that medical tourism might actually lead to improvements in the U.S. health care system. Princeton University health care economist Uwe Reinhardt has observed that "[medical tourism] has the potential of doing to the U.S. healthcare system what the Japanese auto industry did to American carmakers" (Kher 2006). The competition could reduce costs, and as part of that effort, also reduce the many inefficiencies critics find in the administratively heavy U.S. system. Referring to U.S. hospitals, Reinhardt adds "A lot of them still don't know how to schedule their operating rooms efficiently . . . They've never had to. They always get paid, no matter how sloppy they are" (Kher 2006).

In March 2010, U.S. President Barack Obama signed into law the Affordable Care Act (ACA). The law outlines comprehensive insurance health insurance reforms that will roll out over the course of several years. The ACA legislation takes full effect in 2014. The legislation will incorporate changes in insurance regulations to include disallowing lifetime caps and denial of coverage based on preexisting conditions. Millions more Americans will receive insurance coverage. While the expanded coverage can be seen as a plus, financial concerns have also been voiced. Combined with ever-increasing health care costs, these changes many mean increasing costs to insurers.

Commentators are divided as to the impact the ACA will have on medical tourism abroad, and on the U.S. health care system domestically. Some believe that outbound American medical tourism will not be largely impacted by health care reform unless significant and systemic cost control measures occur (Rhea 2009). Others think the ACA might reduce medical tourism by ultimately reducing health care costs within the American system. That means some of the cost-saving incentives currently driving much of the impetus for medical tourism could be reduced. In that scenario, destinations might need to adjust their marketing strategies to continue to attract American travelers.

It is possible that health care reform could provide a boon to the medical tourism industry. Americans will likely still travel for procedures not covered by the reforms, such as plastic surgeries or experimental procedures. If waiting times increase due to the ACA reforms, Americans may elect to travel elsewhere for faster service. Medical tourism could become an even more attractive option to insurers looking for cost-cutting opportunities. Because the reforms may result in Medicare cuts, senior citizens might become more of a target population for medical tourism (Lee, Groves, and Lengfelder 2010). Even before the ACA reforms, the suggestion to allow Medicare recipients to purchase lower-cost health care abroad was already being voiced (Youngman 2009). The new medical landscape in the United States is going to increase the opportunity for medical tourism and cooperation among medical institutions (Lee, Groves, and Lengfelder 2010). Just what that landscape will look like is still being shaped.

References

Abramson, Hilary. "The Best Money Can Buy: Medical Tourism in the U.S.A." *New America Media,* February 2, 2006. Accessed November 20, 2009. http://news.newamericamedia.org/news/view_article. html?article_id = 5b7c206e74b96be675410f6f369b5113.

Altman, S.H., D. Shactman, and E. Eilat. "Could U.S. Hospitals Go The Way of U.S. Airlines?" *Health Affairs* 25, no. 1 (2006): 11–21.

Anonymous. "Operating Profit; Globalisation and Health Care." *The Economist* 388, no. 8593 (2008).

Appleby, Julie. "Latest Destination For Medical Tourism: The U.S." *Kaiser Health News* (July 27, 2010). www.kaiserhealthnews.org/Stories/ 2010/July/07/domestic-medical-tourism.aspx (accessed July 29, 2011).

Bezruchka, Stephen. "Medical Tourism as Medical Harm to the Third World: Why? For Whom?" *Wilderness and Environmental Medicine* 11 (2000): 77–78.

Bookman, Milica Z., and Karla R. Bookman. *Medical Tourism in Developing Countries.* New York, NY: Palgrave Macmillan, 2007.

Centers for Disease Control and Prevention (CDC). "Ten Great Public Health Achievements—United States, 1900–1999." *Morbidity and Mortality*

Weekly Report (MMWR) 48, no. 12 (1999): 241–243. www.cdc.gov/mmwr/preview/mmwrhtml/00056796.htm (accessed February 1, 2011).

Colorado General Assembly Bill 07–1143. www.statebillinfo.com/bills/bills/07/1143_01.pdf (accessed October 27, 2011).

Connell, John. *Medical Tourism.* Cambridge, MA: CABI, 2011.

Council of the European Union. "Directive on Cross-border Healthcare Adopted." February 28, 2011. www.consilium.europa.eu/uedocs/cms_data/docs/pressdata/en/lsa/119514.pdf (accessed September 28, 2011).

Crooks, Valorie A., and Jeremy Snyder. "Regulating Medical Tourism." *The Lancet* 376, no. 9751 (2010): 1465–1466.

Deloitte Center for Health Solutions. "Medical Tourism: Consumers in Search of Value." October 2, 2008. www.deloitte.com/view/en_HR/hr/industries/lifescienceshealthcare/article/964710a8b410e110VgnVCM100000ba42f00aRCRD.htm (accessed November 20, 2009).

Deloitte Center for Health Solutions. "Medical Tourism: Update and Implications—2009 Report." www.deloitte.com/us/medicaltourism (accessed December 7, 2009).

Deloitte Center for Health Solutions. *2011 Survey of Health Care Consumers in the United States: Key Findings, Strategic Implications.* 2011. www.deloitte.com/assets/Dcom-UnitedStates/Local%20Assets/Documents/US_CHS_2011ConsumerSurveyinUS_062111.pdf (accessed September 28, 2011).

Douglas, Darrell E. "Is Medical Tourism the Answer?" *Frontiers of Health Services Management* 24, no. 2 (2007): 35–40.

Dugan, Judy. "Medical Tourism—A Remedy for Insurers?" *Los Angeles Times.* November 3, 2009, A. 21.

Ellin, Abby. "Health Care Goes Global." *Delta Sky Magazine,* November 2009, 112–118.

Esola, Louise. "Emerging Models Aim to Boost Allure of Medical Tourism." *Business Insurance* 43, no. 27 (2009): 12.

Ferreira, Lissett. "Access to Affordable HIV/AIDS Drugs: The Human Rights Obligations of Multinational Pharmaceutical Corporations." *Fordham Law Review* 71, no. 3 (2002): 1133–1179.

Fiore, Kristina. "Medical Tourism: Boom or Bust?" *MedPage Today.* July 3, 2011. www.medpagetoday.com/PublicHealthPolicy/GeneralProfessionalIssues/27386 (accessed September 28, 2011).

Gahlinger, Paul. *The Medical Tourism Travel Guide: Your Complete Reference to Top-Quality, Low-Cost Dental, Cosmetic, Medical Care and Surgery Overseas.* North Branch, MN: Sunrise River, 2008.

Giddens, Anthony. *The Consequences of Modernity*. 1990. Stanford: Stanford University Press.

Helble, Matthias. "The Movement of Patients Across Borders: Challenges and Opportunities for Public Health." *Bulletin of the World Health Organization* 89 (2011): 68–72.

Herrick, Devon M. "Medical Tourism: Global Competition in Health Care." National Center for Policy Analysis. NCPA Policy Report No. 304, November 2007.

Horowitz, Michael D., and Jeffrey A. Rosensweig. "Medical Tourism—Health Care in the Global Economy." *Physician Executive* 33, no. 6 (2007):24–29.

Jenner, Elizabeth Anne. "Unsettled Borders of Care: Medical Tourism as New Dimension in America's Health Care Crisis." *Care for Major Health Problems and Population Health Concerns: Impacts on Patients, Providers and Policy*. Edited by Jennie Jacobs Kronenfeld. Bingley, UK: Emerald Group Publishing Limited, 2008, 235–249.

Johnston, Rory, Valorie A. Crooks, Krystyna Adams, Jeremy Snyder, and Paul Kingsbury. "An Industry Perspective on Canadian Patients' Involvement in Medical Tourism: Implications for Public Health." *BMC Public Health* 11, no. 416 (2011). www.biomedcentral.com/1471–2458/11/416 (accessed July 30, 2011).

Johnston, Rory, Valorie A. Crooks, Jeremy Snyder, and Paul Kingsbury. "What Is Known About the Effects of Medical Tourism in Destination and Departure Countries? A Scoping Review." *International Journal for Equity in Health* 9 (2010): 24–37.

"Jordan: Regional Turmoil Impacts on Medical Tourism." *International Medical Travel Journal* (September 9, 2011). www.imtj.com/news/?EntryId82 = 306471 (accessed September 25, 2011).

Kanchanachitra, Churnrurtai, Magnus Lindelow, Timothy Johnston, Piya Hanvoravongchai, Fely Marilyn Lorenzo, Nguyen Lan Huong, Siswanto Agus Wilopo, and Jennifer Frances dela Rosa. "Human Resources for Health in Southeast Asia: Shortages, Distributional Challenges, and International Trade in Health Services." *Lancet* 377 (2011): 769–781.

Kher, Unmesh. "Outsourcing Your Heart." *Time*. May 21, 2006. www.time.com/time/magazine/article/0,9171,1196429,00.html (accessed July 30, 2011).

Kumar, Rajesh. *Global Trends in Health and Medical Tourism*. New Delhi: SBS Publishers & Distributors Pvt. Ltd., 2009.

Landers, Jim. "No Country Has Perfect System, But There are Lessons to Learn." *McClatchy–Tribune Business News*, September 27, 2009.

Lee, Bob, David Groves, and Julie Lengfelder. "The Changing Landscape of Health Care in the United States and Its Potential Influence Upon Medical Tourism." *International Medical Travel Journal* (2010). www.imtj.com/articles/2010/health-care-in-the-united-states-30600/ (accessed September 1, 2011).

Lee, Kelley, Devi Sridhar, and Mayur Patel. "Bridging the Divide: Global Governance of Trade and Health." *The Lancet* 373 (January 31, 2009): 416–422.

Lindsay, Greg. "Medical Leave." *Fast Company* 125 (May 2008): 109–120.

Lubell, Jennifer. "New Tourist Attractions." *Modern Healthcare* 39, no. 24 (2009): 28–29.

Madhok, Diksha. "Medicine: The Cutting Edge; State of the Art Hospitals, Groundbreaking Research and Major Government Reforms Are All Changing the Face of Healthcare Industry in India." *India Today,* October 12, 2009.

Marlowe, Joseph, and Paul Sullivan. "Medical Tourism: The Ultimate Outsourcing." *HR. Human Resource Planning* 30, no. 2 (2007):8–10.

"MASholidays Eyes 200,000 Medical Tourists In Next Two Years." June 30, 2011. Bernama.com. www.bernama.com/bernama/v5/newsbusiness.php?id = 598084 (accessed September 15, 2011).

McQueen, MP. "Paying Workers to Go Abroad for Health Care." *The Wall Street Journal,* September 30, 2008, B9.

Medical Travel Quality Alliance (MTQUA). "How to Choose a Medical Destination That Is Best Suited for You." No date. www.mtqua.org/countries/how-to-choose-a-medical-destination/ (accessed September 28, 2011).

MedicineNet.com. "Definition of Public Health." No date. www.medterms.com/script/main/art.asp?articlekey = 5120 (accessed July 2, 2011).

Menvielle, Loick. "Medical Tourism: Paradoxes of Globalisation and Ethical Issues." *The Paradoxes of Globalisation.* Edited by Eric Millinot and Nadine Tournois. New York: Palgrave/MacMillan, 2010, 145–165.

"Middle East, North Africa: Medical Tourism Hit Hard by Arab Spring." June 17, 2011. www.imtj.com/news/?EntryId82 = 293867 (accessed September 28, 2011).

Moran, Na'ama. "Medical Tourism on Ships." February 3, 2010. http://seasteading.org/blogs/main/2010/02/03/naama-moran-medical-tourism-ships (accessed July 25, 2011).

Murphy, Tom. "Insurers Aim to Save from Overseas Medical Tourism." *USA Today*, August 22, 2009. Accessed October 21, 2009. www.usatoday. com/news/health/2009–08–22-medical-tourism_N.htm.

Nath, Shyam Varan. "Global Medical Tourism: Dawn of a New Era." *Journal of Information Technology Case and Application Research* 9, no. 3 (2007): 1–5.

Norton, Leslie P. "Medical Tourism Takes Flight." *Barron's* 89, no. 36 (2009): 24–25.

O'Neill, Emma. "Medical Tourism Versus Human Rights." *Voice.* 7, 1 (2011). http://voice.unimelb.edu.au/volume-7/number-1/medical-tourism-versus-human-rights (accessed September 3, 2011).

Organisation for Economic Cooperation and Development (OECD). "International Migration of Health Workers: Improving International Co-Operation to Address the Global Health Workforce Crisis." Policy Brief. February 2010. www.oecd.org/dataoecd/8/1/44783473.pdf (accessed September 15, 2011).

Payer, Lynn. *Medicine and Culture.* New York: Henry Holt, 1996.

Quesada, Jose. "Medical Tourism: An Economic Boost to the United States." *Medical Tourism Magazine* 11 (2009). www.medicaltourismmag. com/magzine_issue.php.

Raja, Kanaga. "Use TRIPS Flexibilities to Reduce HIV Drug Prices, Urge UN Bodies Published in SUNS #7110 dated 17 March 2011." TWN Info Service on Health Issues. 18 March 2011. www.twnside.org.sg/title2/health.info/2011/health20110305.htm (accessed September 4, 2011).

Ratner, Caroline. "Cruise Ship Medical Tourism: Will it Sink or Swim?" Interview with Dr. Uwe Klein. *International Medical Travel Journal.* 2010. www.imtj.com/articles/2010/cruise-ship-medical-tourism-30039/ (accessed July 5, 2011).

Reed, Christie M. "Medical Tourism." *Medical Clinics of North America* 92 (2008): 1433–1446.

Reisman, David. *Health Tourism: Social Welfare Through International Trade.* Cheltenham, UK: Edward Elgar, 2010.

Rhea, S. "Still Packing Their Bags: Health Reform Won't Drastically Alter the Economics of Medical Tourism, But Patients and Providers Can Expect New Opportunities, at Home and Abroad." *Modern Healthcare* 39, no. 30 (2009): 28–30.

Riczo, Steve, and Sarah Riczo. "Globalizing Health Care Through Medical Tourism." *USA Today* 138, no. 2772 (2009): 26–28.

Shetty, Priya. "Medical Tourism Booms in India, But at What Cost?" *The Lancet* 376 (2010): 671–672.

Sicko. Dir. Michael Moore. Dog Eat Dog Films. 2007. Documentary.

Smith, M. K. and Doyle M. "Globalization.' *Encyclopedia of Informal Education*. www.infed.org/biblio/globalization.htm (accessed September 1, 2011).

Smith, Pamela C., and Dana A. Forgione. "Global Outsourcing of Healthcare: A Medical Tourism Decision Model." *Journal of Information Technology Case and Application Research* 9, no. 3 (2007): 19–28.

Smith, Richard D., Carlos Correa, and Cecilia Oh. "Trade, TRIPS, and Pharmaceuticals." *The Lancet* 373 (2009): 684–691.

"Top 10 World's Best Hospitals for Medical Tourists." Medical Travel Quality Alliance (MTQUA). 2010. www.mtqua.org/providers/top-10-worlds-best-hospitals-for-medical-tourists/ (accessed September 1, 2011).

UNAIDS, WHO, and UNDP. "Using TRIPS Flexibilities to Improve Access to HIV Treatment." Policy Brief. March 17, 2011. www.unaids.org/en/media/unaids/contentassets/documents/unaidspublication/2011/JC2049_PolicyBrief_TRIPS_en.pdf (accessed July 29, 2011).

United Nations World Tourism Organization (UNWTO). "About UNWTO?" No date. http://unwto.org/en/about/unwto (accessed July 30, 2011).

United Nations World Tourism Organization (UNWTO). "Global Code of Ethics for Tourism." No date. http://ethics.unwto.org/content/global-code-ethics-tourism (accessed September 28, 2011).

United Nations World Tourism Organization (UNWTO). "Why Tourism?" No date. http://unwto.org/en/content/why-tourism (accessed July 30, 2011).

United States Department of State, Bureau of Consular Affairs, Consular Information Program, Office of American Citizens Services and Crisis Management (ACS). International Travel pages. No date. http://travel.state.gov/travel/travel_1744.html (accessed September 28, 2011).

United States Senate. Special Committee on Aging. *The Globalization of Health Care: Can Medical Tourism Reduce Health Care Costs?* Senate Hearing 109–659. 109th Congress, Second Session. June 27, 2006. Washington, DC. Government Printing Office. http://frwebgate.access.gpo.gov/cgi-bin/getdoc.cgi?dbname = 109_senate_hearings&docid = f:30618.pdf (accessed August 30, 2011).

"USA: Domestic Medical Tourism More Popular with U.S. Employers Than International." *International Medical Travel Journal* (August 18, 2011). www.imtj.com/news/?EntryId82 = 303269 (accessed September 28, 2011).

"USA: Miami Hospitals Seek Medical Tourists." *International Medical Travel Journal* (September 9, 2011). www.imtj.com/news/?EntryId82 = 306475 (accessed September 28, 2011).

"USA: 70% of American Cancer Treatment Centre Patients are Reported to be Domestic Medical Tourists." *International Medical Travel Journal* (August 26, 2011). www.imtj.com/news/?EntryId82 = 304423 (accessed September 28, 2011).

"USA: US Hospitals Promoting Inbound and Domestic Medical Tourism." *International Medical Travel Journal* (January 19, 2011). www.imtj.com/news/?EntryId82 = 269044 (accessed September 28, 2011).

Vequist IV, David G., and Erika Valdez. "Economic Report: Inbound Medical Tourism in the United States." *Medical Tourism Magazine* 11 (August 2009). www.medicaltourismmag.com/magzine_issue.php.

Verrasto, Nick. "Europe Healthcare Directive Could Open Up Travel Market." February 7, 2011. TravelMarket Report. www.travelmarketreport.com/content/publiccontent.aspx?PageID = 1370&articleid = 5078&LP = 1 (accessed September 30, 2011).

West Virginia State Legislature House Bill 4359. www.legis.state.wv.us/Bill_Text_HTML/2006_SESSIONS/RS/Bills/hb4359%20intr.htm (accessed October 1, 2011).

Woodman, Josef. *Patients Beyond Borders: Everybody's Guide to Affordable, World-Class Medical Travel.* Chapel Hill, NC: Healthy Travel Media, 2008.

World Health Organization (WHO). *International Health Regulations 2005,* 2nd ed. 2008. http://whqlibdoc.who.int/publications/2008/9789241580410_eng.pdf (accessed September 15, 2011).

World Health Organization (WHO). "The WHO Global Code of Practice on the International Recruitment of Health Personnel." WHA 63.16. 2010. www.who.int/hrh/migration/code/practice/en/index.html (accessed September 15, 2011).

World Trade Organization (WTO). *Declaration on the TRIPS Agreement and Public Health.* November 20, 2011. www.wto.org/english/thewto_e/minist_e/min01_e/mindecl_trips_e.htm (accessed September 28, 2011).

World Trade Organization (WTO). Standards and Safety. No date. www.wto.org/english/thewto_e/whatis_e/tif_e/agrm4_e.htm (accessed September 28, 2011).

World Trade Organization (WTO). *Technical Information on Technical Barriers to Trade.* No date. www.wto.org/english/tratop_e/tbt_e/tbt_info_e.htm (accessed September 28, 2011).

World Trade Organization (WTO). *Understanding the WTO Agreement on Sanitary and Phytosanitary Measures.* May 1998. www.wto.org/english/tratop_e/sps_e/spsund_e.htm (accessed September 28, 2011).

Youngman, Ian. "How Many Americans Would Consider Medical Tourism?" *International Medical Travel Journal* (2009). www.imtj.com/articles/2009/americans-going-abroad-medical-care-30015/ (accessed September 29, 2011).

4

Chronology

Pre-4th century BC   Egyptian temples are the earliest known institutions providing health care. The primary functions of these temples, however, were religious rather than medical.

The ancient Greeks travel to the Mediterranean hot springs and healing baths. Pilgrims and patients come from all over the Mediterranean to temples of the healing god and son of Apollo, Asclepius (the Greek god of health). Treatments involve rituals, cleansing, offerings, snakes, and drug-induced sleep.

4th century BC   King Pandukabhaya of Sri Lanka has hospitals built around the country. Records in the Mahavamsa (an ancient chronicle of Sinhalese royalty) are the first written evidence of institutions specifically dedicated to treating the sick. Mihintale Hospital in Sri Lanka, the remains of which are still a popular tourist attraction, may be the oldest hospital in the world.

circa 1500 BC   Indian Ayurveda dates back five thousand years. The four Vedas (Rigveda, Yajurveda, Samaveda, and Atharvaveda) are the oldest Hindu literature. Atharvaveda contains medical knowledge in the form of charms, prayers, hymns, and incantations. In addition to health, the content also addresses other aspects of life, such as success

119

and protection from dangers. Its content is the basis of Ayurveda, a perspective that still appeals to medical tourists.

1000 BC
Chinese writings about medicine date at least this far back in history. An extensive body of ancient writings on health and illness will develop that covers prevention, treatment approaches and outcomes, sexuality, folklore, specific conditions and diseases, and physician's duties, among other topics.

700 BC
Cold water bathing for warriors is introduced by the Greeks. Historically, cold water therapies are also used in other cultures. Cold water therapy is still used for medicinal and health purposes, including to boost immune function and circulation.

600–300 BC
The Persians use steam baths and mud baths. Many modern spas also offer both treatments.

The Greek physician Hippocrates lives from approximately 450–380 BC. Known as the "Father of Medicine," he offers a new medical paradigm that sees illness as based on physical, rather than supernatural, causes. He also views the body as a whole system, and makes detailed observations, making him the first person to document several illnesses. His code of ethical behavior for physicians remains the basis of modern medical ethics. Hippocrates also writes about the healing powers of water. This is the earliest known reference to water having healing properties.

circa 230 BC
King Ashoka founds 18 hospitals in India. These hospitals, paid for by the royal treasury, have physicians and nursing staff. Whether these facilities had an actual hospital function has been debated by modern scholars.

200 BC
The Hebrews use water as ritual purification. Rituals involve hand washing or immersion of

the entire body. Water will continue to be used in various forms and ways throughout history in healing and wellness rituals. Some of these rituals are religious or spiritual in nature, while others are not.

By this date, the Dead Sea is already an established source of immersion therapy.

circa 100 BC   Romans create valetudinaria (hospitals) for the care of sick slaves, gladiators, and soldiers. Civilians and the general public were not regularly treated in these facilities.

Massage is practiced at least back to this date in what is now Thailand. Even more ancient texts from other cultures suggest that forms of massage were already used elsewhere.

Greek physicians travel to Rome, where physicians have low status until the arrival of Asclepiades. He becomes a popular physician, founding a medical school possibly influencing Julius Caesar (100 BC–44 BC) to grant citizenship to freed Greek physicians.

1st millennium AD   State-supported hospitals appear in China.

Tourism, including tourism for health reasons, becomes fashionable. Romans, for example, travel to Alexandria, Egypt, Wiesbaden, or the Lipari Islands north of Sicily. They also travel to visit "oracles" (such as the famous Oracle at Delphi) for fortune-telling.

AD 100   A thermal resort is established in the Belgian town of Spa by this date. It becomes so famous that by the 16th century, the term "spa" comes into common usage, referring to thermal spa resorts.

325   Spurred by the growth of Christianity, the First Council of Nicaea orders that every cathedral town have a hospital. Hospitals built by the physician Saint Sampson in Constantinople, and by

Basil, bishop of Caesarea, are among the earliest of these institutions.

Patients bathe at a shrine in Bath, England. Bath's spa has been renovated and is a current destination for modern medical tourists.

500–1500   In Europe, the early part of the Medieval era is a time of monastic medicine. The early Christian church (in Byzantium) officially controls medicine, and believes in religious causes and interventions for illness. Lay practitioners pass along secular healing knowledge. Hospitals are also religious communities where monks and nuns provide care. In addition to institutions that care for a variety of conditions, specialized institutions also care for lepers or pilgrims.

Arab hospitals become teaching centers and physicians are afforded high status. These hospitals link Greek medicine to the later Renaissance.

737   Located near Izumo, Dogo Onsen, Japan's first onsen (hot spring) opens. Today, onsens are spread throughout Japan. These popular destinations, believed to have beneficial health properties due to their mineral content, play a central role in the Japanese tourism industry.

800   Turkish baths are built in the Ottoman Empire. Crusading British knights will use them in 1200.

1000   By now, spas are appearing in Finland, along the Baltic.

1130   Viewing it as a disruption to monasteries, the Council of Claremont forbids monks from practicing medicine. This, combined with the diseases and plagues sweeping Europe, introduces the age of scholastic medicine and the rise of secular practitioners and university medical education. Medicine will become increasingly specialized and tied to education in schools of medicine.

1170   After a conflict with King Henry II, Thomas Becket (the Archbishop of Canterbury) is murdered.

He is martyred and monks rename a Southwark infirmary after him. In 1993 the hospital bearing his name will become famous and merge with Guy's Hospital. Together they will form the Guy's and St. Thomas NHS Foundation Trust.

9th–10th centuries   Spas are established in central Europe in what are now Hungary and the Czech Republic.

Hospitals built in Baghdad employ up to 25 staff physicians and have separate wards for different conditions.

European tourism begins in the form of the medieval pilgrimage, such as the travel taken by the pilgrims portrayed in Chaucer's famous *Canterbury Tales*. Pilgrimages still occur today, with pilgrims traveling to places such as Lourdes or Mecca, among other destinations.

15th century   Public bathing in warm water becomes a concern for some Europeans, amidst fears of spreading diseases such as syphilis, leprosy, and plague. The Bishop of Bath and Wells also declares naked, mixed bathing as immoral.

16th–17th centuries   Water therapy treatments become a popular medical practice. In Italy, sulphurous springs in Abano and mud baths in Padua, Lucca, and Caldero are common destinations.

1553   The first European Spa Directory is published in Venice. It lists more than 200 spas.

1571   In an attempt to keep Britons from traveling to Belgian spas, Queen Elizabeth I popularizes public bathing.

17th century   It becomes fashionable for sons of English nobility and gentry to take extended tours of England as educational experiences. The 18th century will become the golden age of these Grand Tours.

An interest in spa waters, supported by spa visits from European royalty, spawns research on chemical, mineral, and temperature properties. Spa waters are seen as healing, not simply relaxing, during this era. Mineral waters are said to treat a variety of afflictions ranging from gout to liver disorders and bronchitis.

18th century   Modern hospitals begin to appear. They are staffed with physicians and surgeons. The advent of germ theory and modern nursing in the late 1800s will shape and propel the course of modern medicine and the modern hospital.

Health tourism becomes important. In England, it is associated with spas. Visiting spas becomes fashionable for the wealthy, with Bath being the most fashionable spa of the time. Popular spas are also in Buxton, Harrogate, and Tunbridge Wells, among other locations. The upper classes visit these places for the spa waters, as well as for the balls and other entertainment.

In the United States, White Sulphur Springs, Virginia, and Saratoga Springs, New York, are popular sites, attracting visitors from a wider income and social class range than the primarily wealthy visitors to the European spas.

Medicine and travel for health reasons changes with the growth and expansion of the Industrial Revolution, as does virtually every other aspect of life.

Spas will be replaced in popularity by sea bathing, and "hill stations" will become popular after the Industrial Revolution. Many of these hill stations are mountain retreats, such as sanitariums for tuberculosis (TB), or other destinations for rest and recuperation. They are located at altitudes high enough to avoid mosquitoes. TB, also called "consumption," has existed throughout recorded history. Crowded, poor, and unsanitary urban conditions that accompany the growth of the Industrial Revolution increase concerns over TB. Public health efforts and the development of antibiotics curb the incidence of this disease. However, multi-drug resistant TB strains have continued to be an issue worldwide since the 1990s.

1710   Charité Hospital is founded in Berlin, Germany. Originally established to quarantine victims of the plague, the hospital today has several campuses and is one of the largest in Europe.

1719   Peter the Great builds the first resort in Russia, and deems building spas and treatment facilities state priorities. These facilities will be well supported by the Russian aristocrats who travel to resorts that rival their European counterparts.

1724   Guy's Hospital is founded in London from a bequest by the wealthy governor Thomas Guy. In 1993, Guy's will merge with St. Thomas, forming the Guy's and St. Thomas NHS Foundation Trust.

1751   Pennsylvania General Hospital is chartered. Founded by Benjamin Franklin and Dr. Thomas Bond, the hospital is now part of the University of Pennsylvania Health System.

1784   Viennese General Hospital (*Allgemeines Krankenhaus*) opens and becomes the world's largest hospital. The hospital is now the site of the Medical University of Vienna and remains one of the largest hospitals in the world.

Thalassotherapy (the therapeutic use of seawater) becomes popular, especially in France. Sea bathing is later popularized by the Prince Regent (George IV) who travels to Brighton for this treatment. Doctors begin to recommend Brighton for its physical and psychological health benefits and many move there themselves.

1796   Edward Jenner invents the smallpox vaccine. The world's first successful vaccine is an early accomplishment in the emerging interest in public health. Public health implications are a major concern in modern medical tourism.

19th century   Travel brochures begin to advertise health treatments at many locations around the globe.

During this century, the Second Viennese Medical School emerges. Basic medical science expands and specialization advances. The first dermatology, eye, ear, nose, and throat clinics are founded in Vienna.

King George III makes regular visits to Weymouth when he is in poor health. The king suffers from mental illness, which is thought to be related to porphyria. Porphyria is a rare inherited disorder involving problems with hemoglobin (a protein in red blood cells responsible for carrying oxygen).

Early in the century, especially in Sweden, modern massage techniques are being developed. Swedish massage is now a well-known type of therapeutic massage.

The first modern hydrotherapy spa is established in Germany. Hydrotherapy (variously known as water therapy, balneotherapy, and hydrothermal therapy) now has many accepted uses in modern medicine. Depending on the condition to be addressed, it variously involves hot or cold water, ice, or steam.

Wealthy Europeans travel to various destinations on other continents.

In mid-century, the growth of railroad and steamship travel make recreational travel available for the first time to the middle class and laborers.

Most of Europe and the United States have established public and private hospital systems by mid-century. Their use and specialization will increase over the course of the century.

Also by the mid-19th century, physicians are moving to the Harley Street section of London,

England. Patients flock there to see doctors in various specialty areas. Harley Street will continue to be a global destination until the National Health Service is established in 1948. By the early 2000s, Harley Street is revived as a developing site for medical tourism.

1806 The first European-style spa in the United States opens in Saratoga, New York.

1840 The India hill station at Darjeeling becomes the informal summer capital of the Bengal president. It will become known as a sanitarium and health resort. It remains a popular tourist destination today.

1851 The Royal Marsden Hospital is established in London, England. Originally named the Free Cancer Hospital, it is the world's first hospital dedicated to the study and treatment of cancer.

In New York, the first medical school based on principles of water cure—the American Hydropathic Institute—opens. Several other hydropathic schools will open during this decade.

1880 Father Sebastian Kneipp, a Bavarian monk, offers hydrotherapy to the poor. Kneipp will become known as the "Father of Hydrotherapy" He will travel and become a well-known author and advocate for hydrotherapies and other alternative approaches to health and wellness.

Spa treatments for the war wounded and seaside vacations for industrial workers are popularized across Europe.

1900s The popularity of coastal resorts fades until sunbathing (rather than seeking the curative effects of water and sea air) becomes popular on its own.

German doctors use heliotherapy (medical therapy using exposure to sunlight) to treat tuberculosis and rheumatism. Also known as light therapy or phototherapy, versions of heliotherapy have been around since ancient times. Heliotherapy has evolved to incorporate artificial light and has several accepted uses in modern medicine, including the treatment of mood disorders and skin problems such as psoriasis.

1910   In New York City, Elizabeth Arden opens the first day spa. It serves as a finishing school and offers beauty treatments. One hundred years later, these "Red Door Spas" are in 31 locations nationwide, advertising exceptional customer service, quality, and expertise. Their vision is to enhance visitors' lives through "beauty, harmony, and well-being."

1925   The International Congress of Official Tourist Traffic Associations (ICOTT) sets up in The Hague. After World War II, it will be renamed the International Union of Official Travel Organizations (IUOGO) and move to Geneva, Switzerland.

1934   The International Union of Official Tourist Propaganda Organizations (IUOTPO), The Hague, is created.

1937   The words "tourist" and "tourism" are first used by the League of Nations, defined as people traveling abroad for periods of more than 24 hours.

1940   Edmond and Deborah Szekely found the world's first destination fitness resort and spa in Tecate, Baja California, Mexico.

1940s   Although cosmetic dental practices date back to at least hundreds of years BC, modern cosmetic dentistry makes its emergence in California late in the decade. The term "cosmetic dentist" will be coined in the 1990s. Today, dentistry (including cosmetic procedures) is a major and specialized area of medical tourism.

Medical mud is used during World War II to treat wounded soldiers. This approach reflects the ancient history of peloid therapy (mud baths), which derives from the belief that certain muds have therapeutic properties due to their mineral or microorganism content. Many modern spas offer mud treatments, and tourists still travel to spas (for example, in Russia) that specialize in mud treatments.

1947   The IUOTPO converts to the International Union of Official Travel Organizations (IUOTO). The organization is granted consultative status by the United Nations the following year.

1948   The National Health Service is established in Great Britain on July 5.

The General Agreement on Tariffs and Trade (GATT) comes into force. It is later extended by the General Agreement on Trade in Services (GATS), which is established in 1995 after being adopted by the World Trade Organization (WTO).

1950s   Modern spa resorts appear in the United States for the first time. Most are centered in California; they will not begin to spread across the country until the 1990s. The first of these is the Golden Door Spa Resort, which focuses on weight loss and personal fitness.

1952   Christine Jorgensen makes headlines after traveling from the United States to Denmark for sex reassignment surgery. Born George Jorgensen, the World War II soldier will become a celebrity and entertainer. Although people had previously traveled to Europe, Mexico, or Morocco for sex reassignment surgery, Jorgensen becomes the first to do so in a public forum.

1960s   Technical breakthroughs in the United States attract patients with financial means from around the world. The United States becomes a leader in medical innovations.

1963   Plastic surgeon Dr. Ivo Pitanguy establishes his now-famous clinic in Rio de Janeiro, Brazil, after studying similar clinics in the United States and England.

The United Nations convenes a Conference on Tourism and International Travel in Rome. The conference adopts a series of recommendations on definitions, international statistics, international travel formalities, and tourism development.

1965   Amid controversy, Johns Hopkins establishes the Hopkins Gender Identity Clinic and becomes the first U.S. hospital to formally establish a sex reassignment program. Americans can now undergo this surgery domestically, rather than having to travel abroad.

1967   The United Nations declares 1967 as International Tourism Year (ITY). The slogan selected for the year is "Tourism, Passport to Peace."

1969   The Intergovernmental Conference in Sofia, Bulgaria, and the UN General Assembly call for the creation of an intergovernmental organization on tourism.

1970s   American hospital chains begin to expand globally. Locations include the Gulf region, Europe, Latin America, and other targeted areas (e.g., Singapore and Malaysia) that will emerge as major medical tourism destinations.

1974   The cosmetic procedure liposuction (also known as lipoplasty) is invented by Dr. Giorgio Fischer, an Italian gynecologist. Liposuction will become one of the cosmetic procedures regularly sought by medical tourists, who may pay less than half the price for procedures abroad than for procedures performed in the United States.

The Ashram, the first fitness spa, opens in California. It offers a boot camp-styled program of weight loss and fitness programs. Located in the Santa Monica Mountains and readily accessible from Malibu and Los Angeles, the Ashram will develop a celebrity clientele.

1975   The IUOTO becomes the World Tourism Organization (UNWTO). Its first General Assembly is held in Madrid in May.

1978   The world's first successful "test-tube baby," Louise Joy Brown, is born in Great Britain. This heralds the future of in vitro fertilization, and many other infertility treatments to follow. Traveling in search of infertility treatments will grow into the lucrative practice of "reproductive tourism."

1980s   Prestigious medical centers in the United States develop formal programs to attract patients from abroad. These centers include the Mayo Clinic, Johns Hopkins Hospital, and the Cleveland Clinic.

1980   September 27th is celebrated as the first "World Tourism Day." The day becomes the annual recognition of world tourism. The date is chosen because it is the anniversary of the UNWTO Statutes, adopted on September 27, 1970.

American actor Steve McQueen makes headlines when he travels to Mexico to receive cancer treatments that are not approved in the United States. McQueen dies in Ciudad Juárez, Chihuahua, Mexico, a day after undergoing surgery. His celebrity brings attention to alternative and complementary treatments, which are now both the subject of medical research and sought by medical tourists.

1980   The Manila Declaration on World Tourism is adopted by the World Trade Organization. It focuses on guidelines for balance and equality in tourism development to guard against the potential harm tourism can bring to less-developed countries. Controversies still continue to surround the local and regional impact of medical tourism on destination countries.

1984   The U.S. Congress passes the National Organ Transplant Act (NOTA), mandating the establishment and operation of the Organ Procurement and Transplantation Network (OPTN) to maintain a national registry for organ matching. U.S. Code Title 42, Section 273 dealing with organ procurement organizations is the result of NOTA and its amendments.

1985   Focusing on understanding and international cooperation, the Tourism Bill of Rights and Tourist Code is adopted at the UNWTO General Assembly held in Sofia, Bulgaria.

1989   The Inter-Parliamentary Conference on Tourism adopts the Hague Declaration on Tourism. The declaration cites both the 1948 United Nations Universal Declaration of Human Rights and the 1966 United Nations International Covenant on Economic, Social and Cultural Rights. The focus of the declaration is its 10 Articles on international cooperation and the role of leisure and tourism in world peace.

1990   The World Travel and Tourism Council (WTTC) is established. It bills itself as "the global forum for business leaders in the Travel & Tourism industry."

1991   The 44th World Health Assembly, in resolution WHA44.25, endorses the WHO Guiding Principles on Human Organ Transplantation. They will be updated in 2009.

1993   The International Network of Agencies for Health Technology Assessment (INAHTA) is established to facilitate the sharing of health technology assessments. The nonprofit organization has grown to include 53 member agencies from 29 countries, which cooperate to share information.

1994   The World Trade Organization (WTO) is created. It is "the only global international organization dealing with the rules of trade between nations."

1995   The General Agreement on Trade in Services (GATS) comes into force. Adopted by the WTO and negotiated by 120 nations, the GATS continues the previous work of the General Agreement on Tariffs and Trade (GATT), which has been in place since 1948.

1996   The Health Insurance Portability and Accountability Act of 1996 (HIPAA) Privacy and Security Rules passes in the United States. These HIPAA guidelines protect the privacy of personal health information and ensure the electronic security of that information. HIPAA does not apply in most foreign countries (except for limited privacy protection in Europe), so patients should ascertain how their medical records will be handled outside of the United States.

1997   Luxurious medical spas, combining both western and alternative treatments, are introduced by U.S. doctors.

1998   The Swiss association Dignitas is founded. Taking advantage of Swiss laws allowing euthanasia under certain circumstances, Dignitas becomes well known for providing services for "suicide tourists." The controversial organization is later featured in various media, including a 2007 PBS *Frontline* television show titled "The Suicide Tourist" directed by John Zaritsky.

1999   The Joint Commission launches its international affiliate agency, the Joint Commission International (JCI). The Joint Commission International (JCI) provides accreditation for hospitals, laboratories, and other health care facilities that meet its patient safety standards. JCI staff travel to inspect hospitals, applying similar but culturally adjusted standards to the ones used in the United States. The American Medical Association advises anyone traveling overseas for care to select a JCI-accredited facility.

The International Society for Quality in Health Care (ISQua) launches its International

Accreditation Programme (IAP). The IAP "accredits the accreditors" in process improvements aimed at increasing the quality and safety of health care around the world.

California legislation passes, allowing insurers operating in that state to reimburse authorized providers in Mexico.

The Global Code of Ethics for Tourism (GCET) is adopted by the World Tourism Organization. Consisting of 10 articles, these principles promote responsible and sustainable tourism, and cover the economic, social, cultural, and environmental aspects of travel and tourism.

2001　　Norway establishes "The Patient Bridge" to send patients who are waiting for care to Sweden, Germany, and Denmark to cut wait times.

The World Tourism Organization adopts the Seoul Declaration on Peace and Tourism and the Osaka Declaration for the Millennium. These declarations acknowledge the need for mutual cooperation in tourism, to help bridge inequalities and economic, social, cultural, and technological gaps between nations.

2002　　A World Health Assembly Resolution urges the World Health Organization and member states to pay close attention to problems of patient safety.

This year sees the pursuit of global human organ and tissue transplantation safety standards. These efforts include:

- The International Atomic Energy Agency (IAEA) issues a set of International Standards on Tissue Banks. The Standards come from the IAEA because of that organization's interest in the use of radiation to sterilize bone and other tissues.

- The *Guide to Safety and Quality Assurance for Organs, Tissues and Cells* is published by the Council of Europe.

- The European Commission proposes a Directive of the European Parliament and the Council of Ministers. The emphasis is on various quality and safety standards in the use of human tissues and cells.

Ecotourism is the focus of international attention, as this year is declared the International Year of Ecotourism. The World Ecotourism Summit in Quebec, Canada adopts the Quebec Declaration on Ecotourism. In Johannesburg, South Africa, a declaration of the World Summit on Sustainable Development references the sustainable development of tourism.

Commercial surrogacy becomes legal in India. India becomes the leading global destination for commercial surrogacy (one facet of reproductive tourism).

2003   The UNWTO becomes a specialized agency of the United Nations. Approval is granted by United Nations General Assembly resolution A/RES/58/232.

Djerba, Tunisia, hosts the First International Conference on Climate Change and Tourism.

The WTO approves the Sustainable Tourism—Eliminating Poverty (ST-EP) program. As the name of the program suggests, the program seeks to leverage tourism in fighting poverty. It is tied to the UN's Millennium Development Goals, which specifically seek to cut extreme poverty by half by 2015.

2004   Recognizing patient safety as a global health issue, the World Health Organization (WHO) launches the World Alliance for Patient Safety. The organization focuses on international collaborations and action, and continues to offer patient safety improvement programs globally.

The Tourism Policy Forum convenes in Washington, DC, in October. It is followed by the

Washington Declaration on Tourism as a Sustainable Development Strategy. The declaration identifies sustainable tourism as a means of reducing poverty.

Madrid, Spain, hosts the First World Conference on Tourism Communications (TOURCOM), emphasizing the relationship between tourism and the news media.

"Medical tourism" appears as a topic in Wikipedia.

2005   The American Society of Plastic Surgeons (ASPS) is the first medical organization to address medical tourism. The ASPS posts a briefing paper on its website, providing information to patients considering cosmetic surgery abroad.

The World Medical Association (WMA) passes its "Resolution on Organ Donation in China." The resolution "demands that China immediately cease the practice of using prisoners as organ donors."

The U.S. television news show *60 Minutes* airs a brief feature on Bumrungrad International Hospital in Bangkok. The hospital receives more than 3,000 emails from Americans in response. At the end of the decade, Bumrungrad International is named one of the top 10 medical tourist destinations in the world by the Medical Travel Quality Alliance (MTQUA).

2006   In June, the Senate Special Committee on Aging holds hearings on the issue of medical tourism. The Hearing raises concerns, including a lack of affordable insurance and quality, but also recognizes the growth of medical tourism and its potential role in health care cost control. The Chair, Senator Gordon Smith, calls for a task force of experts to explore the impact and safety of lower-cost health care abroad.

In West Virginia, HB 4359 is introduced before the state legislature. It is "A BILL to amend the

Code of West Virginia, 1931, as amended, by adding thereto a new section, designated §5–16–28, relating to establishing a system to reduce the cost of medical care paid by the Public Employees Insurance Agency by providing incentives to covered employees to obtain treatment in low cost foreign health care facilities accredited by the Joint Commission International." The bill is not passed, but is notable because it is the first such bill to ever be introduced in a U.S. state legislature.

Stem cell research (tied to stem cell therapies sought by some medical tourists) takes a step forward when scientists learn how to "reprogram" specialized cells to behave like embryonic stem cells. These cells are called induced pluripotent cells, or iPS cells.

Tehran, in the Islamic Republic of Iran, hosts the First International Conference on Tourism and Handicrafts. A later report will note that, although Iran was once a health care destination, wars, a lack of government support, and visa issues have negatively impacted the country's medical tourism.

Hip resurfacing, a less-invasive alternative to hip replacement, is approved in the United States. American patients can now obtain this procedure at home rather than having to travel.

In May, the European Court of Justice rules in the Watts Case. The court finds in favor of Yvonne Watts, a British citizen seeking reimbursement for a hip replacement she obtained in France after a year's wait at home. The court rules a year to be an "undue delay." This case is important in the rights of EU citizens to seek care in other EU member nations.

Malaysia legalizes the advertising of local hospitals. All ads must be approved by the Medical Advertisements Board (MAB) under the Ministry of Health. Exaggerated claims are disallowed.

2007
The Colorado General Assembly entertains Bill 07–1143. This bill seeks to establish "incentives for state employees who are covered under a state self-insured group benefits plan who elect to obtain medical care in an accredited foreign health care facility when the cost of such care is lower in the foreign facility than in a covered U.S. facility." The bill is postponed indefinitely.

HealthCare Trip, a 501 (c) (3) nonprofit service of HealthCare Tourism International, launches as an information portal and service specifically for health travel safety.

China issues the "Provisions on Human Organ Transplant" on May 1, prohibiting organ transplants for foreign visitors. The action is taken in response to charges of rampant illegal organ trafficking in the country.

On June 15, the world implements the International Health Regulations (IHR). Legally binding in 194 countries, these regulations recognize that germs know no political boundaries and can be readily spread by international trade and travel in an increasingly globalized world. The IHR aim to support public health measures with minimal interference to international traffic and trade. (www.who.int/ihr/about/en/).

Cordoba, Spain, hosts the First International Conference on Tourism, Religions and Dialogue of Cultures.

American film director Michael Moore releases *Sicko*. The controversial documentary, which criticizes the high cost of the U.S. for-profit heath care system, features a group of medical tourists who travel to Cuba for care.

2008
The Center for Medical Tourism Research is established in the H-E-B School of Business and Administration at the University of the Incarnate Word in San Antonio, Texas. Current research is wide-ranging and includes the marketing aspects

of medical tourism, quality and continuity of care, attitudes toward medical tourism, sociocultural aspects, economic aspects, and legal issues.

More than 150 scientists, government officials, ethicists, and other representatives meet in Istanbul, Turkey to address many of the increasing and serious problems surrounding transplant tourism. The result is *The Declaration of Istanbul on Organ Trafficking and Transplant Tourism.*

Thailand introduces the Procedural Act for Consumer Protection Cases. This law upholds patients' rights in medical negligence cases, providing compensation in a timely manner.

The American Medical Association (AMA) releases its "Guidelines on Medical Tourism." These principles advocate that medical tourism be voluntary. They also stress the importance of seeking care in accredited facilities and following HIPAA guidelines, and they discuss financial considerations, continuity of care, and patient rights and safety.

2009   The American College of Surgeons releases its (ST-65) Statement on Medical and Surgical Tourism. Among the points in its position are emphases on quality care (including seeking accredited facilities with credentialed providers), informed decision making, follow-up care concerns, and financial issues.

2010   In March 2010, U.S. President Barak Obama signs into law the Affordable Care Act (ACA). The law outlines comprehensive health insurance reforms that will roll out over the course of several years. The ACA legislation takes full effect in 2014. The impact this will have on medical tourism is debated.

The Medical Travel Quality Alliance (MTQUA) lists the world's 10 best medical tourism destinations. The rankings are based on quality, outcomes, patient management and marketing, value, safety and security, transparency, and service. The top-ranked hospitals are:

- Fortis Hospital in Bangalore, India (formerly Wockhardt Hospitals)
- Gleneagles Hospital in Singapore
- Prince Court Medical Centre in Kuala Lumpur, Malaysia
- Shouldice Hospital in Toronto, Canada
- Shoen-Kliniken in Munich, Germany
- Bumrungrad International in Bangkok, Thailand
- Bangkok Hospital Medical Center in Bangkok, Thailand
- Wooridul Spine Hospital in Seoul, Korea
- Clemenceau Medical Center in Beirut, Lebanon
- Christus Muguerza Super Specialty Hospital in Monterrey, Mexico

U.S. researchers begin the first official trial using human embryonic stem cells in patients with spinal cord injuries.

An outcome of the European Medical Travel Conference 2010 in Italy is the Venice Declaration on Medical Travel. Issued by the European medical travel industry, the Declaration supports the rights of European Union citizens to travel to receive health care, and it addresses service, quality, and patient safety.

On May 21, the 63rd World Health Assembly adopts the WHO Global Code of Practice on the International Recruitment of Health Personnel. The Code aims to establish principles and practices for ethical health care recruitment and discourage active recruitment of health care workers from countries already facing personnel shortages. The intent is to strengthen the struggling health care systems in these countries.

The British medical journal *The Lancet* reports that 37 medical tourists from the United Kingdom who underwent surgery in India were infected with a "superbug" dubbed NDM-1 (which stands for New Delhi metallobeta-lactamase 1). India complains about the potentially negative implications of using New Delhi as part of the bug's name. The report causes concern for India specifically, but also for the medical tourism industry more generally.

2011   In May, voters in Zurich, Switzerland, defeat a proposal to restrict euthanasia access to foreigners, allowing suicide tourism to continue in that country.

To meet the domestic need for organ donation, China offers drivers the opportunity to register as organ donors when they renew their driver's license. Financial incentives are also considered. Critics say the approach follows a Western model that discounts Chinese burial customs.

The 1st International Congress on Ethics and Tourism, organized by the Spanish General Secretariat of Tourism and Domestic Trade and the World Tourism Organization (UNWTO), convenes in Madrid, Spain.

The European Union Directive on Cross-Border Healthcare is passed. The directive specifies that patients may cross national borders to receive health care in European Union member states other than their home country. The home country is required to pay as much of the patient's bill as it would have paid had the patient received care at home. It reflects previous European Court of Justice rulings (e.g., the 2006 Watts case).

References

American College of Surgeons. "[ST-65] Statement on Medical and Surgical Tourism." *Bulletin of the American College of Surgeons* 94, no. 4

(2009). www.facs.org/fellows_info/statements/st-65.html (accessed October 10, 2011).

"Chinese Organ Donation Plans Slammed." *HuffPost World*. September 5, 2011. www.huffingtonpost.com/2011/04/26/china-organ-donor-incentives_n_853794.html (accessed September 5, 2011).

Connell, John. *Medical Tourism*. Cambridge, MA: CABI, 2011.

Horowitz, Michael D., and Jeffrey A. Rosensweig. "Medical Tourism—Health Care in the Global Economy." *Physician Executive* 33, no. 6 (2007): 24–29.

"IRAN: Why Medical Tourism Has Not Taken off in Iran." February 18, 2011. www.imtj.com/news/?EntryId82 = 274934 (accessed September 15, 2011).

Kumar, Rajesh. *Global Trends in Health and Medical Tourism*. New Delhi: SBS Publishers & Distributors Pvt. Ltd., 2009.

Kumarasamy, Karthikeyan K., Mark A. Toleman, Timothy R. Walsh, Jay Bagaria, Fafhana Butt, Ravikumar Balakrishnan, Uma Chaudhary, Michel Doumith, Christian G. Giske, Seema Irfan, Padma Krishnan, Anil V. Kumar, Sunil Maharjan, Shazad Mushtaq, Tabassum Noorie, David L. Paterson, Andrew Pearson, Claire Perry, Rachel Pike, Bhargavi Rao, Ujjwayini Ray, Jayanta B. Sarma, Madhu Sharma, Elizabeth Sheridan, Mandayam A. Thirunarayan, Jane Turton, Supriya Upadhyay, Marina Warner, William Welfare, David M. Livermore, and Neil Woodford. "Emergence of a New antibiotic Resistance Mechanism in India, Pakistan, and the UK: A Molecular, Biological, and Epidemiological study." *The Lancet* 10, no. 9 (2010): 597–602.

"Medical Tourism Shivers After NDM1 Superbug Report." August 17, 2010. *PhoCusWright Connect*. http://connect.phocuswright.com/2010/08/medical-tourism-shivers-after-ndm1-superbug-report/ (accessed October 10, 2011).

Reed, Christie M. "Medical Tourism." *Medical Clinics of North America* 92 (2008): 1433–1446.

Reisman, David. *Health Tourism: Social Welfare Through International Trade*. Cheltenham, UK: Edward Elgar, 2010.

Smith, Melanie, and Laszlo Puczko. *Health and Wellness Tourism*. Oxford: Butterworth-Heinemann, 2008.

"Top 10 World's Best Hospitals for Medical Tourists." *Medical Travel Quality Alliance* (MTQUA). 2010. www.mtqua.org/providers/top-10-worlds-best-hospitals-for-medical-tourists/ (accessed September 1, 2011).

Weiss, Gregory L., and Lynne E. Lonnquist. *The Sociology of Health, Healing, and Illness*. Boston: Prentice Hall, 2012.

Weiss, Harry B., and Howard R. Kemble. *The Great American Water-Cure Craze.* Trenton, NJ: The Past Times Press, 1967.

Wexler, Laura. "Identity Crisis." *Style.* January/February 2007. www.baltimorestyle.com/index.php/style/features_article/fe_sexchange_jf07 (accessed October 10, 2011).

World Health Organization (WHO). "Human Organ and Tissue Transplantation." May 2, 2003. www.who.int/ethics/topics/human_transplant_report/en/index2.html (accessed August 29, 2011).

World Health Organization (WHO). *International Health Regulations 2005,* 2nd ed. 2008. http://whqlibdoc.who.int/publications/2008/9789241580410_eng.pdf (accessed September 15, 2011).

World Health Organization (WHO). "The WHO Global Code of Practice on the International Recruitment of Health Personnel." WHA 63.16. 2010. www.who.int/hrh/migration/code/practice/en/index.html (accessed September 15, 2011).

World Medical Association (WMA). "Resolution on Organ Donation in China." 173rd WMA Session Council. May. www.wma.net/en/30publications/10policies/30council/cr_5/index.html (accessed September 10, 2011).

World Tourism Organization (UNWTO). "History." No date. http://unwto.org/en/about/history (accessed July 30, 2011).

5

Medical Care Providers— Organizational Biographies

The selected biographies offered here are of medical care service providers around the world. This listing includes only a sample of providers in each country—it is not a complete listing. Included are many of the world's top-rated hospitals, as well as providers that represent unique, growing, or popular services. An exhaustive list of medical care providers around the globe would be impossible to compile. The inclusion or exclusion of any organization in this listing should not be considered a reflection on, endorsement of, or recommendation regarding the provider or its business practices.

Asia

India

Apollo Hospitals
No. 21, Greams Lane
Off. Greams Road
Chennai 600 006
India
Tel: + 91-44-2829 0200/2829 3333
E-mail: enquiry@apollohospitals.com
Website: www.apollohospitals.com/

Founded by a U.S.-trained cardiologist, the Apollo Hospital chain is one of the largest health care groups in Asia. It boasts 8,500 beds across 54 hospitals. It has also partnered to build the 200-bed Apollo Bramwell Hospital in Mauritius. Apollo Hospital–Chennai

145

is the flagship hospital in the group, established in 1983. It now has 60 departments and is a well-established medial tourism destination for procedures including orthopedics, transplants, and cardiac surgery. It was the first hospital in South India to receive Joint Commission International (JCI) accreditation. Seven of the Apollo hospitals now have earned JCI accreditation.

Fortis Hospital, Bangalore
Fortis Hospital Bannerghatta
154/9, Bannerghatta Road,
Opp. IIM-B, Bangalore—560 076.
India
Tel: +91-80-66214444 / 22544444/9663367253
E-mail: enquiries@fortishospitals.in
Website: www.fortishospitals.com/bangalore/overview.html

Fortis Hospital (formerly Wockhardt) was selected by the Medical Travel Quality Alliance (MTQUA) as the top hospital on its list of the Top 10 World's Best Hospitals for Medical Tourists in 2010. The Fortis system consists of 39 hospitals across India, with 12 of those facilities located in Mumbai, Bangalore, and Kolkata. It offers more than 5,000 hospital beds and claims to have conducted 48,000 surgical procedures in 2010 alone. The 400-bed Fortis Hospital Bangalore (formerly known as Wockhardt Super-Specialty Hospital) was designed in consultation with Harvard Medical International (HMI) using a patient-centric design. It received JCI accreditation in 2008. Clinical specialties include heart care, brain and spine care, bone and joint care, nephrology, urology, and minimal access surgeries. ("Fortis Hospital Bangalore," Patients Beyond Borders website, n.d.).

Max Super-Specialty Hospital
International Patient Services
Max Healthcare Limited
1, Press Enclave Road, Saket
New Delhi—110017
India
Tel: 91-11-26515050
E-mail: ips@maxhealthcare.com
Website: www.maxhealthcare.in/

Max Healthcare operates eight hospitals in Delhi, providing 930 beds and more than 1,500 physicians and 3,500 support staff.

Specialties advertised to international patients include: aesthetic and cosmetic surgeries, bariatric procedures, heart surgeries, cancer treatments, eye and dental care, reproductive medicine, as well as neurologic, orthopedic, and pediatric surgery. Offices have been opened in Afghanistan, Bangladesh, and Nigeria to serve international patients from those areas. The two super-specialty hospitals at Sakat, New Delhi, have received India's National Accreditation Board for Hospital & Healthcare Providers (NABH) certification in patient care.

Shroff Eye Hospital and LASIK Center
222, S. V. Road
Bandra (West), Next to old Bandra Talkies
Mumbai 400 050
India
Tel: (+91-22) 6692 1000
E-mail: safalashroff@lasikindia.in
Website: www.lasikindia.in/

First established in 1919, Shroff Eye became the first JCI-accredited eye hospital in India. It uses an advanced laser not yet approved in the U.S. (at this writing) for LASIK procedures. (LASIK is a method of reshaping the external surface of the cornea. It corrects various degrees of nearsightedness, astigmatism and farsightedness.) Other eye treatments are also provided.

Malaysia

Prince Court Medical Centre
39 Jalan Kia Peng
50450 Kuala Lumpur
Malaysia
Tel: (Malaysia) 1-800-88-PCMC; (International)+603 2160 0000
E-mail: corporate.affairs@princecourt.com
Website: www.princecourt.com/

The Medical Travel Quality Alliance (MTQUA) put Prince Court Medical Centre in third place on its list of the Top 10 World's Best Hospitals for Medical Tourists in 2010. This 300-bed private health care facility is owned by Petronas, Malaysia's national petroleum company. The hospital has collaborative relationships with an international management team from VAMED GmbH in Vienna,

Austria, as well as the Medical University of Vienna International (MUVI). JCI lists the Prince Court Medical Center as having been accredited in 2008.

Tropicana Medical Centre (TMC)
11, Jalan Teknologi,
Taman Sains Selangor 1,
PJU 5, Kota Damansara,
47810 Petaling Jaya,
Selangor Darul Ehsan
Malaysia
Tel: +60362871111
E-mail: patientenquiries@tropicanamedicalcentre.com
Website: www.tropicanamedicalcentre.com/

The 180-bed Tropicana Medical Centre is the center of TMC Life Sciences Berhad. It advertises an aesthetically pleasing ambiance and several centers of excellence. The TMC Fertility Centre (originally established in 1994 as the Damansara Fertility Centre) was the pioneer of those centers. Other centers of excellence address heart and vascular issues, the kidneys and diabetes, imaging and imaging surgery, women and children, and aesthetics and cosmetic services (including cosmetic dentistry).

Philippines

St. Luke's Medical Center (SLMC)
279 E. Rodriguez Sr. Boulevard
Quezon City
1112 Philippines
Tel: (632) 723-0101; (632) 723-0301
E-mail: info@stluke.com.ph
Website: www.stluke.com.ph/

Founded in 1903 as a dispensary clinic, St. Luke's Medical Center (SLMC) has grown to comprise a 650-bed hospital, ten institutes, eight departments, and twenty-three centers. Additionally, SLMC has over 1,700 hospital-affiliated medical consultants providing services in more than 450 private clinics. It has international affiliations with New York-Presbyterian Hospital, the Columbia University College of Physicians and Surgeons, the Weill Cornell

Medical College of Cornell University, and Memorial Sloan-Kettering Cancer Center. St. Luke's was first accredited by JCI in 2003. It has since been reaccredited in 2006 and 2009. It was the first hospital in the Philippines and the second in Asia to receive JCI accreditation.

Singapore

Alexandra Hospital
378 Alexandra Road
Singapore 159964
Tel: +6564722000
E-mail: enquiries@juronghealth.com.sg
Website: www.alexhosp.com.sg/

Alexandra Hospital was formerly the British Military Hospital. In that era, it was the first southeast Asian hospital to successfully perform a limb reattachment. It received its current name when it was turned over to the Singaporean government and opened to the public in 1971. The hospital became JCI-accredited in 2005, and was reaccredited in 2008 and 2011.

Gleneagles Hospital
6A Napier Road
Singapore 258500
Tel: 65 6473 7222
E-mail: ppac@parkway.sg
Website: www.parkwayhealth.com/hospitals/gleneagles_ hospital/

The 272-bed private Gleneagles Hospital was selected by the Medical Travel Quality Alliance (MTQUA) as the second-place hospital on its list of the Top 10 World's Best Hospitals for Medical Tourists in 2010. Gleneagles is part of Parkway Health, a group that includes 16 hospitals with more than 3,000 beds in Asia. The hospital became JCI-accredited in 2006, and was reaccredited in 2009. Gleneagles advertises its specialty areas as cardiology, gastroenterology, obstetrics and gynecology, oncology, orthopedics, and liver transplants. The Asian Center for Liver Diseases and Transplantation (ACLDT) was established at Gleneagles in 1994 ("Gleneagles Hospital," Patients Beyond Borders website, n.d.).

National Cancer Center, Singapore (NCCS)
11 Hospital Drive
Singapore 169610
Tel: +6564368000
E-mail: through the online form at: http://www.nccs.com.sg/
Contact/index.asp
Website: www.nccs.com.sg/

Singapore's institutional home for cancer experts, the National Cancer Center, Singapore (NCCS), provides a range of holistic cancer care. The largest number of oncologists in Singapore are housed at the NCCS. The hospital serves more than two-thirds of the country's public medical oncology cases. It received JCI accreditation in 2010.

Raffles Hospital
585 North Bridge Road
Singapore 188770
Tel: (65) 6311 1666
E-mail: rafflesipc@raffleshospital.com
Website: www.rafflesmedicalgroup.com/

Raffles Hospital is owned and operated by Raffles Medical Group (RMG), the largest private group practice in Singapore. Hospital services include 35 disciplines and 20 specialist centers. Calling itself "the ideal sanctuary for rest and recovery," Raffles advertises hospital rooms that rival those in five-star hotels, including suites ranging from singles to six-bedrooms. International patients from more than 100 countries comprise just over one-third of the hospital's patients. Its core markets are Indonesia and Malaysia, with increasing business from other areas, including the Russian Far East. It received JCI accreditation in 2008.

South Korea

Wooridul Spine Hospital
Seoul Wooridul Hospital
676 Gwahae-dong
Gangseo-gu
Seoul, Korea
Tel: 82-2-513-8385

E-mail: wipc@wooridul.co.kr
Website: www.wooridul.com/

Wooridul Spine Hospital was selected by the Medical Travel Quality Alliance (MTQUA) (MTQUA) as the eighth-ranked hospital on its list of the Top 10 World's Best Hospitals for Medical Tourists in 2010. The hospital bills itself as "The Specialized General Hospital with Spine Total Care System" and "The World's Leading Spine Hospital of Minimally Invasive Spine Surgery." Since its establishment in 1982, the hospital staff have performed 80,000 spine procedures and had published more than 165 journal articles as of 2009. Since 2006, the Wooridul International Patients Center (WIPC) has been serving international medical tourists. More than 1,100 international patients from 64 countries were treated in 2009.

Taiwan

Chang Bing Show Chwan Memorial Hospital
No. 6, Lugong Rd.
Lugang Town
Changhua County 505
Taiwan
Tel: +886-4-781-2012; 886-921-975-153
E-mail: showimc@gmail.com
Website: www.cbshow.org.tw/en

Chang Bing Show Chwan Memorial Hospital is part of the eight-hospital, 3,000-bed Show Chwan health care system in Taiwan. Its international medical center was established in 2009, the same year the hospital received JCI accreditation. Rather than following a traditional hospital model, the design is a "health park." Together with treatment facilities, it offers an art gallery, movie theater, museum, restaurants, retail stores, and recreational facilities. Chang Bing Show Chwan Memorial Hospital has several international affiliations ("Chang Bing Show Chwan Memorial Hospital," Patients Beyond Borders website, n.d.).

Min-Sheng General Hospital
22F #168 Jin-Kuo Rd 330
Taoyuan City
Taoyuan County
Taiwan R.O.C.

Tel: (US) 1-626-376-5113; (Taiwan) +88633179599, extension 2076 or 2080
E-mail: missioncare.tw@gmail.com
Website: www.missioncare.com.tw/

Min-Sheng General Hospital of Missioncare, Inc., is a 600-bed facility. Specializations are minimally invasive spine, open heart, and bariatric surgeries. This was the first Taiwanese hospital to receive JCI accreditation in 2006, and it was reaccredited in 2009. The hospital's acute myocardial infarction (AMI), type 2 diabetes, and chronic kidney disease programs are also each certified by JCI.

Taipei Medical University—Municipal Wan Fang Hospital
No. 111
Section 3
Hsing-Long Road
Taipei 116
Taiwan, R.O.C
Tel: +886229307930
E-mail: through the online form at: www.wanfang.gov.tw/ W402008web_new/english/Contact.asp
Website: www.wanfang.gov.tw/W402008web_new/english/index. html

This 800-bed facility is a regional teaching hospital. It offers centers for medication consulting, stem cell research, community medicine research, trauma prevention and treatment, pain treatment, women's tumor prevention and treatment, and traditional medicine. Wan-Fang Hospital is the first civilian-run hospital owned by the Taipei City government. It was JCI-accredited in 2006 and again in 2009.

Thailand

Bangkok Hospital Medical Center
2 Soi Soonvijai 7
New Petchaburi Road
Bangkok, Thailand 10310
Tel: (+66) 2310-3000
E-mail: info@bangkokhospital.com
Website: www.bangkokhospital.com/

Bangkok Hospital Medical Center was selected by the Medical Travel Quality Alliance (MTQUA) as the seventh-ranked hospital on its list of the Top 10 World's Best Hospitals for Medical Tourists in 2010. Bangkok Hospital began in 1972 as a 100-bed facility, Thailand's first private medical institution. Bangkok Hospital Group has now grown to include 13 locations across the country, making it Thailand's largest hospital operator. The hospital earned JCI accreditation in 2007, and was reaccredited in 2010.

Bumrungrad International
33 Sukhumvit 3 (Soi Nana Nua)
Wattana,
Bangkok, Thailand 10110
Tel: +662 667 1000
E-mail: info@bumrungrad.com
Website: www.bumrungrad.com/thailandhospital

Bumrungrad International was selected by the Medical Travel Quality Alliance (MTQUA) as the sixth-ranked hospital on its list of the Top 10 World's Best Hospitals for Medical Tourists in 2010. The hospital opened as a 200-bed facility in 1980. Today, with 554 beds and 30 specialty centers, Bumrungrad is now the largest private hospital in southeast Asia. It was also the first JCI-accredited hospital in Asia. Bumrungrad has been JCI accredited since 2002, and was reaccredited in 2011. It is also the first non-U.S. hospital to receive two JCI Disease or Condition-Specific Care Certifications for its Primary Stroke and Heart Attack Programs. Medical tourism is a major focus of the hospital. Of the 1 million patients treated there each year, more than 400,000 are international medical tourists, hailing from 190 countries around the globe and aided by more than 150 interpreters and other customer service providers. Bumrungrad has been featured as a medical tourism destination in several media outlets, including CBS's *60 Minutes* (which popularized the hospital), NBC's *Today Show, Time,* and *Newsweek.*

Caribbean

Antigua

Crossroads Centre
P.O. Box 3592
St. John's

Antigua, West Indies
Tel: 1-268-562-0035; (USA and Canada) 1-888-452-0091
E-mail: info@crossroadsantigua.org
Website: http://crossroadsantigua.org/

Founded in 1998 by Eric Clapton (a British singer and recovering addict and alcoholic), the 32-bed Crossroads Centre's mission "is to provide treatment and education to the chemically dependent person, their families and significant others." This is accomplished through residential, family, and aftercare programs. Approximately 75 percent of the clientele are Americans, and 30 percent are women.

Barbados

Barbados Fertility Centre
Seaston House
Hastings
Bridgetown
Barbados
bb15154
Tel: +12464357467
E-mail: contact@barbadosivf.com
Website: www.barbadosivf.com/

This clinic is housed in a renovated plantation house. Satellite offices are located in Trinidad, Antigua, and St. Maarten. Barbados Fertility Centre offers a variety of fertility treatments, particularly in vitro fertilization (IVF). Published IVF success rates are up to 71 percent for certain procedures. The clinic was JCI accredited in 2007, and reaccredited in 2011.

Curacao

Curacao Dialysis Center
Klipstraat, Otrobanda
Willemstad
Curacao, Netherlands Antilles
Tel: (011) 5999 434 7777
E-mail: info@curacao-dialysis.com
Website: www.curacao-dialysis.com/

The Curacao Dialysis Center is part of the Kura Hulanda Project, which consists of the center; a five-star hotel, spa, and casino; and the Museum Kura Hulanda, which houses a collection of slave-related artifacts and replicas, African artifacts, and Caribbean exhibits. The center received its ISO 9001:2008 Certificate in June 2010.

Puerto Rico

HIMA–HEALTH
Puerto Rico
PO Box 4980
Caguas, Puerto Rico
00726
Tel: (787) 653-6060
E-mail: through the online form at: http://himahealth.com/contact/
Website: www.himahealth.com/

HIMA•San Pablo Group has 1,059 licensed acute care beds in HIMA•San Pablo Caguas, Bayamón, Humacao, and Fajardo. Its health care model is designed specifically for medical tourists. HIMA is organized around the technology and expertise in its centers of excellence, which include a neurological center, cardiovascular institute, orthopedics, and oncology. Its hospitals are accredited by the Joint Commission on the Accreditation of Health Care Organizations (JCAHO), and its physicians are largely U.S. trained and board certified.

Central and South America

Brazil

Hospital Israelita Albert Einstein (HIAE)
Avenida Albert Einstein
627/701—Morumbi—SP—05651–901—Brazil
Tel: +551121511301; +551121510817
E-mail: international@einstein.br
Website: http://apps.einstein.br/english/

Founded in 1971, Hospital Israelita Albert Einstein (HIAE) focuses on services ranging from prevention to rehabilitation. HIAE lists among its "knowledge collaborators" a number of well-known U.S., European, and Israeli medical institutions, as well as several public health collaborators from around Brazil. In 1999, HIAE became the first hospital outside of the United States to receive accreditation from JCI. It has been reaccredited every three years since that time. In 2006, the facility embarked on an extensive modernization and building project as part of a Leadership in Energy and Environmental Design (LEED) accreditation. The new facility meets the U.S.-based Green Building Council (GBC) requirements for environmentally correct building construction.

Ivo Pitanguy Clinic
Rua Dona Mariana
65 Botafogo
Rio de Janeiro
22280–020 Brazil
Tel: +552122669500
E-mail: contact through the online form at: www.pitanguy.com.
    br/contato.asp
Website: /www.pitanguy.com.br/default.asp?i=2

This world-famous 14-bed private clinic was founded in 1963 by Professor Ivo Pitanguy, an early leader in the field of plastic surgery. Surgeons from around the world travel to study his techniques at the associated Pitanguy Institute. This is the only known facility in which two patients receive simultaneous surgery in the same operating room at the same time. However, infection rates are reportedly low. Visitors are cautioned that the neighborhood surrounding the clinic is dangerous and crime rates in the city are high ("Ivo Pitanguy Clinic," Patients Without Borders website, n.d.).

Costa Rica

CIMA San José
Escazú, Costa Rica
Tel: (US toll free) +18665403382; +526622590900
E-mail: intlpatientservices@cimamedicalvaluetravel.com
Website: www.cimamedicalvaluetravel.com/sjos

Hospital CIMA San José opened in 2000. Owned and operated by the Texas-based International Hospital Corporation, it provides a full range of diagnostic, emergency medical, and surgical services. Medical tourists often choose the hospital for cosmetic, eye, hip, and knee surgery. It was JCI-accredited in 2008. It is also accredited by the U.S. Department of Veterans Affairs ("CIMA San José," Patients Without Borders website, n.d.).

Clinica Biblica Hospital
1st & 2nd Street
14th & 16th Avenue
PO Box 1307-1000
San José, Costa Rica
Tel: (506) 2522-1000
E-mail: info@clinicabiblica.com
Website: www.clinicabiblica.com/eng/index.php

Clinica Biblica Hospital was founded in 1929. The private hospital's stated mission is to be "a general Hospital that provides excellent medical care with high quality and resolution capacity, in harmony with the environment, with Christian principles and with the strong commitment of strengthening Social Action Programs for those most in need." The hospital is located downtown in the country's capital city. Approximately 20 percent of its patients hail from outside of Costa Rica. Clinica Biblica is affiliated with the following American hospitals: Mount Sinai, Florida; Tulane Medical Center, New Orleans; and Oschner Clinic, New Orleans. It was first accredited by JCI in 2007 and again in 2010.

Europe

Czech Republic

Na Homolce Hospital
Nemocnice Na Homolce
Roentgenova 2/37
150 30 Praha 5
Czech Republic
Tel.: +420 257 271 111
E-mail: hospital@homolka.cz
Website: www.homolka.cz/en-CZ/home.html

The focus of Na Homolce Hospital is the treatment of cardiovascular and neurological-neurosurgical diseases. It is housed in a building that was originally a medical facility for high-ranking communist officials during the 1980s (known at that time as the State Institute of National Health, or Sanopz). In 1989 it became a public medical facility with its current areas of emphasis. JCI noted that Na Homolce Hospital is "one of the most modern hospitals in Europe." It was first JCI-accredited in 2005, and was again reaccredited in 2008 and 2011. ("Na Homolce Hospital" 2011).

Germany

Schoen-Kliniken
Head Office
Schön Klinik Verwaltung GmbH
Seestraße 5a
83209 Prien am Chiemsee
Munich, Germany
Tel: 08051 695-0
E-mail: contact through the online form at: www.schoen-kliniken.
    com/ptp/service/kontakt/skv/index.php.en?contact = active
Website: www.schoen-kliniken.com/ptp/

Schoen-Kliniken was selected by the Medical Travel Quality Alliance (MTQUA) as the fifth-ranked hospital on its list of the Top 10 World's Best Hospitals for Medical Tourists in 2010. The 4,200-bed hospital group specializes in orthopedics, neurology, psychosomatic medicine, surgery, and internal medicine. International patients include many travelers from Arab countries and Russia.

Turkey

Anadolu Medical Center
Cumhuriyet mahallesi 2255 sokak no:3
Gebze 41400 Kocaeli
Turkey
Tel: +902164444276
E-mail: through the online form at: www.anadolumedicalcenter.
    com/en/we-are-listening.aspx
Website: www.anadolumedicalcenter.com/en/Default.aspx

The Anadolu Medical Center is affiliated with Johns Hopkins Medicine in Baltimore, Maryland. Specialties include dental care, women's health, and cancer care. The oncology center is accredited through the European Society for Medical Oncology (ESMO). The center advertises "culturally appropriate" personalized service through its International Services Department. The medical center facilitated more than 3,000 medical visits by patients from more than 60 countries in 2010.

Middle East and Africa

Israel

IVF Haifa
12 Yair Katz Street
Haifa, Israel
Tel: +972 9 866.5314
E-mail: ivfisrael@gmail.com
Website: www.ivf.co.il/eindex.htm

This clinic began in 1996 as the first private IVF program in Northern Israel. The clinic offers in vitro fertilization and other state-of-the-art assisted reproductive technologies (ART). It advertises that a 2- to 3-week stay is often involved. The clinic also offers a sperm bank service, as well as an egg donation program in Kiev, Ukraine.

Jordan

King Hussein Cancer Center
Queen Rania Al Abdullah Street
P.O.Box: 1269, Amman 11941
Hashemite Kingdom of Jordan
Tel: +96265300460
E-mail: info@khcc.jo
Website: www.khcc.jo/

The King Hussein Cancer Center is the only specialized cancer center in Jordan and the wider region. It treats both adult and pediatric patients, providing an option for cancer patients from Arab countries who want to be treated in a familiar language and cultural setting. The hospital received JCI accreditation in 2006 and reaccreditation in 2009. The Oncology Program was separately accredited by JCI in 2007 and again in 2011.

Lebanon

Clemenceau Medical Center
Clemenceau St
Minet el Hosn
Beirut, Lebanon
Tel: +961 1 372888
E-mail: info@cmc.com.lb
Website: www.cmc.com.lb/

Clemenceau Medical Center was selected by the Medical Travel Quality Alliance (MTQUA) as the ninth-ranked hospital on its list of the Top 10 World's Best Hospitals for Medical Tourists in 2010. It offers 101 operating beds and "a 5-star hotel ambiance." Specialties include a wide range of conditions. The hospital is affiliated with Johns Hopkins Medicine International. It received JCI accreditation in 2009.

South Africa

Netcare Olivedale Hospital
Cnr Pres Fouche/Windsor Way
Olivedale
Johannesburg
South Africa
Tel: + 27 11 777-2000
E-mail: Deborah.Sieff@netcare.co.za; and through online form at:
    www.olivedaleclinic.co.za/contact.asp
Website: www.olivedaleclinic.co.za/

The 265-bed Netcare Olivedale Hospital is a member of South Africa's Netcare Group of Hospitals. Netcare is the largest private hospital and doctor network in the country. It offers a range of services, but claims specialties in obstetrics and gynecology, cardiology and cardio-thoracic surgery, orthopedics, nephrology, pediatrics, and oncology, among other areas.

United Arab Emirates

American Hospital Dubai
Oud Metha Road

P.O. Box 5566
Dubai, UAE
Tel: +97143367777
E-mail: through the online forms at: www.ahdubai.com/contact/
contactinfo.aspx
Website: www.ahdubai.com

The 143-bed American Hospital Dubai advertises that it was planned, designed, built, and equipped specifically to meet American standards of health care. Its mission is "to provide high quality American standard healthcare that will meet the needs and exceed the expectations of the people of Dubai, the UAE and the surrounding Gulf States." In 2000, it became the first Middle Eastern hospital to receive JCI accreditation. It has been reaccredited consistently since then. The hospital's medical laboratory was also the first private laboratory in the Middle East to receive accreditation from the College of American Pathologists (CAP). American Hospital Dubai encompasses four centers of excellence in total joint replacement, cardiac care, cancer care, and diabetes care.

Dubai Healthcare Center (DHCC)
P.O. Box 66566
Dubai
United Arab Emirates
Tel: +97143245555
E-mail: info@dhcc.ae
Website: www.dhcc.ae//

Occupying more than 4 million square feet in the heart of Dubai, Dubai Healthcare Center (DHCC) was launched in 2002. It has grown to encompass two hospitals and more than 90 outpatient medical centers and diagnostic laboratories, as well as 2,000 licensed professionals. Partners Harvard Medical International (PHMI) collaborated in establishing the DHCC Center for Healthcare Planning and Quality (CPQ).

North America

Canada

Shouldice Hospital
7750 Bayview Avenue
Thornhill, Ontario,

Canada L3T 4A3
Tel: 905-889-1125
E-mail: postoffice@shouldice.com
Website: www.shouldice.com/

Shouldice Hospital was selected by the Medical Travel Quality Alliance (MTQUA) as the fourth-ranked hospital on its list of the Top 10 World's Best Hospitals for Medical Tourists in 2010. The 89-bed surgical hospital was founded in 1947. Its specialization is hernia repair. Shouldice surgeons perform more than 7,000 hernia repairs annually. The hospital claims a 99.5 percent lifetime success rate for primary inguinal hernias, with the lowest recorded rate of infection, complications, and recurrence in the world.

Mexico

Christus Muguerza Super Specialty Hospital
Avenida Hidalgo Pte. 2525 Colonia Obispado
Monterrey, Nuevo Leon
Mexico 64060
Tel: +528183993400
E-mail: internationalpatients@christusmuguerza.com.mx
Website: www.christusmuguerza.com.mx/

Christus Muguerza Super Specialty Hospital was selected by the Medical Travel Quality Alliance (MTQUA) as the tenth-ranked hospital on its list of the Top 10 World's Best Hospitals for Medical Tourists in 2010. The hospital is part of a health care system that consists of 7 hospitals, 27 medical attention centers, 2 rehabilitation and therapy centers, and 7 social assistance clinics, in addition to ambulances. It is also affiliated with the U.S. CHRISTUS Health System. The hospital's first JCI accreditation was in 2007. It received reaccreditation in 2010.

United States

Cancer Treatment Centers of America (CTCA)
Corporate Administration
1336 Basswood Road
Schaumburg, Illinois 60173
USA
Tel: (patients) +18009319299; (general inquiries) +18473427400

E-mail: through the online form at: www.cancercenter.com/
contact-us/email.cfm
Website: www.cancercenter.com/

Cancer Treatment Centers of America (CTCA) offer a holistic, Patient Empowered Care model labeled the "Mother Standard of
care" (so-named after the founder's mother died from cancer).
CTCA cancer hospitals are located in Zion, Illinois; Philadelphia,
Pennsylvania; Tulsa, Oklahoma; and Goodyear, Arizona. There is
also an outpatient practice in Seattle, Washington. The CTCA hospitals are accredited by the Joint Commission and other professional organizations.

Cleveland Clinic
9500 Euclid Avenue
Cleveland, Ohio 44195
USA
Tel: +18002232273; (international patient center) +001 216.444. 8184
E-mail: through the online form at: https://my.clevelandclinic.
org/webcontact/webmail.aspx
Website: http://my.clevelandclinic.org/

Now ranked as one of America's top hospitals by *U.S. News and
World Report*, the Cleveland Clinic was founded in 1921. (Its heart and
heart surgery program has ranked in first place since 1995.) In 2011,
Cleveland Clinic was Ohio's second largest employer. In addition
to a main urban campus, 10 community hospitals, and 16 suburban
family health and ambulatory surgery centers, it also has facilities
in Florida, Nevada, Canada, and Abu Dhabi. Cleveland Clinic
opened its Global Patient Services department in 1975. The department initially dealt with domestic medical tourism, but
now hosts thousands of inbound medical tourists annually
(Lambier 2009).

Jackson Memorial Hospital
1611 NW 12th Avenue
Miami, Florida 33136-1096
USA
Tel: 305-585-1111
E-mail: through the contacts listed at: http://www.jhsmiami.org/
body.cfm?id = 23
Website: www.jhsmiami.org/

Jackson Memorial Hospital is part of the Jackson Health System. The hospital is the center of a 68-acre medical campus that is the major teaching facility for the University of Miami-Miller School of Medicine. Nationally ranked programs there include ophthalmology; neurology and neurosurgery; ear, nose and throat; urology; and nephrology or kidney disorders. It houses both a Kidney Transplantation Center and the Ryder Trauma Center. Jackson Memorial International has an International Patient Reception Center, which is open 24 hours a day to assist patients who are traveling to the United States for medical services.

Johns Hopkins Medicine International (JHI)
The Johns Hopkins Hospital
600 N. Wolfe Street
Baltimore, Maryland 21287
USA
Tel: +14109558032
E-mail: international@jhmi.edu
Website: www.hopkinsmedicine.org/international/

The Johns Hopkins Hospital has been the number-one ranked hospital in the United States for the last 21 years by *U.S. News and World Report* in its annual "America's Best Hospitals" survey. Its medical specialties are also top-ranked and include cancer, head and neck diseases, heart and vascular issues, neurology and neurosurgery, orthopedic surgery, transplantation, and urology. JHI has affiliations with Amcare Labs International, Inc., Anadolu Medical Center (Turkey), Clemenceau Medical Center (Lebanon), Clínica Las Condes (Chile), and Tokyo Midtown Medical Center (Japan). It also has agreements involving hospital management and clinical operations, as well as strategic collaborations with other organizations elsewhere around the globe.

Mayo Clinic
200 First Street S.W.
Rochester, Minnesota 55905
USA
Tel: +15072842511
E-mail: through the online form at: www.mayoclinic.org/contact/
    #form
Website: www.mayoclinic.com/

In addition to the original Minnesota clinic, the Mayo Clinic also has U.S. locations in Florida and Arizona. It has representative offices in Canada, Ecuador, Guatemala, and Mexico. Every year, more than 1 million patients are treated at the Mayo Clinics. Patients come from all 50 states and nearly 150 countries outside of the United States for care.

Memorial Sloan-Kettering Cancer Center (MSKCC)
General address
1275 York Avenue
New York, New York 10065
USA
E-mail: publicaffairs@mskcc.org

Bobst International Center
160 East 53rd Street
Rockefeller Outpatient Pavilion, 11th floor
New York, New York 10022
USA
E-mail: intnlprg@mskcc.org
Tel: 212-639-4900 or toll-free 888-675-7722
Website: www.mskcc.org/

Memorial Sloan-Kettering provides comprehensive cancer care at several locations across the New York metropolitan area, including Manhattan, Brooklyn, Westchester County, and New Jersey, as well as on Long Island. In 2010, there were more than half a million outpatient visits to these facilities. MSKCC is a top-ranked hospital in the *U.S. News and World Report* rankings and its specialists treat more than 400 different types of cancer each year. The center is also a leader in research, and education and training programs. International patients traveling to the United States are assisted through the Bobst International Center.

Partners Harvard Medical International (PHMI)
131 Dartmouth Street, 5th Floor
Boston, Massachusetts 02116-5134
USA
Tel: +1 617-535-6400
E-mail: info@phmi.partners.org
Website: www.phmi.partners.org/

Formerly known as Harvard Medical International, this organization was founded by Harvard Medical School in 1994 "to enable the school to share its tradition of excellence with institutions around the world." It is part of the Partners HealthCare System, which includes Massachusetts General Hospital and Brigham and Women's Hospital. Both are top-ranked institutions where Harvard Medical School students train. PHMI has worked in more than 40 countries, and has "significant experience" in Europe, Asia, and the Middle East.

Philadelphia International Medicine (PIM)
1835 Market Street
10th Floor
Philadelphia, PA 19103
Tel: 215-563-4733
E-mail: general information contact through the online form at:
   www.philadelphiamedicine.com/About_PIM/Contact.
   aspx#reqform
Website: www.philadelphiamedicine.com/

Philadelphia International Medicine (PIM) is a U.S. medical consortium consisting of the Alfred I. duPont Hospital for Children, Fox Chase Cancer Center, Temple University Hospital, and Thomas Jefferson University Hospital. PIM was founded in 2000, with a stated mission to "assist international patients seeking high quality, cost-effective medical care; create partnerships with leading international hospitals in areas of training, research and staff development; and seek opportunities to improve health care abroad through consulting and hospital management." Its three area specialties are patient care services, education, and hospital management and development. Annually, PIM attracts several thousand patients, many of them from the Caribbean, the Middle East, and Brazil. The medical consortium generates millions of dollars for the Philadelphia economy (Abramson 2006).

Shady Grove Fertility Center
15001 Shady Grove Road
Suite 400
Rockville, Maryland 20850
USA
Tel: 1-888-761-1967

E-mail: through the online form at: www.shadygrovefertility.com/
    webform/contact-us
Website: www.shadygrovefertility.com/

The Shady Grove Fertility Center is the largest fertility center in
the United States. It has 17 locations (13 full service and 4 satellite) in Maryland; Northern Virginia; Harrisburg, Pennsylvania;
and Washington, DC. Patients from all 50 states and 35 countries
travel to this center for fertility services. The advertised IVF success rates are "among the very best in the nation." Published patient satisfaction rates are over 90 percent.

Stanford Hospital & Clinics
International Medical Services
300 Pasteur Drive
Room H-1111
Stanford, California 94305
USA
Telephone: (650) 723-8561
E-mail: ims@stanfordmed.org
Website: http://stanfordhospital.org/forPatients/patientServices/
    internationalMedicalServices.html

The International Medical Services (IMS) is a program of the Stanford Hospital & Clinics. The program, designed to serve inbound
medical tourists to the United States, is "committed to providing
international patients and their families with the highest quality
medical care and support services to ensure a pleasant experience" at the Stanford facilities.

Texas Medical Center
2450 Holcombe Blvd.
Suite 1
Houston, Texas 77021
USA
Tel: +17137916161
E-mail: through the online form at: http://forms.texasmedicalcenter.
    org/tmc/
Website: www.texasmedicalcenter.org/

The largest medical center in the world with 49 member institutions, Texas Medical Center hosted 18,000 international patients

in 2010. Its services are provided through several patient care institutions, with targeted programs that are specifically designed to assist patients who are traveling to the area for care. These include the Texas Children's Hospital, the University of Texas M. D. Anderson Cancer Center, and the Texas Heart Institute. Texas Medical Center also has affiliations with institutions in Mexico, Guatemala, El Salvador, Venezuela, Spain, Turkey, the United Arab Emirates, China, and Japan (Moreno 2009).

University of Michigan Health System
1500 E. Medical Center Drive
Ann Arbor, Michigan 48109
USA
Tel: 734-936-6641
E-mail: through the links at: www.med.umich.edu/umhs/contact-us/index.html
Website: www.med.umich.edu/

The University of Michigan, in conjunction with several area hospitals (Detroit Medical Center, Henry Ford Health System, and St. John Health System), began an online marketing campaign in 2008 to attract international patients to the United States (Greene 2009). Its close proximity to Canada makes it an attractive destination for some Canadian visitors.

University of Pittsburgh Medical Center (UPMC)
200 Lothrop Street
Pittsburgh, PA 15213-2582
USA
Tel: 412-647-UPMC (8762); 1-800-533-UPMC (8762)
E-mail: through the contact online at: www.upmc.com/contact/Pages/contact-us.aspx; or the Global Care program directly at GlobalCare@upmc.edu
Website: www.upmc.com/

With more than 54,000 employees, the University of Pittsburgh Medical Center (UPMC) is Pennsylvania's largest employer. The UPMC system consists of more than 20 hospitals and 400 clinical locations in the United States. Specializations include transplantation, cancer, neurosurgery, psychiatry, orthopedics, and sports medicine. In addition to treating international patients at its U.S. locations through its Global Care program, the UPMC has several international ventures, including those in China, Cyprus, Ireland, Italy, Japan, Qatar, and the United Kingdom.

Weill Cornell Medical College
1300 York Avenue
New York, New York 10065
USA
Tel: (212) 746-5454
E-mail: through the online form at: http://weill.cornell.edu/visitors
/contact-us.html
Website: http://weill.cornell.edu

In addition to being a destination for medical tourists in its own right, Cornell University's medical school, Weill Cornell Medical College has developed a number of U.S. and international affiliations. These include affiliations in France, Tanzania, Turkey, and South Korea, as well as the Weill Medical College in Qatar.

References

Abramson, Hilary. "The Best Money Can Buy: Medical Tourism in the U.S.A." *New America Media*, February 2, 2006. accessed November 20, 2009. http://news.newamericamedia.org/news/view_article. html?article_id = 5b7c206e74b96be675410f6f369b5113.

Greene, Jay. "Southeast Michigan Hospitals Advertise for International Patients." *Crain's Detroit Business*. June 26, 2009. www.crainsdetroit.com/article/20090626/HEALTH/906269974/southeast-michigan-hospitals-advertise-for-international-patients (accessed November 16, 2011).

Lambier, Cayla. "American Hospitality—Inbound Medical Tourism at International Standards." *Medical Tourism Magazine* 11 (August 4, 2009). www.medicaltourismmag.com/article/American-Hospitality.html (accessed November 16, 2011).

Medical Travel Quality Alliance (MTQUA). "How to Choose a Medical Destination That Is Best Suited for You." No date. www.mtqua.org/countries/how-to-choose-a-medical-destination/ (accessed September 28, 2011).

Moreno, Rosanna. "Five Essentials for a Successful Inbound Medical Tourism Practice." *Medical Tourism Magazine* 11 (August 4, 2009). www.medicaltourismmag.com/article/five-essentials-for-a-successful.html (accessed November 16, 2011).

"Na Homolce Hospital." Joint Commission International. www.jointcommissioninternational.org/Na-Homolce-Hospital/ (accessed November 16, 2011).

Patients Beyond Borders website. www.patientsbeyondborders.com/ (accessed November 2011).

Woodman, Josef. *Patients Beyond Borders: Everybody's Guide to Affordable, World-Class Medical Travel.* Chapel Hill, NC: Healthy Travel Media, 2008.

6

Data and Documents

This chapter includes some of the latest research and facts on medical tourism. It describes the number and nature of medical tourists, as well as some of the leading destinations to which they travel. Also included are statements from professional organizations that offer guidance to help consumers make educated choices as they travel for medical care. More detailed information about these facts can be found throughout the rest of the book.

Data

- An estimated 750,000 Americans traveled abroad for medical care in 2007 (Deloitte 2009). Most traveled to Mexico and Latin America (Herrick 2010).
- The number of American medical tourists is expected to rise by 35 percent a year through 2012, jumping to 15.75 million by 2017 (Deloitte Medical Tourism Update 2009). After that, numbers may fall, as medical tourism destinations reach their maximum capacities.
- The worldwide medical tourism market is an estimated $78.5 billion, and is expected to grow to $100 billion by 2012 (Herrick 2007; "Medical Tourism" 2010).
- Asia's medical tourism industry is one of the fastest growing in the world. Thailand expected 2 million medical tourists in 2010, with an annual growth rate of 14 percent. In 2008, foreign patients generated an estimated US$6 billion for Thailand (Anonymous 2009). India's

FIGURE 6.1
Percentages of Americans Willing to Travel for Medical Care

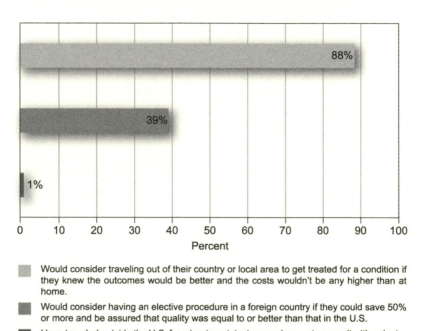

Would consider traveling out of their country or local area to get treated for a condition if they knew the outcomes would be better and the costs wouldn't be any higher than at home.

Would consider having an elective procedure in a foreign country if they could save 50% or more and be assured that quality was equal to or better than that in the U.S.

Have traveled outside the U.S. for a treatment, test, procedure, or to consult with a doctor in the last 12 months.

Source: Deloitte Center for Health Solutions. "Medical Tourism: Consumers in Search of Value." Deloitte Center for Health Solutions. "Medical Tourism: Update and Implications — 2009 Report."

medical tourism is a $30 billion industry, and is expected to reach $150 billion by 2017 (Madhok 2009). Singapore hopes to greet 1 million foreign patients by 2012, up from 350,000 in 2007 (Norton 2009).

- Americans spent $2.1 billion overseas for health care in 2008. As a result, health care providers in the United States lost $15.9 billion in revenues (Deloitte 2009).
- More than 400,000 foreign tourists received health care in the United States in 2008, generating almost $5 billion in revenue. By 2011, incoming medical tourists were expected to reach 800,000 (Deloitte 2009).

TABLE 6.1
Medical Specialties by Destination

Addiction recovery	Antigua, Barbados
Cardiovascular care	India, South Korea, Malaysia, Philippines, Singapore, Thailand, Turkey, United Arab Emirates
Cosmetic and plastic surgery	Argentina, Brazil, Costa Rica, Mexico, South Africa, Thailand, Turkey
Dentistry	Costa Rica, Czech Republic, Hungary, Mexico, South Africa, Thailand
Fertility treatments	Antigua, Barbados, Israel, Singapore, Thailand, Turkey
Neurology and spine	India, South Korea, Singapore, Thailand
Orthopedic (including hip and knee replacements and hip resurfacing)	India, South Korea, Malaysia, Singapore, Thailand, United Arab Emirates
Oncology (cancer)	India, Jordan, South Korea, Singapore, Thailand, Turkey, United Arab Emirates
Stem cell research	Singapore, Thailand
Sex reassignment surgery	Thailand
Weight loss surgery	Brazil, India, Malaysia, Mexico, Panama, Singapore, South Africa, Taiwan, Thailand
Wellness/holistic/alternative treatments	India, South Korea, Malaysia, Singapore, South Africa, Thailand

Sources: Deloitte Center for Health Solutions. "Medical Tourism: Consumers in Search of Value." Woodman, Josef. *Patients Beyond Borders: Everybody's Guide to Affordable, World-Class Medical Travel.* Chapel Hill, NC: Healthy Travel Media, 2008.

- When Americans were surveyed about their interest in medical tourism, 88 percent said they would consider going out of their country or local area for treatment, if they could be assured that the outcomes would be better and the costs were no higher than in their local care centers (Deloitte 2009). Figure 6.1 and Figure 6.2 show the percentages of patients who would be likely to travel for medical care overall, and by generation.
- Medical tourists plan their travel based on the procedure they want, rather than the destination. Table 6.1 highlights a number of medical specialties, and the countries known for those specialties. Leading medical tourism destinations and their respective number of health care facilities accredited by the Joint Commission International (JCI) are featured in Table 6.2. A list of JCI-accredited health facilities around the world is included in Table 6.3.

TABLE 6.2
JCI-Accredited Facilities in Leading Tourism Destinations

Country	Number of JCI-Accredited Facilities
Antigua	0
Argentina	0
Barbados	1
Brazil	11
Costa Rica	3
Czech Republic	4
Hungary	0
India	15
Israel	3
Malaysia	6
Jordan	5
Mexico	8
Philippines	3
Singapore	16
South Africa	0
South Korea	3
Taiwan	9
Thailand	9
Turkey	37
United Arab Emirates	35

Source: Joint Commission International. "Joint Commission International (JCI) Accredited Organizations." www.jointcommissioninternational.org/JCI-Accredited-Organizations/.

TABLE 6.3
International Health Facilities Accredited by JCI

Country	JCI-Accredited Health Facilities
Austria	Institut fur medizinische und chemische — Labordiagnostik — Villach Landerskrankenhaus Villach — Villach Neurologisches Therapiezentrum Kapfenberg GmbH — Kapfenberg Sonderkrankenanstalt fur Rehabilitation, Thermenhof Warmbad GmbH — Warmbad-Villach

continued

TABLE 6.3 (Continued)

Country	JCI-Accredited Health Facilities
Bangladesh	Apollo Hospital, Dhaka — Dhaka
Barbados	Barbados Fertility Centre — Christ Church
Bermuda	Bermuda Hospitals Board – Department of Pathology — Paget
Brazil (jointly accredited by JCI and the Consortium for Brazilian Accreditation)	AMIL Resgate Saude — Rio de Janeiro AMIL Total Care – Barra da Tijuca — Rio de Janeiro AMIL Total Care – Berrini — Sao Paulo Amil Total Care – Botafogo — Rio de Janeiro Associação do Sanatório Sírio – Hospital do Coração — Sao Paulo Centro de Transplante de Medula Óssea (CEMO) – INCA — Rio de Janeiro Hospital Alemão Oswaldo Cruz — Sao Paulo Hospital Copa D'OR — Rio de Janeiro Hospital do Câncer II – INCA — Rio de Janeiro Hospital do Cancer III – INCA — Rio de Janeiro Hospital do Cancer III – INCA — Rio de Janeiro Hospital do Cancer IV-INCA — Rio de Janeiro Hospital Israelita Albert Einstein — Sao Paulo Hospital Moinhos de Vento — Porto Alegre Hospital Sao Vicente de Paulo — Rio de Janeiro Hospital Sirio Libanes – Sociedade Beneficente de Senhoras — Sao Paulo Instituto Estadual de Hematologia – Hemorio — Rio de Janeiro Instituto Nacional de Traumato e Ortopedia – Unidade Hospitalar-Into — Rio de Janeiro PRONEP – Rio de Janeiro PRONEP – Sao Paulo Sociedade Hospital Samaritano — Sao Paulo
Chile	Clinica Alemana de Santiago S.A. — Santiago Clinica Las Condes — Santiago
China	Beijing United Family Hospital and Clinics — Beijing Clifford Hospital — Guangzhou, Guangdong Province Shanghai United Family Hospital and Clinics — Shanghai Sir Run Run Shaw Hospital — Hangzhou Zhejiang Province TEDA International Cardiovascular Hospital — TEDA, Tianjin
Colombia	Fundación Cardiovascular de Colombia – Instituto del Corazón — Floridablanca, Santander Hospital Universitario Fundacion Santa Fe de Bogota — Bogota
Costa Rica	Hospital CIMA, San Jose — San Jose Hospital Clinica Biblica — San Jose Hospital La Catolica — Guadalupe, San Jose
Cyprus	Near East University Faculty of Dentistry — Lefkosa (TRNC)

continued

TABLE 6.3 (Continued)

Country	JCI-Accredited Health Facilities
Czech Republic	Central Military Hospital — Prague Institute of Hematology and Blood Transfusion — Prague Masarykův onkologicky ustav — Brno Na Homolce Hospital — Prague
Denmark	Amager Hospital — Copenhagen Bispebjerg Hospital — Copenhagen Frederiksberg Hospital — Frederiksberg Hvidovre Hospital — Hvidovre Rigshospitalet — Copenhagen Sankt Hans Hospital — Roskilde
Egypt	Dar Al Fouad Hospital — Giza Magrabi Eye Hospital — Cairo
Ethiopia	International Clinical Laboratories — Addis Ababa
Germany	DRK Kliniken Berlin — Berlin Klinikum Chemnitz gGmbH — Chemnitz Kreiskrankenhaus Greiz GmbH — Greiz Städtisches Klinikum Görlitz gGmbH — Gorlitz
Greece	Diagnostic and Therapeutic Center of Athens HYGEIA S.A. — Marousi
India	Ahalia Foundation Eye Hospital — Palakkad/Kerala Apollo Hospitals, Bangalore — Bangalore Apollo Hospitals, Chennai — Chennai Apollo Hospitals, Hyderabad — Hyderabad Apollo Gleneagles Hospital, Kolkata — Kolkata Asian Heart Institute — Mumbai Fortis Hospital — Mohali Fortis Escorts Heart Institute — New Delhi Grewal Eye Institute — Chandigarh Indraprastha Apollo Hospital — New Delhi Moolchand Hospital — New Delhi Satguru Partap Singh Apollo Hospital — Punjab Shroff Eye Hospital — Mumbai Sri Ramachandra Medical Centre — Chennai, Tamil Nadu Fortis Hospitals — Bangalore (formerly Wockhardt Hospital, Bangalore) Fortis Hospitals — Mulund (formerly Wockhardt Hospital, Mulund, Mumbai)
Indonesia	Siloam Hospital Lippo Karawaci — Lippo Karawaci
Ireland	Aut Even Hospital — Kilkenny Barrington's Hospital Limited — Limerick Beacon Dermatology — Dublin Beacon Hospital — Sandyford, Dublin

continued

TABLE 6.3 (Continued)

Country	JCI-Accredited Health Facilities
Ireland	Aut Even Hospital — Kilkenny
	Barrington's Hospital Limited — Limerick
	Beacon Dermatology — Dublin
	Beacon Hospital — Sandyford, Dublin
	Beacon Hospital Cancer Centre — Dublin
	Beacon Renal — Dublin
	Blackrock Clinic — Dublin
	Aut Even Hospital — Kilkenny
	Barrington's Hospital Limited — Limerick
	Beacon Dermatology — Dublin
	Beacon Hospital — Sandyford, Dublin
	Beacon Hospital Cancer Centre — Dublin
	Beacon Renal — Dublin
	Blackrock Clinic — Dublin
	Bon Secours Hospital — Cork
	Bon Secours Hospital — Dublin
	Bon Secours Hospital — Galway
	Bon Secours Hospital — Tralee
	Eurocare Health Care Ltd T/A Whitfield Clinic Medical Centre — Waterford
	Galway Clinic — County Galway
	Hermitage Medical Clinic — Dublin
	Mater Private Hospital — Dublin
	Mount Carmel Hospital — Dublin
	Sports Surgery Clinic — Dublin
	St. Joseph's Hospital — Sligo
	St. Vincent's Private Hospital — Dublin
	UPMC Whitfield Cancer Centre — Waterford
Israel	Ha EMEK Medical Center — Afula
	Meir Medical Center — Kefar-Saba
	Soroka University Medical Center — Beer Sheva
Italy	Azienda Ospedaliero – Universitaria — Trieste
	Azienda Ospedaliera Istituti Clinici di Perfezionamento — Milano
	Casa di Cura Villa San Benedetto Menni — Albese con Cassano
	CDI Centro Diagnostico Italiano S.P.A. — Milan
	Centro Medico San Biagio SRL — Fossalta di Portogruaro (Venice)
	Ceinge Biotecnologie Avanzate Scarl — Napoli
	European Institute of Oncology – Istituto Europeo de Oncologia — Milan
	Giannina Gaslini Institute — Genoa
	Hospital Bassini — Milan
	Humanitas Gavazzeni — Bergamo
	IRCCS Istituto Clinico Humanitas — Milan (formerly Humanitas Mirasole S.P.A.)
	IRCCS Centro San Giovanni di Dio FATEBENEFRATELLI — Brescia

continued

TABLE 6.3 (Continued)

Country	JCI-Accredited Health Facilities
Italy	Istituto Clinico Mater Domini — Castellanza Istituto Mediterraneo per I Trapianti e le Terapie ad Alta Specializzazione — Palermo Ospedale Pediatrico Bambino Gesu — Rome Presidio Ospedaliero Oglio-Po — Vicomoscano Santa Chiara Hospital — Trento
Japan	Kameda Medical Center — Kamogawa City, Chiba
Jordan	Al-Essra Hospital — Amman Jordan Hospital & Medical Center — Amman King Abdullah University Hospital — Ibid King Hussein Cancer Center — Amman The Specialty Hospital — Amman
Kingdom of Saudi Arabia	King Faisal Specialist Hospital and Research Centre — Jeddah King Faisal Specialist Hospital and Research Centre — Riyadh King Khaled Eye Specialist Hospital — Riyadh Magrabi Eye and Ear Center — Dammam Magrabi Eye and Ear Hospital — Jeddah Mouwasat Hospital — Dammam Mouwasat Hospital — Jubail Mouwasat Hospital — Qatif Riyadh Care Hospital — Riyadh Royal Commission Medical Center — Yanbu Saad Specialist Hospital — Al-Khobar Saud Al-Babtain Cardiac Center (SBCC) — Eastern Province/Dammam Saudi Aramco Medical Services Organization — Dhahran Saudi German Hospital — Aseer Saudi German Hospital — Jeddah Saudi German Hospital — Riyadh Saudi German Hospitals Group — Madinah Sultan Bin Abdulaziz Humanitarian City — Riyadh
Korea, Republic of (South Korea)	Korea University Anam Hospital — Seoul Severance Hospital, Yonsei University College of Medicine — Seoul The Gachon Brain Health Center — Incheon
Lebanon	American University of Beirut Medical Center — Beirut Clemenceau Medical Center — Beirut
Malaysia	International Specialist Eye Centre — Kuala Lumpur Intitut Jantung Negara (also known as National Heart Institute) — Kuala Lumpur Pentai Hospital — Kuala Lumpur Penang Adventist Hospital — Jalan Burma Prince Court Medical Centre — Kuala Lumpur Sime Darby Medical Centre Subang Jaya Sdn. Bhd. — Subang Jaya
Mexico	The American British Cowdray Medical Center IAP – Observatorio Campus — Mexico City The American British Cowdray Medical Center IAP – Santa Fe Campus — Mexico City

continued

TABLE 6.3 (Continued)

Country	JCI-Accredited Health Facilities
Mexico	Christus Muguerza Alta Especialidad — Monterrey Clinica Cumbres Chihuahua — Chihuahua Hospital CIMA Hermosillo — Hermosillo, Sonora Hospital CIMA Monterrey — San Pedro Garza Garcia N.L. Hospital San Jose Tec de Monterrey — Monterrey Hospital Y Clinica OCA, S.A. de C.V. — Monterrey, Nuevo Leon
Pakistan	Aga Khan University Hospital — Karachi
Philippines	Chong Hua Hospital — Cebu City St. Luke's Medical Center — Quezon City The Medical City — Pasig City
Portugal	Centro Hospitalar do Tâmega e Sousa, EPE — Guilhufe Centro Hospitalar do Alto Ave, EPE — Unidade de Guimaraes — Creixomil, Guimaraes
Qatar	Al Amal Hospital — Doha Al Khor Hospital — Doha Hamad General Hospital — Doha Home Healthcare Services — Doha Rumailah Hospital — Doha Women's Hospital — Doha
Singapore	Alexandra Hospital Changi General Hospital Institute of Mental Health/Woodbridge Hospital Johns Hopkins Singapore International Medical Centre KK Women's and Children's Hospital National Healthcare Group Polyclinics National Heart Centre of Singapore National Skin Cenre National University Hospital Parkway Hospitals Singapore Pte Ltd — East Shore Hospital Parkway Hospitals Singapore Pte Ltd — Gleneagles Hospital Parkway Hospitals Singapore Pte Ltd — Mount Elizabeth Hospital Raffles Hospital Private Limited Singapore General Hospital Singapore National Eye Center (SNEC) Tan Tock Seng Hospital
Spain (accredited jointly by JCI and the Fundacion Avedis Donabedian)	ABS Vandellòs — L'Hospitalet (formerly Centre d'Atencio Primaria Hospitalet Vandellos) — Tarragona) Centre d'Atencio Primaria de La Selva — Catalunya Centre d'Atencio Primaria Salou — Tarragona Centro de Salud de El Llano — Asturias Centro de Salud de Moreda — Asturias Centro de Salud de Otero — Oviedo Centro Medico Teknon — Barcelona Clinica Universitaria de Navarra — Navarra

continued

TABLE 6.3 (Continued)

Country	JCI-Accredited Health Facilities
Spain (accredited jointly by JCI and the Fundacion Avedis Donabedian)	Hospital Costa del Sol — Marbella Hospital de Benalmádena — Benalmádena (Malaga) Hospital Valle del Nalon — Asturias Institut Guttmann — Hospital de Neurorrehabilitació — Barcelona Instituto Balear de Oftalmologia — Mallorca Llar Caixa Terrassa-Fundacio Privada Present Torres Falguera — Barcelona Residència d'Avis d'Asco — Tarragona Residència Geriatrica Montsacopa — Girona Residència per a Gent Gran "El Villar" — Tarragona
Switzerland	Ospedale Regionale Di Locarno — Locarno
Taiwan	Chang Bing Show Chwan Memorial Hospital — Lugang Town, Changhua Changhua Christian Hospital — Changhua E-DA Hospital — Kaohsiung Koo Foundation Sun Yat-Sen Cancer Center — Taipei Min-Sheng General Hospital — Tao-Yuan Shuang Ho Hospital — Taipei Medical University — Jhonghe City, Taipei County Taipei Medical University Hospital — Taipei Taipei Medical University- Wan Fang Medical Center — Taipei Tungs' Taichung MetroHarbor Hospital-Wuchi Campus — Taichung
Thailand	Bangkok Hospital Medical Center — Bangkok Bangkok Hospital Pattaya — Chonburi Bangkok Hospital Phuket — Phuket BNH Hospital — Bangkok Bumrungrad International — Bangkok Chiangmai Ram Hospital — Chiangmai Samitivej Srinakarin Hospital — Bangkok Samitivej Sriracha Hospital — Chonburi Samitivej Sukhumvit Hospital — Bangkok
Turkey	Acibadem Bakirkoy Hospital — Bakirkoy-Istanbul Acibadem Bursa Hospital — Bursa Acibadem Kadikoy Hospital — Kadikoy-Istanbul Acibadem Kocaeli Hospital — Kocaeli-Izmit Acibadem Kozyatagi Hospital — Kozyatagi-Istanbul Alman Hastanesi/Deutsches Krankenhaus — Istanbul American Hospital, A.S. — Istanbul Anadolu Medical Center — Kocaeli Ankara Guven Hospital — Ankara Bayindir Hospital — Ankara BSK Metropark Hospital — Cukurova Sisli (Caglayan) Florence Nightingale Hospital — Sisli, Istanbul Cukurova University Medical Faculty — Adana Dunya Eye Hospital — Istanbul Ege Saglik Hastanesi — Izmir

continued

TABLE 6.3 (Continued)

Country	JCI-Accredited Health Facilities
Turkey	Gayrettepe Florence Nightingale Hospital — Gayrettepe, Istanbul
	Hacettepe University Adult Hospital — Ankara
	Hisar Intercontinental Hospital — Istanbul
	International Hospital — Yesilkoy-Istanbul
	Istanbul Memorial Hospital — Istanbul
	Kadiköy Florence Nightingale Hospital — Istanbul
	Kent Hastanesi — Izmir
	Medical Park Healthcare Group — Antalya Hospital — Antalya
	Medical Park Healthcare Group — Bahcelievler Hospital — Istanbul
	Medical Park Healthcare Group — Bursa Hospital — Bursa
	Medial Park Healthcare Group — Goztepe Hospital — Istanbul
	Medline Alarm Saglik Hizmetleri A.S. — Istanbul
	Mesa Hastanesi — Ankara
	Ortopedia Hospital — Adana
	Ozel Medicana Hospital Camilca — Istanbul
	Ozel Medicana Hospitals Bahcelievler — Istanbul
	Sema Hastanesi — Dragos, Maltepe
	TDV Ozel 29 Mayis Hastanesi — Ankara
	Turkish Red Crescent Society Middle Anatolia Regional Blood Center — Ankara
	Uludag Universitesi Saglik Kuruluslan — Bursa
	Yeditepe University Faculty of Dentistry — Gozetepe, Istanbul
	Yeditepe University Hospital — Istanbul
United Arab Emirates	Al Corniche Hospital — Abu Dhabi
	Al Noor Hospital-Airport Road Branch — Abu Dhabi
	Al Noor Hospital-Al Ain Branch — Abu Dhabi
	Al Noor Hospital-Khalifa Branch — Abu Dhabi
	Al Rahba Hospital — Abu Dhabi
	Al Wasi Maternity & Paediatric Hospital — DOHMS — Dubai
	American Academy of Cosmetic Surgery Hospital — Dubai
	American Hospital Dubai — Dubai
	Belhoul European Hospital L.L.C. — Dubai
	Belhoul Specialty Hospital — Dubai
	Biosytech Medical Laboratory — Dubai
	Dubai Hospital-DOHMS — Dubai
	Dubai Medical Laboratory (DML) — Dubai
	Dr. Rustom's Medical & Day Care Surgery Centre — Dubai
	Emirates Hospital — Dubai
	Gulf Diagnostic Center Hospital — Abu Dhabi
	Histopathology and Specialty Laboratory — Dubai
	Imperial College London Diabetes Centre — Abu Dhabi
	International Modern Hospital — Dubai
	Khalifa A Ambulatory Healthcare Center — Abu Dhabi
	Lifeline Hospital — Abu Dhabi
	MEDCARE Hospital L.L.C. — Dubai

continued

TABLE 6.3 (Continued)

Country	JCI-Accredited Health Facilities
United Arab Emirates	MEDCARE Hospital L.L.C.—Dubai
	Medinova Diagnostic Centre—Dubai
	New Medical Centre Specialty Hospital—Dubai
	New Medical Centre Specialty Hospital—Al Ain
	Oasis Hospital—Al Ain
	RAK Hospitak—Ras Al Khaimah
	Rashid Hospital-DOHMS—Dubai
	Sheikh Khalifa Medical City—Abu Dhabi
	Tawam Hospital—Al Ain
	Thalassemia Center-DOHMS—Dubai
	Welcare Hospital Pathology Laboratory—Dubai
	Zulekha Hospital—Dubai
	Zulekha Hospital—Sharjah
	Zulekha Medical Center—Al Qusais
Vietnam	Cao Thang Eye Hospital—Ho Chi Minh City
Yemen	Saudi German Hospital—Sanaa

Source: Joint Commission International. "Joint Commission International (JCI) Accredited Organizations."

- Virtually every type of medical procedure is available abroad. Table 6.4 lists medical specialties that are available, by hospital.
- Americans can save 30 to 90 percent in costs by traveling to other countries for their medical care (Deloitte 2009). Tables 6.5 and 6.6 illustrate some of the potential cost savings, by country. The costs of health care abroad are generally far lower than they are in the United States. For example, a heart bypass that can exceed $120,000 in the United States costs just a fraction of that—$9,000—in India.
- If insurance companies were to cover medical tourism, the potential cost savings to Americans could be $20 billion (Chordas 2009).
- Nearly half of Americans find out about medical tourism via the Internet, and nearly three-quarters research their destination online (*Medical Tourism Magazine* 2009). Figures 6.3, 6.4, 6.5, and 6.6 highlight medical tourists' reasons for traveling and how they research their destinations. Figures 6.7, 6.8, and 6.9 show how they rate their experiences.

TABLE 6.4
International Hospitals, by Medical Specialty

Country	Hospitals	Specialties	JCI Accredited
Antigua	Holberton Hospital	Radiology, pathology, surgery, pediatrics	No
	Crossroads Centre	Addiction recovery	No
Barbados	Bay View Hospital	Cardiology and cardiothoracic surgery, orthopedic surgery, urology, general surgery, neurosurgery, ophthalmology	No
	Barbados Fertility Centre	Fertility treatments	Yes
Brazil	Ivo Pitanguy Clinic	Plastic surgery	No
	Hospital Israelita Albert Einstein	Cardiology, neurology, oncology, organ transplants	Yes
	Sociedad Hospital Samaritano	Highly complex orthopedic, pediatric, cardiac, cancer, neurological, and video-assisted surgeries	Yes
Costa Rica	CIMA Hospital San José	Orthopedics, cosmetic and reconstructive surgery, laparoscopic surgery, urology, otolaryngology	Yes
	Hospital Clínica Bíblica	Cardiology, cosmetic and reconstructive surgery, ophthalmology, orthopedics	Yes
Czech Republic	Na Homolce Hospital	Cardiovascular, neurology, general medical care	Yes
	European Dental Center	Cosmetic dentistry, orthodontics, dental implants	No
	Laderma Clinic	Cosmetic surgery	No
Hungary (*These are just two of the hundreds of dental clinics in Hungary)	Marident	Porcelain veneers, tooth implants, oral surgery, other dental services	No
	Villányi Dent	Aesthetic dentistry, orthodontics, other dental services	No
India	Apollo Hospitals	Neurology, endocrinology, gastroenterology, orthopedics, oncology	Yes (Apollo Hospitals Bangalore, Chennai, Hyderabad)
	Fortis Escorts Heart Institute	Cardiology	Yes
	Shroff Eye Hospital	Ophthalmology	Yes
Israel	Sheba Medical Center	Cardiology, oncology, fertility treatments	No
	Hadassah University Medical Center	Oncology, hematology, bone marrow transplant, orthopedic surgery	No
Jordan	Jordan Hospital and Medical Center	Nuclear medicine, cardiology, endocrinology, fertility treatments, obesity treatments	Yes
	King Hussein Cancer Center	Oncology	Yes
	Specialty Hospital	Cardiovascular surgery, neurosurgery, kidney transplantation, joint replacement, plastic surgery	Yes

continued

TABLE 6.4 (Continued)

Country	Hospitals	Specialties	JCI Accredited
Malaysia	International Specialist Eye Centre	Ophthalmology	Yes
	Institute Jantang Negara (National Heart Institute)	Cardiovascular and thoracic medicine	Yes
	Pentai Hospital Kuala Lampur	Health screenings, preventive care, oncology, fertility treatments, obesity surgery	Yes
Mexico	Christus Muguerza Alta Especialidad Hospital	Cardiovascular surgery, orthopedics, ophthalmology, general surgery	Yes
	Hospital CIMA Hermosillo and Monterrey	Obstetrics, pediatrics, dialysis, cardiology	Yes
Philippines	St. Luke's Medical Center	Blood and marrow transplant, oncology, liver and kidney diseases	Yes
	The Medical City	Obstetrics and gynecology, ophthalmology, orthopedics, otolaryngology	Yes
Singapore	Parkway Hospital Gleneagles	Cardiology, gastroenterology, liver transplant, oncology, orthopedics	Yes
	Johns Hopkins Singapore International Medical Centre	Oncology, complex medical procedures	Yes
	KK Women's and Children's Hospital	High-risk obstetrics, pediatric bone marrow transplantation and open heart surgery	Yes
	National Cancer Centre	Oncology	Yes
	National Dental Centre	Dentistry	Yes
	National Heart Centre	Cardiology	Yes
	National Eye Centre	Ophthalmology	Yes
	National Skin Centre	Dermatology	Yes
	Raffles Hospital	Oncology, dentistry, cardiology, surgery, Chinese medicine	Yes
South Africa	Cape Town Medi-Clinic	Cardio-thoracic surgery, dentistry, dermatology, general surgery, neurology, orthopedics, plastic surgery	No
	Netcare Rosebank Hospital	Cardiology, gastroenterology, neurosurgery, plastic and reconstructive surgery	No
South Korea	Korea University Anam Hospital	Cryosurgery, cardiovascular surgery, oncology, health screenings	Yes
	Severence Hospital, Yonsei University Health System	Oncology, diabetes treatment, health screenings	Yes
Taiwan	Min-Sheng General Hospital	Kidney disease, diabetes, cardiovascular surgery, eye surgery, weight-loss surgery	Yes
	Taipei Medical University — Wan Fang Hospital	Neurosurgery, cardiology, orthopedics, infertility treatments, cosmetic surgery	Yes

continued

TABLE 6.4 (Continued)

Country	Hospitals	Specialties	JCI Accredited
Taiwan	E-Da Hospital	Esophageal and voice reconstruction, joint replacement, laparoscopic weight-loss surgery, gamma knife radiosurgery	Yes
Thailand	Bangkok Hospital Medical Center Bumrungrad International Samitivej Sukhumvit	Orthopedic surgery, neurology, oncology, pulmonary disease, complimentary and alternative medicine, gastroenterology, cardiology, kidney disease Cardiology, radiation and radiology, plastic surgery, orthopedics Oncology, dermatology, ophthalmology, cardiology, kidney and liver disease, wellness	Yes Yes Yes
Turkey	Acibadem Healthcare Group	Oncology, neurosurgery, cardiology, cardiovascular surgery, infertility treatment, neurology, orthopedics, plastic surgery, dentistry, ophthalmology	Yes (Acibadem Bakirkoy, Bursa, Kadikoy, Kocaeli, and Kozyatagi hospitals are accredited)
	Andalou Medical Center	Cardiac care, diagnostic/imaging, neurology, oncology, women's health	Yes
	Medical Park Healthcare Group	Organ transplantation, bone marrow transplantation, oncology, brain and nerve surgery, orthopedics, cardiac surgery, ophthalmology, plastic surgery	Yes (Antalya, Bahcelievler, Bursa, and Goztepe are accredited)
United Arab Emirates	American Hospital Dubai	Cardiology, neuroscience, oncology, joint replacements, endocrinology, gastroenterology	Yes
	Dubai Hospital	Endocrinology, nephrology, nuclear medicine, obstetrics, oncology, ophthalmology, orthopedics, urology	Yes
	Zulekah Hospitals	Cardiology, orthopedics, minimally invasive surgeries, respiratory medicine	Yes (Zulekha Hospital Dubai, Sharjah, and Al Qusais)

Note: This table includes only a small percentage of hospitals in each country — it is not a complete listing.
Source: Woodman, Josef. *Patients Beyond Borders: Everybody's Guide to Affordable, World-Class Medical Travel.* Chapel Hill, NC: Healthy Travel Media, 2008. Joint Commission International. "Joint Commission International (JCI) Accredited Organizations."

TABLE 6.5

Comparative Costs for Medical Procedures in the U.S. vs. Other Countries

Procedure	U.S. Cost	India	Thailand	Singapore	Costa Rica	Israel	Jordan	Mexico
Heart bypass	$122,000–$177,000	$9,000–$10,000	$12,000	$20,000	$24,000	$25,000	$9,500–$15,000	$27,000
Heart bypass with valve replacement	$159,000–$230,000	$9,500	$10,500	$13,000	$30,000	$25,000	$12,000–$15,000 (plus valve)	$28,000–$35,000
Hip replacement	$43,000–$63,000	$9,000	$12,000	$12,000	$8,000–$11,000	$18,000	$5,000–$8,000 (plus joint prosthesis)	$8,000–$14,000
Knee replacement	$40,000–$58,000	$9,000	$10,000	$13,000	$8,000–$11,000	$11,000–$18,000	$5,000–$8,000 (plus joint prosthesis)	$7,000–$15,000

TABLE 6.6

Comparative Costs For Cosmetic and Dental Surgery Procedures in the U.S. vs. Other Medical Tourism Destinations

Procedure	U.S. Cost	Brazil	Czech Republic	India	Mexico	Singapore
Breast augmentation	$8,000	$4,500–$5,000	$4,000–$5,700	$3,000–$5,000	$3,900–$4,200	$5,000–$10,000
Facelift	$15,000	$3,500–$4,000	$3,000–$4,500	$3,000–$5,700	$5,800–$11,300	$5,000–$10,000
Liposuction	$13,500	$650 (per region)	$3,000–$4,000	$1,000–$3,000	$2,300–$4,500	$3,000–$10,000
Dental crown	$750–$1,000	$230	Price information not available	$360	$339–$650	$275–$325
Porcelain veneers	$800–$1,200	$230	$540–$630	$420	$180–$600	$250–$300
Dental implant	$1,900–$5,000	$460	$750–$1,250	$1,100	$985–$1,800	$2,500–$3,200

Sources: Woodman, Josef. *Patients Beyond Borders: Everybody's Guide to Affordable, World-Class Medical Travel.* Chapel Hill, NC: Healthy Travel Media, 2008. Uni, James A. "Medical and Surgical Tourism: The New world of Health Care Globalization and What it Means for the Practicing Surgeon." *American College of Surgeons Nora Institute for Surgical Patient Safety.* Kumar, Rajesh. *Global Trends in Health and Medical Tourism.* New Delhi: SBS Publishers & Distributors Pvt. Ltd., 2009.

FIGURE 6.2
Percent of people who are willing to travel to a foreign country
for an elective procedure, by generation

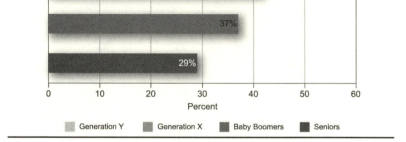

Percent of people who are willing to travel to a foreign country
for an elective procedure, by generation

51%

42%

37%

29%

Percent

■ Generation Y   ■ Generation X   ■ Baby Boomers   ■ Seniors

Source: Deloitte Center for Health Solutions. "Medical Tourism: Consumers in Search of Value." Deloitte Center for Health Solutions. "Medical Tourism: Update and Implications — 2009 Report."

FIGURE 6.3, 6.4
How Medical Tourists Research Their Travel

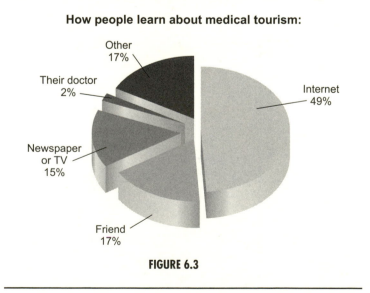

How people learn about medical tourism:

Other
17%

Their doctor
2%

Internet
49%

Newspaper
or TV
15%

Friend
17%

FIGURE 6.3

Source: "MTA Releases First Patient Surveys on Medical Tourism." *Medical Tourism Magazine.* June 1, 2009.

FIGURE 6.3, 6.4 (continued)
How Medical Tourists Research Their Travel

How People Research Their Information on Destinations and Hospitals

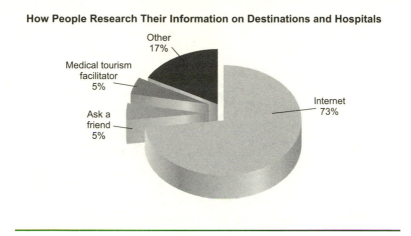

Source: "MTA Releases First Patient Surveys on Medical Tourism." *Medical Tourism Magazine.* June 1, 2009.

FIGURE 6.5, 6.6
Why Medical Tourists Travel

Reasons why medical tourists travel

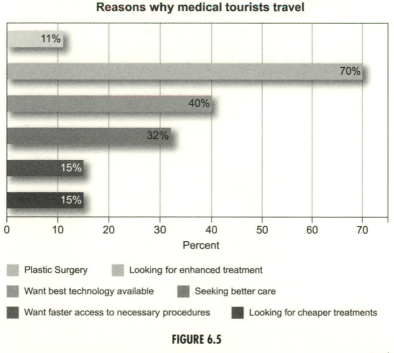

Plastic Surgery   Looking for enhanced treatment

Want best technology available   Seeking better care

Want faster access to necessary procedures   Looking for cheaper treatments

FIGURE 6.5

continued

FIGURE 6.5, 6.6 (continued)
Why Medical Tourists Travel

Type of procedure for which medical tourists travel:

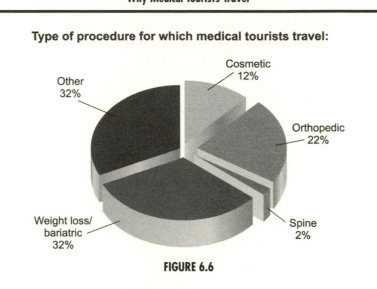

FIGURE 6.6

Sources: "MTA Releases First Patient Surveys on Medical Tourism." *Medical Tourism Magazine.* June 1, 2009. Prashad, Sharda. "The World Is Your Hospital." *Canadian Business 81,* no. 12/13 (August 18, 2008): 62–64.

FIGURE 6.7, 6.8, 6.9
Medical Tourists' Satisfaction with Their Medical Care

How medical tourists rate the hospital at which they received medical care:

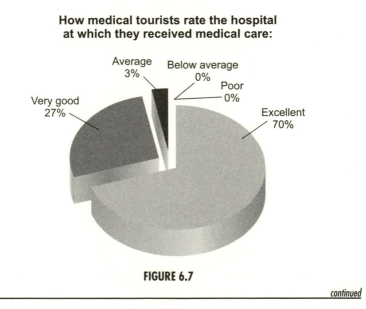

FIGURE 6.7

continued

FIGURE 6.7, 6.8, 6.9 (continued)
Medical Tourists' Satisfaction with Their Medical Care

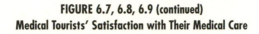

**Did you feel the service you received
was more personalized than in the U.S.?**

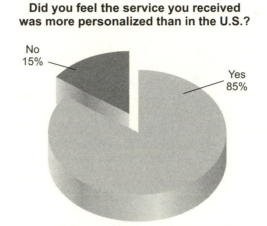

No
15%

Yes
85%

FIGURE 6.8

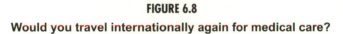

Would you travel internationally again for medical care?

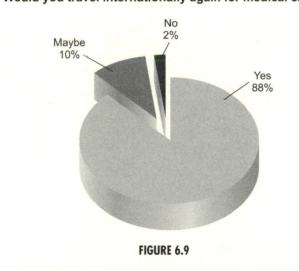

No
2%

Maybe
10%

Yes
88%

FIGURE 6.9

Documents

American College of Surgeons Statement on Medical and Surgical Tourism

In recognition of the explosive growth of the medical tourism industry, the American College of Surgeons—a scientific and educational association of surgeons that is dedicated to improving surgical care—developed an official statement on medical tourism. The statement is designed to inform patients about the implications of traveling abroad for medical care, including the potential risks and legal ramifications.

The College's governing board, the Board of Regents, approved the nine-point position statement in February 2009. It was published in the April 2009 issue of the Bulletin of the American College of Surgeons.

Reprinted with permission from the *Bulletin of the American College of Surgeons*, Vol. 94, No. 4, April 2009.

Medical tourism is a term denoting travel across international borders for the express purpose of receiving medical care.

Residents of the U.S. may choose to pursue medical care abroad for a variety of reasons, including a real or perceived lack of services available at home; limitations imposed by payors or regulatory agencies on access to certain specialists, treatment protocols, equipment, or services; prolonged waiting periods; lower costs of care; and personal reasons, such as a desire to travel.

Medical care outside the U.S. involves a number of risks. Some of the intangible risks include variability in the training of medical and allied health professionals; differences in the standards to which medical institutions are held; potential difficulties associated with treatment far from family and friends; differences in transparency surrounding patient discussions; the approach to interpretation of test results; the accuracy and completeness of medical records; the lack of support networks, should longer-term care be needed; the lack of opportunity for follow-up care by treating physicians and surgeons; and the exposure to endemic diseases prevalent in certain countries. Language and cultural barriers may impair communication with physicians and other caregivers. Finally, compensation for liability associated with injury may be difficult to obtain.

The American College of Surgeons has adopted the following position with respect to medical tourism.

The ACS encourages patients to seek care of the highest quality and supports their rights to select their surgeons and health care institutions without restriction.

The ACS encourages its Fellows to assist all patients in reaching informed decisions concerning medical care, whether at home or abroad.

The ACS advises patients to consider the medical, social, cultural, and legal implications of seeking medical treatment abroad prior to deciding on a venue of care. In the event of proven medical liability for injury, viable means for the recovery of damages should be in place. Patients should be aware that many of the means for legal recourse available to citizens in the U.S. are not universally accessible in other countries.

The ACS encourages patients electing to receive treatment abroad to seek care at health care institutions that have met the standards for accreditation established by recognized accrediting organizations. Examples of recognized accrediting organizations include The Joint Commission International (U.S.) and the Trent International Accreditation Scheme (U.K.). Patients should be aware, however, that accreditation standards are not uniform and that standards set locally can vary from place to place around the world.

The ACS encourages patients electing treatment abroad to seek care from surgeons and anesthesiologists certified in their specialties through a process equivalent to that established by the member boards of the American Board of Medical Specialties.

The ACS encourages patients receiving treatment abroad to obtain a complete set of medical records prior to returning home so that the details of their care are immediately available to their physicians and surgeons in the U.S. Follow-up care at home should be organized prior to travel whenever possible.

The ACS encourages patients contemplating medical tourism to understand the special risks of combining long international flights and certain vacation activities with anesthesia and surgical procedures.

The ACS opposes the imposition of provisions for mandatory referral of patients by insurers to health care institutions outside the U.S., unless such provisions are clearly and explicitly stated in the insurance contract and accepted by the subscriber. The ACS opposes the addition of provisions for mandatory referral abroad for patients with insurance contracts already in force, absent the subscribers' fully informed consent. In any circumstance, mandatory care abroad should be verifiably equivalent in quality to care available in the U.S.

The ACS supports the view that payors referring patients for mandatory treatment abroad should be responsible for the coordination and reimbursement of follow-up care in the U.S., including the management of postoperative complications, readmissions, rehabilitation, and long-term care.

International Society of Aesthetic Plastic Surgery Guidelines for Plastic Surgery Tourists

*The International Society of Aesthetic Plastic Surgery (ISAPS) is an or-
ganization made up of more than 1,600 board-certified plastic surgeons
in 86 countries. Its members help consumers make the safest choices
about cosmetic surgery. After receiving numerous questions from consumers and professionals regarding international travel for cosmetic
surgery, the ISAPS decided to create the first guidelines for plastic surgery tourism. These guidelines help tourists make informed choices before planning their trip overseas.*

Reprinted by permission of the International Society of Aesthetic Plastic
Surgery.

The Key Guidelines for Plastic Surgery Travelers

What Is the Surgeon's Training?

A gynecologist performing a breast augmentation or a dermatologist
doing a face lift are not an appropriate choices.

Is the Plastic Surgeon Certified?

The ISAPS website lists the names and addresses of over 1,600 certified
plastic surgeons in 84 countries.

Is the Plastic Surgeon's Facility Certified?

Ask for certification information and who the certifying body is.

Does Your Personal Health Insurance Cover You Outside Your Country?

Most health insurance providers do not cover individuals for surgery
performed outside their own country. Consider obtaining International
Medical Coverage that may be available through your insurance agent.

What About Aftercare?

Patients should stay in the area where the surgery was performed for
at least one week, depending on the procedure. Find out in advance
where you will stay and if this facility is prepared to care for your post
operative needs.

What About Complications?

What doctor will care for you at home if you have complications and
who will pay for secondary or revision procedures?

Do the Key Personnel at the Surgeon's Office Speak Your Language Fluently?

If you cannot be easily understood, be prepared for complications.

With Whom Are You Communicating?

You should be talking directly with the doctor's staff and the doctor. A travel agent should only make travel and accommodations arrangements.

Is the Surgeon a Member of Recognized National and International Societies?

ISAPS membership is by invitation and is granted to applicants only after extensive screening.

Have You Checked for References?

Ask for names and contact information of patients who have recently had a similar procedure and contact them about their experience with the surgeon, their staff, aftercare facilities and post-operative follow up.

Centers for Disease Control and Prevention. The Pre-Travel Consultation: Counseling and Advice for Travelers

The Centers for Disease Control and Prevention (CDC) has published this advice for medical travelers in Chapter 2 of its Yellow Book. *This consumer guide, which is published once every two years, is meant to help international travelers with the potential health implications of their travels abroad. The following is an excerpt from the* Yellow Book.

The complete book can be found on the CDC's website: http://wwwnc.cdc.gov/travel/content/yellowbook/home-2010.aspx. The author of Chapter 2 is Christie R. Reed.

Introduction

Travel for the purpose of obtaining health care abroad has received a great deal of attention in the popular media recently—even Wikipedia has recently devoted a section to the practice (*http://en.wikipedia.org/wiki/Medical_tourism*). However, it is not the only form of "medical tourism." The term has also been applied to travel by health-care professionals for the purpose of providing health care. The extent of either form of travel is not well characterized, but the overarching issues for both types of travelers, their primary health-care providers, and travel medicine providers are outlined below.

Travel to Obtain Care

Data from the annual U.S. Department of Commerce in-flight survey during 2003–2006 show an overall annual increase in the number of trips taken by U.S. residents for which at least one purpose was health care. In 2006, there were approximately half a million overseas trips in which health treatment was at least one purpose of travel. Common cited procedures include:

Dentistry

Reproductive procedures

Surgeries (cosmetic, joint replacement, and cardiac)

Lower cost is often mentioned as the motivation for this type of medical tourism, and an entire industry has grown up around this phenomenon. One can search for a provider and research accreditation status of the facility online, opt for an online concierge service that will make all the arrangements or, more recently, find that health insurance coverage may include the option of "outsourced" health care.

The dynamic nature of the field was described in a recent round-table discussion in Merrell et al.,

> In recent years, standards have been rising in other parts of the world even faster than prices have surged in the U.S. Many physicians abroad trained in the U.S. and the Joint Commission International (JCI) applies strict standards to accreditation of offshore facilities. Those facilities use the same implants, supplies, and drugs as their U.S. counterparts. However, a heart bypass in Thailand costs $11,000 compared to as much as $130,000 in the U.S. Spinal fusion surgery in India at $5,500 compares to over $60,000 in the U.S.

However, the quality of facilities, assistance services, and care is neither uniform nor regulated; thus, in most instances, responsibility for assessing suitability of an individual program or facility lies solely with the traveler.

Guidelines for Travelers Seeking Care Abroad

Potential patients should consider that, whatever procedure is being contemplated, travelers undergoing medical treatment outside their accustomed environment are almost always at a disadvantage, particularly if there are complications. Concerns are—

- Resolution of financial issues if costs escalate, such as in the case of complications.
- Language and cultural differences may impede accurate interpretation of both verbal and nonverbal communication.
- Religious and ethical differences may be encountered over issues such as heroic efforts to preserve life or limb or in care of the terminally ill.
- Lack of familiarity with the local medical system, limited access to past medical history, unfamiliar drugs and medicines.
- Legal recourse may be fairly limited, difficult to obtain, or nonexistent.
- Follow-up care back in the United States may be more difficult to arrange and may be fraught with problems, should there be complications.

Potential patients should consider the guiding principles developed by the American Medical Association for employers, insurance companies, and other entities that facilitate or offer incentives for care outside the United States, although in some circumstances it is unclear how realistic they may be [see American Medical Association Guidelines for Patients Traveling Overseas for Medical Care above]. These principles stipulate that international care must be voluntary and provided by accredited institutions; financial incentives should not inappropriately limit or restrict patient options; there should be continuity of care, including coverage of costs upon return; patients should be informed of their rights and legal recourse before travel; patients should have access to licensing, outcome, and accrediting information when seeking care; medical record transfers should comply with Health Insurance Portability and Accountability Act (HIPAA) guidelines; and patients should be informed of potential risks of combining surgical procedures with long flights and vacation activities. The American Society for Plastic Surgery emphasizes plastic surgery is "real" surgery and outlines the issues every patient undergoing surgery should consider, whether at home or abroad, on their website at www.plasticsurgery.org/patients_consumers/patient_safety/Medical-Tourism.cfm. Several clusters of mycobacterial wound infections in travelers returning from cosmetic procedures abroad have been published. Similarly, the American Dental Association provides informational documents, including: "Traveler's Guide to Safe Dental Care" through the Global Dental Safety Organization for Safety and Asepsis Procedures at www.osap.org and "Dental Care Away from Home" at www.ada.org/public/manage/care/index.asp.

Individuals researching accreditation status should note that, although facilities may be part of a chain, they are surveyed and accredited individually. They should also check the duration of the accreditation and validate that the information is current by consulting the public portion of the appropriate accrediting agency website.

Pre-Travel Advice for the Medical Tourist

As discussed in the Planning for Healthy Travel section in Chapter 1, patients who do elect to travel should consult a travel health-care practitioner for advice tailored to individual health needs, preferably at least 4–6 weeks in advance of travel. This is particularly true for patients considering invasive procedures, who should consult as soon as travel is considered to allow for assessment of hepatitis B vaccination status (see the Hepatitis B section earlier in this chapter). Hepatitis B and C viruses and HIV are examples of blood-borne infections that can be transmitted via contaminated equipment, from infected health-care providers during invasive procedures, via transfusion of blood or blood products, or through transplantation of tissue or organs that have not been properly screened. Prevalence rates of these viruses vary considerably around the world and are generally higher in developing parts of the world than in the United States. U.S. policies address hepatitis B vaccination status of health-care workers, but these policies are not uniform worldwide and there are no currently licensed vaccines for hepatitis C and HIV. Blood transfusion programs in the United States and other developed areas rely on voluntary, nonremunerated donors; screen the donated blood for a variety of potentially blood-borne pathogens; and are closely regulated. Standards in other parts of the world vary. Based on data from 2000–2001, the latest available on the WHO Global Database on Blood Safety (www.who.int/bloodsafety/global_database/en/), 70 countries did not test all donated blood for the three major blood-borne viruses, HIV and hepatitis B and C.

Organ Transplantation

Organ transplantation in the United States is also a voluntary, closely monitored process coordinated by the United Network for Organ Sharing (www.optn.org). The need for transplantable organs, however, far exceeds the available supply worldwide. Travel to a country with less rigorous methods of distribution for the purpose of obtaining a transplant has been termed "transplant tourism" or "organ trafficking." Recently, there have been reports in the media of investigations and arrests associated with "rings" that use unscrupulous methods to obtain organs. In 2004, the World Health Assembly Resolution 57.18

encouraged member countries to protect vulnerable populations. Some countries have begun experimenting with controlled programs to relieve the shortage, support the health of the donor, and remove incentives for clandestine operations. A revised set of eleven WHO Guiding Principles on Human Cell, Tissue and Organ Transplantation will be presented to the World Health Assembly in 2009 (www.who. int/transplantation/).

Travel for the Purpose of Delivering Health Care

There are many structured opportunities for health-care profession-als, students, or trainees to participate in established programs in developing areas of the world that are mutually beneficial to both the local population and the traveler. Travel by health-care workers in their professional capacity should be governed by the principle of *Primum non nocere*, or "first, do no harm." The traveling health-care worker should have sufficient experience or be at a stage in training to be able to contribute labor, knowledge, and skills to the host com-munity. Benefits to the traveling health-care worker include exposure to patients with tropical diseases and conditions that are not com-monly seen or are at a more advanced stage than in the country of residence; local diagnostic skills which are often less dependent on technology; and new cultures and new ways of thinking, in addition to any personal gratification. Many medical schools and universities have established reciprocal relationships with institutions in devel-oping areas in which there is an exchange of students and faculty. A variety of organizations match volunteers with local needs for skills-building or to address specific problems. Doctors Without Borders/ Médecins Sans Frontières (MSF), which received the Nobel Peace Prize in 1999 for humanitarian efforts around the world, requires a minimum 6-month commitment from physicians and a shorter com-mitment for surgeons. Interventional programs such as dentistry or surgery simultaneously provide reparative or reconstructive services to the population and train local staff to perform the procedures and provide follow-up care, often donating excess supplies. Other ongoing volunteer relationships exist between faith-based or service organizations and local communities. The involvement of the local health establishment is key to determining needs and maximiz-ing benefit to the local population, as well as educating the visitors on local customs and medical issues and providing translation, if needed, to adequately assess the patients, obtain consent, and advise on postprocedure care.

These forms of international capacity-building should be differenti-ated from—medicine that is practiced on local populations ad hoc by independent travelers to areas that seem to have no system of health care, the development of adventure holidays sold to groups of doctors specifically for the purposes of research or providing health care in the absence of prior consultation, and students or trainees who travel to "gain practical experience" beyond their training with minimal supervision or absence of structured learning, or practitioners performing outside the area of their expertise.

The acts performed in a life-threatening emergency are justified, but if a local health-care system exists there should still be follow-up with the nearest local provider. Health-care professionals contemplating an international clinical experience should also consult the Humanitarian Aid Workers section in Chapter 8 for a discussion of emotional and physical fitness to participate, preparation, and after-care issues.

The Primary Health-Care Provider

Primary health-care providers play a crucial role in several aspects of medical tourism. For un- or under-insured patients who cannot afford their prescribed course of treatment, the primary care provider may be asked to provide counsel regarding international treatment options, assist with vetting available options, optimize patient status prior to travel, or coordinate care on return. Each provider will need to assess individually his or her ability to address travel health issues or refer to a travel medicine provider.

Clinicians who care for immigrant populations should also be aware that the majority of health-seeking travelers in 2004 were current U.S. citizens born outside the United States, followed by non-U.S. citizens. Health-care needs, such as dentistry, are often included in visits home, due to familiarity with care in the country of origin, the high cost of health care in the United States, and lack of insurance coverage in these populations. There are also recent reports that patients on transplant waiting lists may also travel abroad for the procedure and return to the developed country of residence for continued care, often requiring immediate hospitalization and intense initial management with little documentation. Options for dialysis care are also increasing in developing areas; thus patients requiring this level of care may return home for visits and obtain local care. Acute hepatitis B infections have been diagnosed in patients returning to developed countries from both scenarios. Clinicians providing care to immigrant populations should consider routinely inquiring about future or recent travel home to visit friends and relatives, whether health care will be sought or occurred during travel and advise accordingly (see the VFR section in Chapter 8).

Travel Medicine Providers

Patients who plan to seek medical care abroad may not divulge this activity during the consultation. The desire for anonymity may be a reason for seeking procedures, such as cosmetic surgery or sex-change operations, abroad. As previously mentioned, cost is often an issue, and patients may be uncomfortable self-disclosing. Clinicians may find that routine discussion of hepatitis B vaccination with all patients in the context of risk due to tattoo, sex, emergency medical care, and invasive procedures offers an environment for patients to initiate further discussion.

Health-care providers may also find that the medical industry and associated resources that are rapidly expanding in the developing world related to medical tourism intersect directly with the medical care options for patients with pre-existing illness who travel, emergency care for travelers, and health-care options for expatriates.

United Nations World Tourism Organization (UNWTO) Global Code of Ethics for Tourism

With international tourism (including medical tourism) growing exponentially, the UN World Tourism Organization (UNWTO) felt that a Code of Ethics was needed to ensure that tourism remains a sustainable endeavor that is beneficial to both travelers and their host countries. To that end, the UNWTO developed a 10-point code that helps safeguard the resources and residents of tourism destinations around the world. The Global Code of Ethics was enacted during the General Assembly in Santiago, Chile, on October 1, 1999.

Used by permission. © UNWTO, 9284402710.

Principles

Article 1 Tourism's Contribution to Mutual Understanding and Respect between Peoples and Societies

(1) The understanding and promotion of the ethical values common to humanity, with an attitude of tolerance and respect for the diversity of religious, philosophical and moral beliefs, are both the foundation and the consequence of responsible tourism; stakeholders in tourism development and tourists themselves should observe the social and cultural traditions and practices of all peoples, including those of minorities and indigenous peoples and to recognize their worth;

(2) Tourism activities should be conducted in harmony with the attributes and traditions of the host regions and countries and in respect for their laws, practices and customs;

(3) The host communities, on the one hand, and local professionals, on the other, should acquaint themselves with and respect the tourists

who visit them and find out about their lifestyles, tastes and expectations; the education and training imparted to professionals contribute to a hospitable welcome;

(4) It is the task of the public authorities to provide protection for tourists and visitors and their belongings; they must pay particular attention to the safety of foreign tourists owing to the particular vulnerability they may have; they should facilitate the introduction of specific means of information, prevention, security, insurance and assistance consistent with their needs; any attacks, assaults, kidnappings or threats against tourists or workers in the tourism industry, as well as the willful destruction of tourism facilities or of elements of cultural or natural heritage should be severely condemned and punished in accordance with their respective national laws;

(5) When travelling, tourists and visitors should not commit any criminal act or any act considered criminal by the laws of the country visited and abstain from any conduct felt to be offensive or injurious by the local populations, or likely to damage the local environment; they should refrain from all trafficking in illicit drugs, arms, antiques, protected species and products and substances that are dangerous or prohibited by national regulations;

(6) Tourists and visitors have the responsibility to acquaint themselves, even before their departure, with the characteristics of the countries the characteristics of the countries they are preparing to visit; they must be aware of the health and security risks inherent in any travel outside their usual environment and behave in such a way as to minimize those risks;

Article 2 Tourism as A Vehicle for Individual and Collective Fulfillment

(1) Tourism, the activity most frequently associated with rest and relaxation, sport and access to culture and nature, should be planned and practised as a privileged means of individual and collective fulfillment; when practised with a sufficiently open mind, it is an irreplaceable factor of self-education, mutual tolerance and for learning about the legitimate differences between peoples and cultures and their diversity;

(2)Tourism activities should respect the equality of men and women; they should promote human rights and, more particularly, the individual rights of the most vulnerable groups, notably children, the elderly, the handicapped, ethnic minorities and indigenous peoples;

(3) The exploitation of human beings in any form, particularly sexual, especially when applied to children, conflicts with the fundamental aims of tourism and is the negation of tourism; as such, in accordance with international law, it should be energetically combated with the cooperation of all the States concerned and penalized without concession by the national legislation of both the countries visited and the countries of the perpetrators of these acts, even when they are carried out abroad;

(4) Travel for purposes of religion, health, education and cultural or linguistic exchanges are particularly beneficial forms of tourism, which deserve encouragement;

(5) The introduction into curricula of education about the value of tourist exchanges, their economic, social and cultural benefits, and also their risks, should be encouraged;

Article 3 Tourism, A Factor of Sustainable Development

(1) All the stakeholders in tourism development should safeguard the natural environment with a view to achieving sound, continuous and sustainable economic growth geared to satisfying equitably the needs and aspirations of present and future generations;

(2) All forms of tourism development that are conducive to saving rare and precious resources, in particular water and energy, as well as avoiding so far as possible waste production, should be given priority and encouraged by national, regional and local public authorities;

(3) The staggering in time and space of tourist and visitor flows, particularly those resulting from paid leave and school holi- days, and a more even distribution of holidays should be sought so as to reduce the pressure of tourism activity on the environment and enhance its beneficial impact on the tourism industry and the local economy;

(4) Tourism infrastructure should be designed and tourism activities programmed in such a way as to protect the natural heritage composed of ecosystems and biodiversity and to preserve endangered species of wildlife; the stakeholders in tourism development, and especially professionals, should agree to the imposition of limitations or constraints on their activities when these are exercised in particularly sensitive areas: desert, polar or high mountain regions, coastal areas, tropical forests or wetlands, propitious to the creation of nature reserves or protected areas;

(5) Nature tourism and ecotourism are recognized as being particularly conducive to enriching and enhancing the standing of tourism, provided they respect the natural heritage and local populations and are in keeping with the carrying capacity of the sites;

Article 4 Tourism, a User of the Cultural Heritage of Mankind and a Contributor to its Enhancement

(1) Tourism resources belong to the common heritage of mankind; the communities in whose territories they are situated have particular rights and obligations to them;

(2) Tourism policies and activities should be conducted with respect for the artistic, archaeological and cultural heritage, which they should protect and pass on to future generations; particular care should be devoted to preserving and upgrading monuments, shrines and museums

as well as archaeological and historic sites which must be widely open to tourist visits; encouragement should be given to public access to privately-owned cultural property and monuments, with respect for the rights of their owners, as well as to religious buildings, without prejudice to normal needs of worship;

(3) Financial resources derived from visits to cultural sites and monuments should, at least in part, be used for the upkeep, safeguard, development and embellishment of this heritage;

(4) Tourism activity should be planned in such a way as to allow traditional cultural products, crafts and folklore to survive and flourish, rather than causing them to degenerate and become standardized;

Article 5 Tourism, a Beneficial Activity for Host Countries and Communities

(1) Local populations should be associated with tourism activities and share equitably in the economic, social and cultural benefits they generate, and particularly in the creation of direct and indirect jobs resulting from them;

(2) Tourism policies should be applied in such a way as to help to raise the standard of living of the populations of the regions visited and meet their needs; the planning and architectural approach to and operation of tourism resorts and accommodation should aim to integrate them, to the extent possible, in the local economic and social fabric; where skills are equal, priority should be given to local manpower;

(3) Special attention should be paid to the specific problems of coastal areas and island territories and to vulnerable rural or mountain regions, for which tourism often represents a rare opportunity for development in the face of the decline of traditional economic activities;

(4) Tourism professionals, particularly investors, governed by the regulations laid down by the public authorities, should carry out studies of the impact of their development projects on the environment and natural surroundings; they should also deliver, with the greatest transparency and objectivity, information on their future programmes and their foreseeable repercussions and foster dialogue on their contents with the populations concerned;

Article 6 Obligations of Stakeholders in Tourism Development

(1) Tourism professionals have an obligation to provide tourists with objective and honest information on their places of destination and on the conditions of travel, hospitality and stays; they should ensure that the contractual clauses proposed to their customers are readily understandable as to the nature, price and quality of the services they commit themselves to providing and the financial compensation payable by them in the event of a unilateral breach of contract on their part;

(2) Tourism professionals, insofar as it depends on them, should show concern, in co- operation with the public authorities, for the security and safety, accident prevention, health protec- tion and food safety of those who seek their services; likewise, they should ensure the existence of suitable systems of insurance and assistance; they should accept the reporting obligations prescribed by national regulations and pay fair compensation in the event of failure to observe their contractual obligations;

(3) Tourism professionals, so far as this depends on them, should contribute to the cultural and spiritual fulfillment of tourists and allow them, during their travels, to practise their religions;

(4) The public authorities of the generating States and the host countries, in cooperation with the professionals concerned and their as- sociations, should ensure that the necessary mechanisms are in place for the repatriation of tourists in the event of the bankruptcy of the enter- prise that organized their travel;

(5) Governments have the right—and the duty—especially in a crisis, to inform their nationals of the difficult circumstances, or even the dangers they may encounter during their travels abroad; it is their responsibility however to issue such information without prejudicing in an unjustified or exaggerated manner the tourism industry of the host countries and the interests of their own operators; the contents of travel advisories should therefore be discussed beforehand with the authori- ties of the host countries and the professionals concerned; recommenda- tions formulated should be strictly proportionate to the gravity of the situations encountered and confined to the geographical areas where the insecurity has arisen; such advisories should be qualified or can- celled as soon as a return to normality permits;

(6) The press, and particularly the specialized travel press and the other media, including modern means of electronic communication, should issue honest and balanced information on events and situations that could influence the flow of tourists; they should also provide ac- curate and reliable information to the consumers of tourism services; the new communication and electronic commerce technologies should also be developed and used for this purpose; as is the case for the media, they should not in any way promote sex tourism;

Article 7 Right to Tourism

(1) The prospect of direct and personal access to the discovery and enjoyment of the planet's resources constitutes a right equally open to all the world's inhabitants; the increasingly extensive participation in national and international tourism should be regarded as one of the best possible expressions of the sustained growth of free time, and obstacles should not be placed in its way;

(2) The universal right to tourism must be regarded as the corollary of the right to rest and leisure, including reasonable limitation of working hours and periodic holidays with pay, guaranteed by Article 24 of the Universal Declaration of Human Rights and Article 7.d of the International Covenant on Economic, Social and Cultural Rights;

(3) Social tourism, and in particular associative tourism, which facilitates widespread access to leisure, travel and holidays, should be developed with the support of the public authorities;

(4) Family, youth, student and senior tourism and tourism for people with disabilities, should be encouraged and facilitated;

Article 8 Liberty of Tourist Movements

(1) Tourists and visitors should benefit, in compliance with international law and national legislation, from the liberty to move within their countries and from one State to another, in accordance with Article 13 of the Universal Declaration of Human Rights; they should have access to places of transit and stay and to tourism and cultural sites without being subject to excessive formalities or discrimination;

(2) Tourists and visitors should have access to all available forms of communication, internal or external; they should benefit from prompt and easy access to local administrative, legal and health services; they should be free to contact the consular representatives of their countries of origin in compliance with the diplomatic conventions in force;

(3) Tourists and visitors should benefit from the same rights as the citizens of the country visited concerning the confidentiality of the personal data and information concerning them, especially when these are stored electronically;

(4) Administrative procedures relating to border crossings whether they fall within the competence of States or result from international agreements, such as visas or health and customs formalities, should be adapted, so far as possible, so as to facilitate to the maximum freedom of travel and widespread access to international tourism; agreements between groups of countries to harmonize and simplify these procedures should be encouraged; specific taxes and levies penalizing the tourism industry and undermining its competitiveness should be gradually phased out or corrected;

(5) So far as the economic situation of the countries from which they come permits, travelers should have access to allowances of convertible currencies needed for their travels;

Article 9 Rights of the Workers and Entrepreneurs in the Tourism Industry

(1) The fundamental rights of salaried and self-employed workers in the tourism industry and related activities, should be guaranteed under

the supervision of the national and local administrations, both of their States of origin and of the host countries with particular care, given the specific constraints linked in particular to the seasonality of their activity, the global dimension of their industry and the flexibility often required of them by the nature of their work;

(2) Salaried and self-employed workers in the tourism industry and related activities have the right and the duty to acquire appropriate initial and continuous training; they should be given adequate social protection; job insecurity should be limited so far as possible; and a specific status, with particular regard to their social welfare, should be offered to seasonal workers in the sector;

(3) Any natural or legal person, provided he, she or it has the necessary abilities and skills, should be entitled to develop a professional activity in the field of tourism under existing national laws; entrepreneurs and investors—especially in the area of small and medium-sized enterprises—should be entitled to free access to the tourism sector with a minimum of legal or administrative restrictions;

(4) Exchanges of experience offered to executives and workers, whether salaried or not, from different countries, contributes to foster the development of the world tourism industry; these movements should be facilitated so far as possible in compliance with the applicable national laws and international conventions;

(5) As an irreplaceable factor of solidarity in the development and dynamic growth of international exchanges, multinational enterprises of the tourism industry should not exploit the dominant positions they sometimes occupy; they should avoid becoming the vehicles of cultural and social models artificially imposed on the host communities; in exchange for their freedom to invest and trade which should be fully recognized, they should involve themselves in local development, avoiding, by the excessive repatriation of their profits or their induced imports, a reduction of their contribution to the economies in which they are established;

(6) Partnership and the establishment of balanced relations between enterprises of generating and receiving countries contribute to the sustainable development of tourism and an equitable distribution of the benefits of its growth;

Article 10 Implementation of the Principles of the Global Code of Ethics for Tourism

(1) The public and private stakeholders in tourism development should cooperate in the implementation of these principles and monitor their effective application;

(2) The stakeholders in tourism development should recognize the role of international institutions, among which the World Tourism

Organization ranks first, and non-governmental organizations with competence in the field of tourism promotion and development, the protection of human rights, the environment or health, with due respect for the general principles of international law;

(3) The same stakeholders should demonstrate their intention to refer any disputes concerning the application or interpretation of the Global Code of Ethics for Tourism for conciliation to an impartial third body known as the World Committee on Tourism Ethics.

International Society for Stem Cell Research Patient Handbook on Stem Cell Therapies: Appendix I of the Guidelines for Clinical Translation of Stem Cell Research (Sections 9, 10, and 11)

Americans travel abroad for a number of different reasons, including lower-cost medical care and access to treatments not available in the United States. The therapeutic use of stem cells—the precursor cells that develop into all of the different organs and tissues in the body—is still highly controversial in the United States. Although President Barack Obama loosened some previous restrictions on the use of federal funding for embryonic stem cell research, the use of stem cells for medical purposes is still in its infancy in the United States.

Many other countries have far less stringent policies on the use of stem cells for treatment. As a result, some foreign clinics are marketing high-cost, yet still unproven stem cell therapies to medical tourists. A 2008 study found that the average price of these treatments was $21,500 (O'Reilly 2009). In response to these marketing practices, the International Society for Stem Cell Research in December 2008 released its own guidelines on stem cell therapies, which are designed to protect consumers from fraudulent and potentially dangerous claims. The three questions included here are specific to stem cell treatments.

Copyright of the *ISSCR Patient Handbook on Stem Cell Therapies* is held by the International Society for Stem Cell Research.

9. How Do I Know If an Approved Stem Cell Therapy Is Safe?

No medical treatment can ever be described as completely safe. There are risks involved with all medical treatment, some small, some great. These risks, even if they are small, should be explained clearly to you by a medical professional.

10. What Should I Look For If I Am Considering Stem Cell Therapy?

You need to be sure that there is good scientific evidence that the treatment is safe and effective, and that your rights as a patient are being respected. To begin, ask for evidence that:

- Preclinical studies (see question 5) have been published, and reviewed and repeated by other experts in the field.
- The providers have approval from an independent committee such as an Institutional Review Board (IRB) or Ethics Review Board (ERB) to make sure the risks are as low as possible and are worth any potential benefits, and that your rights are being protected.
- The providers have approval from a national or regional regulatory agency, such as the Food and Drug Administration (FDA) or the European Medicines Agency (EMEA) for the safe conduct of clinical trials or medical use of a product for this disease.

Some smaller research studies may not need this level of regulatory approval, but must have approval from an independent review committee (see above) and support from the clinical and administrative leadership where the procedure will be done.

11. What Should I Be Cautious About If I Am Considering Stem Cell Therapy?

This is not a comprehensive list but some major warning signs include:

Claims based on patient testimonials. Patients want to believe so much that a treatment is helping them that they can convince themselves that it has. They may even have experienced some recovery unrelated to the treatment. Unless there has been carefully evaluated clinical research it is very difficult to know what is a true effect of the treatment and what you can expect.

Multiple diseases treated with the same cells. Unless the diseases are related, such as all being diseases of the blood, different diseases, such as Parkinson's disease and heart disease, would be expected to have very different treatments. Also, you want to be treated by a doctor that is a specialist in your disease.

The source of the cells or how the treatment will be done is not clearly documented. This should be clearly explained to you in a treatment consent form (see question 8). In addition, there should be a 'protocol' that outlines the treatment in detail to the medical practitioner. The protocol is the 'operating manual' for the procedure. While it may not be made available to you automatically, you should be able to request this. For a clinical trial or experimental treatment, protocols should have been reviewed for scientific merit by independent experts and approved by an ethics committee to ensure that the rights and well-being of the participants will be respected. Ask who has approved this protocol and when the approval expires.

Claims there is no risk. There is always risk involved with treatment. Information about the possible risks should be available from preclinical or earlier clinical research.

High cost of treatment or hidden costs. It is not customary for someone to pay to be in a clinical trial (other than perhaps travel and other personal expenses). Consider whether you should pay for a treatment that is unproven. Furthermore, ask about the costs of emergency medical care if something goes wrong, particularly if you are outside your own country. Find out what costs your national health program or health insurance provider will cover, in what circumstances and in what countries.

References

American Medical Association. "AMA Guidelines on Medical Tourism." www.ama-assn.org/ama1/pub/upload/mm/31/medicaltourism.pdf (accessed March 15, 2010).

Anonymous. "Thailand's Medical Tourism Growth Rate Continues to Increase." *PR Newswire,* November 6, 2009.

Chordas, Lori. "Heading for Home." *Beat's Review* 110, no. 5 (September 2009): 40–43.

Deloitte Center for Health Solutions. "Medical Tourism: Consumers in Search of Value." October 2, 2008. www.deloitte.com/view/en_HR/hr/industries/lifescienceshealthcare/article/964710a8b410e110VgnVCM10 0000ba42f00aRCRD.htm (accessed November 20, 2009).

Deloitte Center for Health Solutions. "Medical Tourism: Update and Implications—2009 Report." www.deloitte.com/assets/Dcom-UnitedStates/Local%20Assets/Documents/us_chs_Medical Tourism_111209_web.pdf (accessed February 27, 2010).

Herrick, Devon M. "Medical Tourism: Global Competition in Health Care." National Center for Policy Analysis. NCPA Policy Report No. 304, November 2007.

International Society for Stem Cell Research. "Guidelines for the Clinical Translation of Stem Cells." December 3, 2008. www.isscr.org/clinical_trans/pdfs/ISSCRGLClinicalTrans.pdf (accessed March 16, 2010).

Joint Commission International. Joint Commission International (JCI)-Accredited Organizations. www.jointcommissioninternational.org/JCI-Accredited-Organizations/ (accessed March 15, 2010).

Kamps, Louisa. "State-of-the-Art Hospitals from Bangkok to Cape Town Are Luring American Travelers with Low Prices and Packages That Include Side Trips to Local Attractions. But Are They Safe?" *Travel and Leisure.com.* July 2006. www.travelandleisure.com/articles/the-medical-vacation/1# (accessed November 20, 2009).

Kumar, Rajesh. *Global Trends in Health and Medical Tourism.* New Delhi: SBS Publishers & Distributors Pvt. Ltd., 2009.

Madhok, Diksha. "Medicine: The Cutting Edge; State of the Art Hospitals, Groundbreaking Research and Major Government Reforms Are All Changing the Face of Healthcare Industry in India." *India Today,* October 12, 2009.

"Medical Tourism to Become USD 100 Billion Industry by 2012: Report." *Times of India,* December 11, 2010. http://timesofindia.indiatimes.com/business/international-business/Medical-tourism-to-become-USD-100-billion-industry-by-2012-Report/articleshow/7082258.cms (accessed January 11, 2012).

Medical Tourism Magazine. "MTA Releases First Patient Surveys on Medical Tourism." June 1, 2009. www.medicaltourismmag.com/issue-detail.php?item = 224&issue = 10 (accessed December 16, 2009).

Norton, Leslie P. "Medical Tourism Takes Flight." *Barron's* 89, no. 36 (September 7, 2009): 24–25.

O'Reily, Kevin B. "Guidelines Target Stem Cell Medical Tourism." February 2, 2009. www.ama-assn.org/amednews/2009/02/02/prsb0202.htm (accessed March 16, 2010).

Prashad, Sharda. "The World is Your Hospital." *Canadian Business* 81, no. 12/13 (August 18, 2008): 62–64.

Uni, James A. "Medical and Surgical Tourism: The New World of Health Care Globalization and What It Means for the Practicing Surgeon." www.surgicalpatientsafety.facs.org/news/medicaltourism.html (accessed December 17, 2010).

United Nations Environment Programme. "World Tourism Organisation Global Code of Ethics for Tourism." www.unep.org/bpsp/Tourism/WTO%20Code%20of%20Conduct.pdf (accessed March 16, 2010).

Woodman, Josef. *Patients Beyond Borders: Everybody's Guide to Affordable, World-Class Medical Travel.* Chapel Hill, NC: Healthy Travel Media, 2008.

7

Directory of Organizations

AABB
8101 Glenbrook Road
Bethesda, MD 20814-2749
USA
Tel.: +1-301-907-6977
E-mail: through the online form at: www.aabb.org/about/who/
    Pages/ContactUs.aspx
Website: www.aabb.org/

AABB's mission is to advance the practice and standards of transfusion medicine and cellular therapies, while maintaining a focus on optimizing patient and donor care and safety. The AABB accreditation program addresses the facility quality and operational systems involved in collecting, processing, testing, distributing, and administering blood and blood products.

Accreditation Canada
(formerly the Canadian Council on Health Services Accreditation—
    CCHSA)
Head Office
1150 Cyrville Road
Ottawa, Ontario, Canada
K1J 7S9
Tel.: 613-738-3800 or 1-800-814-7769 (within Canada)
E-mail: International@accreditation.ca
Website: www.accreditation.ca/en/

Accreditation Canada is a not-for-profit, independent organization providing external peer reviews based on national standards of excellence. Experienced professionals assess services across more than 30 sectors of health care quality and delivery. Individuals receiving care can look for an Accreditation Canada certificate on the walls of a health care organization. Certificates are awarded only to organizations that have met national standards of excellence. Accreditation Canada is, itself, accredited by the International Society for Quality in Health Care (ISQua).

African Society for Quality in Healthcare (ASQH)
7 Hamadan Street
Giza Square
Flat no. 17
Al Mohandes Tower
Al Haram
Giza, Egypt
Box 12211
Tel.: 0121099369; 0235686775; 0233757203
E-mail: info@asqh.org
Website: www.asqh.org/

With more than 65,000 members around the world, the African Society for Quality in Healthcare (ASQH) bills itself as "the world's largest community of experts and the leading authority on quality in healthcare." As the name suggests, the focus of the organization is establishing and improving quality African health care.

Agency for Healthcare Research and Quality (AHRQ)
Office of Communications and Knowledge Transfer
540 Gaither Road, Suite 2000
Rockville, MD 20850
USA
Tel.: 1-301-427-1104
E-mail: through the online form at the Frequently Asked Questions
    page: https://info.ahrq.gov/cgi-bin/ahrq.cfg/php/enduser/
    std_alp.php
Website: www.ahrq.gov/

This agency is the health services research arm of the U.S. Department of Health and Human Services (HHS). It includes research centers and provides funding for issues such as quality improvement and patient safety, outcomes and effectiveness of care, clinical practice and technology assessment, and health care organization and delivery systems. This information can then be translated into policy and practice. The site contains consumer guides for patients along with a wealth of other information on health care quality for other audiences.

American College of Obstetricians and Gynecologists (ACOG)
PO Box 96920
Washington, DC 20090-6920
USA
Tel.: 202-638-5577
E-mail: from the online directory at: www.acog.org/from_home/ proxy/
Website: www.acog.org/

This professional organization is involved in advocacy, education, and practice management efforts. The information available on ACOG's website is for both medical professionals and patients. The site contains links to news, medical information, and much more.

American College of Surgeons (ACS)
633 N Saint Clair Street
Chicago, IL 60611-3211
USA
Tel.: 312-202-5000; (toll free) 800-621-4111
E-mail: postmaster@facs.org
Website: www.facs.org/

Founded in 1913, the American College of Surgeons (ACS) is a scientific and educational association of surgeons. By setting high practice and educational standards, ACS seeks to improve the quality of care for surgical patients. Members of the organization are called "Fellows" and identified by the letters FACS (Fellow, American College of Surgeons) after their name.

American Dental Association (ADA)
211 East Chicago Ave.
Chicago, IL 60611-2678
USA

Tel.: 1-312-440-2500
E-mail: select the desired contact through the online form at: www.
 ada.org/22.aspx
Website: www.ada.org/

The American Dental Association was founded in 1859. It is now the oldest and largest national dental society in the world. The association is committed to promoting oral health and access to care, as well as ethics, science, and professional advancement. Information on the website is provided for both dental professionals and patients.

American Dental Society of Europe (ADSE)
Dr. Alastair MacDonald
2 Clifton Street, Glasgow
G3 7LA
Scotland
Tel.: 011 44 141 331 0088
E-mail: through the online form at: www.ads-eu.org/index.php?
 menuID = 3
Website: www.ads-eu.org/

American dentists working in Europe founded the American Dental Society of Europe (ADSE) in 1873 as a forum in which to exchange professional ideas. The organization claims to be second in longevity only to the Red Cross. Members of the society are all dentists working in Europe who remain true to the original purpose of the organization. The ADSE website also contains a dental referral directory and links to other dental organizations.

American International Health Alliance (AIHA)
1250 Eye Street, NW, Suite 350
Washington, DC 20005
USA
Tel.: 202-789-1136
E-mail: through the online form at: www.aiha.com/en/ContactUs
 /Contact_Us.asp
Website: www.aiha.com/en/

This alliance, together with its partnerships and programs, responds to a broad range of global health care issues in developing and transitioning countries. It seeks to leverage U.S. health care expertise to help institutions abroad expand their knowledge and introduce new models of care.

American Medical Association (AMA)
515 N. State Street
Chicago, IL 60654
USA
Tel.: 800-621-8335
E-mail: through the online forms at: https://extapps.ama-assn.org/
contactus/contactusMain.do
Website: www.ama-assn.org/

The American Medical Association (AMA) has existed since 1847. Its mission is "to promote the art and science of medicine and the betterment of public health." It currently seeks to accomplish this mission through an emphasis on five areas: access to care; quality of care; cost of health care; prevention and wellness; and payment models. The AMA website contains a wide variety of information for physicians (including medical residents and medical students), as well as patients.

American Telemedicine Association (ATA)
1100 Connecticut Avenue, NW, Suite 540
Washington, DC 20036
USA
Tel.: 1-202-223-3333
E-mail: info@americantelemed.org
Website: www.americantelemed.org/

The tagline of the American Telemedicine Association (ATA) is "quality healthcare through telecommunications technology." To this end, the organization acts as an international resource and advocate on the use of advanced remote medical technologies. The ATA's mission includes education, networking and collaboration, policy development and dissemination, as well as financial and customer support.

Association of Private Hospitals of Malaysia (APHM)
No. 43 2nd Floor
Jalan Mamanda 9 Ampang Point
68000 Ampang Selangor, Malaysia
Tel.: 603-4252-0278
Website: www.hospitals-malaysia.org/

This association represents more than 100 private hospitals and medical centers throughout the country of Malaysia. It undertakes a number of activities to help raise the standard of Malaysian health care, including networking and dialoguing with public sector agencies (including the Ministry of Health Malaysia), training, and promoting medical tourism.

Association of Travel Insurance Intermediaries (ATII)
10 Victoria Road South
Southsea
Hampshire
PO5 2DA
United Kingdom
Tel.: +448456180333
E-mail: info@atii.co.uk or chairman@atii.co.uk
Website: www.atii.co.uk/

The nonprofit Association of Travel Insurance Intermediaries (ATII) represents tour operators and travel agents on matters related to travel insurance. The association expects its more than 30 members to uphold professional insurance standards. The public can find information about members and their contact information on the ATII website.

Australian Council on Healthcare Standards (ACHS)
5 Macarthur Street
Ultimo
NSW, Australia
Tel.: + 61 2 9211 9633
E-mail: achs@achs.org.au
Website: www.achs.org.au

This independent, not-for-profit organization represents governments, consumers, and peak health bodies from throughout Australia. It identifies itself as Australia's leading health care assessment and accreditation provider.

Australian General Practice Accreditation Limited (AGPAL)
Street Address:
Level 1
20 Railway Terrace
Milton QLD 4064, Australia

Postal address:
PO Box 2058
Milton BC QLD 4064, Australia
Tel.: 1300 362 111
E-mail: info@agpal.com.au
Website: www.agpal.com.au/

Established in 1997, the not-for-profit Australian General Practice Accreditation Limited (AGPAL) is one of eight country-specific accrediting organizations. AGPAL is also an International Society for Quality in Health Care (ISQua) member. Accreditation is the organization's core business.

British Standards Institute (BSI)
389 Chiswick High Road
London
W4 4AL
United Kingdom
Tel.: +44 (0)20 8996 9001
E-mail: cservices@bsigroup.com
Website: www.bsi-global.com

This London-based organization provides independent assessment and management systems certification for clients around the globe. One of BSI's areas of activity focuses on the assessment and certification of management systems and medical devices.

CARF International
6951 E. Southpoint Road
Tucson, AZ 85756
USA
Tel.: 1-520-325-1044; (toll free) 1-888-281-6531
E-mail: through the online form at: www.carf.org/contact-us/
Website: www.carf.org/

CARF was founded in 1966 as the Commission on Accreditation of Rehabilitation Facilities. It is an independent, nonprofit organization that accredits a range of health and human services. These include aging services, behavioral health (including opioid treatment programs), child and youth services, vision rehabilitation, and medical rehabilitation.

Case Management Society of America (CMSA)
6301 Ranch Drive
Little Rock, AR 72223
USA
Tel.: 1-501-225-2229
E-mail: cmsa@cmsa.org (client services)
Website: www.cmsa.org/

This nonprofit association is dedicated to supporting and developing the case management profession. Founded in 1990, the Case Management Society of America (CMSA) has grown to serve more than 11,000 members, 20,000 subscribers, and 75 chapters. The society provides educational forums, networking opportunities, and legislative advocacy, and it establishes standards to advance the profession.

Center for Medical Tourism Research (CMTR)
Center Director
David G. Vequist IV, Ph.D.
4301 Broadway, CPO #460
San Antonio, Texas, 78209
USA
Tel.: 1-210-805-5825
E-mail: vequist@uiwtx.edu
Website: www.uiw.edu/medicaltourism/

The Center for Medical Tourism Research (CMTR) conducts research to "support the development of thought leadership, best practices, lessons learned, and policy formulation in the new industries of Health Tourism, Wellness Tourism, Dental Tourism, Medical Tourism, and Retirement Tourism." Founded and directed by David George Vequist IV, PhD, the center is located in the H-E-B School of Business & Administration at the University of the Incarnate Word in San Antonio, Texas. The website provides links to a range of information on medical tourism issues, much of which is accessible to consumers.

Centers for Disease Control and Prevention (CDC)
1600 Clifton Road
Atlanta, GA 30333
USA
Tel.: 1-800-232-4636
E-mail: cdcinfo@cdc.gov
Website: www.cdc.gov/

The Atlanta-based Centers for Disease Control and Prevention (CDC) is the U.S. public health authority focusing on health promotion, disease prevention, and threat preparedness. The center's website and publications provide a wealth of information for inbound and outbound travelers on a wide variety of health conditions, as well as environmental health, safety and preparedness, traveler's health, and more. Information is provided for the public, health professionals, students, educators, researchers, members of the media, policy makers, and businesses. The CDC also offers multimedia content.

CHKS Healthcare Accreditation Quality Unit
CHKS Ltd
1 Arden Court
Arden Road
Alcester, Warwickshire, B49 6HN, United Kingdom
Tel.: + 44 (0)1789 761600
E-mail: through the online form at: www.chks.co.uk/index.
   php?id = 11
Website: www.chks.co.uk/

CHKS is an International Society for Quality in Healthcare (ISQua) member organization. Based in the United Kingdom, CHKS works with all health care sectors. These include everything from National Health Service Trusts to international health agencies across Europe.

Council for Health Services Accreditation of Southern Africa (COHSASA)
Postal address:
PO Box 676
Howard Place
7450, South Africa
Street address:
Office Suite No 13–15 First Floor,
Lonsdale Building
Lonsdale Way
Pinelands
7405, South Africa
Tel.: +27215314225
E-mail: info@cohsasa.co.za
Website: www.cohsasa.co.za/

This organization is accredited by the International Society for Quality in Health Care (ISQua). It works with health care facilities to meet and maintain quality standards and to help them make improvements where necessary.

Customs and Border Protection (CPB)
U.S. Department of Homeland Security
300 Pennsylvania Avenue, N.W.
Washington, DC 20229
USA
Tel.: 1-877-227-5511 (for U.S. callers); 703-526-4200 (for international callers)
E-mail: through the online forms at: https://help.cbp.gov/app/answers/detail/a_id/1207
Website: www.customs.gov/xp/cgov/travel/

The Customs and Border Protection (CBP) is responsible for the safety of the approximately 1 million travelers who cross U.S. borders daily. The CPB site provides information travelers need before departing, and upon re-entering the United States.

Data Bank
PO Box 10832
Chantilly, VA 20153-0832
USA
Tel.: 1-800-767-6732; (outside US) 1-703-802-9380
E-mail: help@npdb-hipdb.hrsa.gov
Website: www.npdb-hipdb.hrsa.gov/

The Data Bank is made up of the National Practitioner Data Bank (NPDB) and the Healthcare Integrity and Protection Data Bank (HIPDB). The NPDB opened in September 1990. It serves as a repository of information on all licensure actions taken against U.S. health care practitioners and entities. The HIPDB was established several years later to combat fraud and abuse in health insurance and health care delivery. It collects data related to medical malpractice payments and adverse actions taken against physicians, dentists, and other licensed health care practitioners. The U.S. Congress created the Data Bank as a confidential information clearinghouse that alerts, or "flags," information regarding the professional credentials of health care practitioners, providers, and suppliers.

The goals are to improve health care quality, protect the public, and reduce health care fraud and abuse in the United States.

DNV
Veritasveien 1
Postal address:
1363
Høvik, Oslo
Norway
Tel.: +4767579900
E-mail: through the online form at: www.dnv.com/contactus/
Website: www.dnv.com/moreondnv/profile/about_us/

DNV is a Norwegian-based company that traces its history back to 1864. Its services include hospital accreditation, primary stroke center certification, and critical access hospital accreditation.

European Medical Tourism Alliance (EuMTA)
Andrassy ut 61
H-1062 Budapest, Hungary
Tel.: + 36 1 321 8579
E-mail: info@eumta.org
Website: www.eumta.org/

This nonprofit alliance focuses on strengthening the medical travel industry. It does so by representing various medical tourism entities, working to harmonize industry activities, acting as an industry forum, and improving patients' ability to freely choose a medical provider.

European Society for Quality in Health Care (ESQH)
St. Camillus Hospital
Shelbourne Road
Limerick
Ireland
Tel.: +353 61 483315
E-mail: no general e-mail address published for nonmembers
Website: www.esqh.net/

The European Society for Quality in Health Care (ESQH) consists of National Societies for Quality in Healthcare from almost two dozen (primarily European) countries. The organization convenes member workshops on specific topics, with the goal of improving the quality of European health care.

European Union (EU)
Council of the European Union
Rue de la Loi 175
B-1048 Brussels, Belgium
Tel.: +32 2 281 61 11
E-mail: through the online form at:
www.consilium.europa.eu/contacts/info-public.aspx?lang=en
Website: http://europa.eu/index_en.htm

General inquiries are handled through a central information service for EU-related questions. The service is Europa Direct:

http://europa.eu/europedirect/index_en.htm

Tel.: +32-2-299 96 96

E-mail: through the online form at: http://europa.eu/europedirect/write_to_us/mailbox/index_en.htm

Webchat: http://europa.eu/europedirect/web_assistance/index_en.htm

In 1951, economic integration began between Belgium, Germany, France, Italy, Luxembourg, and the Netherlands. Today, the European Union (EU) is comprised of 27 member nations, which cooperate on issues related to development, environmental policy, human rights, and more. Seventeen of these member nations share the same currency—the euro. (At this writing, the 27 member countries are: Austria, Belgium, Bulgaria, Cyprus, Czech Republic, Denmark, Estonia, Finland, France, Germany, Greece, Hungary, Ireland, Italy, Latvia, Lithuania, Luxembourg, Malta, Netherlands, Poland, Portugal, Romania, Slovakia, Slovenia, Spain, Sweden, and the United Kingdom.)

Global Health Council
1111 19th Street, NW—Suite 1120
Washington, DC 20036
USA

Tel.: 202-833-5900
E-mail: information@globalhealth.org
Website: http://web.globalhealth.org/

The Global Health Council describes itself as "the world's largest and most diverse membership alliance dedicated to improving the health of the 2 billion people who live on less than $2 a day." It tackles a variety of global health issues through conferences and other networking and collaboration activities. The Global Health Council also advocates with legislators and publishes research, among other activities.

Global Health Workforce Alliance
Global Health Workforce Alliance Secretariat
World Health Organization
20 avenue Appia
1211 Geneva 27, Switzerland
Tel.: +41 22791 2621
E-mail: ghwa@who.int
Website: www.who.int/workforcealliance/en/

The Alliance was created in 2008 as a means to address the global shortage in health care workers, particularly in developing countries. Around the globe, 57 countries have "critical shortages" of health care workers. Thirty-six of these countries are in Africa. The Alliance Secretariat is administered by the World Health Organization (WHO). The Alliance itself consists of partners from national governments, international agencies, and financial institutions, as well as researchers, educators, and others who are interested in finding solutions to the crisis.

Health Information and Quality Authority (HIQA)
Unit 1301
City Gate
Mahon, Cork
Ireland
Tel.: +353212409300
E-mail: info@hiqa.ie
Website: www.hiqa.ie/

This independent Irish organization is responsible for setting safety and quality standards for health and social care services. Additionally, the Health Information and Quality Authority

(HIQA) monitors compliance, carries out investigations and national health technology assessments (HTA), and advises on information sharing and collection.

Health Technology Assessment International (HTAi)
HTAi Secretariat
1200, 10405 Jasper Avenue
Edmonton, Alberta, Canada T5J 3N4
Tel.: 1-780-448-4881
E-mail: info@htai.org
Website: www.htai.org

As the name of this organization suggests, Health Technology Assessment International (HTAi) is a global organization that supports professionals who are involved in health technology assessment (HTA). (As defined on the organization's website, "HTA is a field of scientific research to inform policy and clinical decision-making around the introduction and diffusion of health technologies.") HTAi helps facilitate informed decision-making involving medical innovations and resources.

HealthCare Tourism International and HealthCare Trip
US Office:
HealthCare Tourism International, Inc.
595 Loyola Drive
Los Altos, CA 94024
USA
Tel.: 310-928-3611 (within USA) or (00) 1-310-928-3611 (outside
 USA)
E-mail: health@healthcaretrip.org
Website: www.healthcaretrip.org/

HealthCare Trip is a U.S.-based nonprofit service of HealthCare Tourism International. It is the "first 501 (c) (3) nonprofit organization specifically for health travel safety." The organization's goals include protecting patient rights, as well as focusing on quality care, business practices, standards, and credentialing processes within the global health industry. The organization claims that it has assumed unbiased accreditation responsibility for all major groups in the health care industry—from hotels to recovery facilities, medical tourism booking agencies, and other resources.

Infectious Diseases Society of America (IDSA)
1300 Wilson Boulevard
Suite 300
Arlington, VA 22209
USA
Tel.: 703-299-0200
E-mail: through the online form at: www.idsociety.org/Contact_
    Us.aspx
Website: www.idsociety.org/

Members of the Infectious Diseases Society of America (IDSA) include physicians, scientists, and other health care professionals. The organization focuses on health improvement through "promoting excellence in patient care, education, research, public health, and prevention relating to infectious diseases."

Institute of Medicine (IOM)
500 Fifth Street, NW
Washington, DC 20001
USA
Tel.: 1-202-334-2352
E-mail: iomwww@nas.edu
Website: www.iom.edu/

The U.S. Institute of Medicine (IOM) was established in 1970 as the health arm of the National Academy of Sciences. The IOM's mission is to serve "as adviser to the nation to improve health." The organization answers health and health care questions to assist in decision-making that pertains to the nation's health.

International Association of Medical Assistance for Travelers (IAMAT)
U.S. Headquarters:
IAMAT
1623 Military Rd. #279
Niagara Falls, NY 14304-1745
USA
Tel.: 716-754-4883
E-mail: through the online form at: www.iamat.org/contact.cfm
Website: www.iamat.org/

This "advocate for travelers' health" was established in 1960. The association states that its mission is to provide "impartial and accurate travel health advice and to coordinate an international network of qualified medical practitioners to assist travelers in need of emergency medical care during their trip." It accomplishes this by offering health education for travelers, providing a medical directory network, and giving educational scholarships and grants on travel medicine to doctors and nurses from low-income countries.

International Association of Medical Regulatory Authorities (IAMRA)
Roxanne Huff
IAMRA Secretariat
400 Fuller Wiser Road, Suite 300
Euless, Texas 76039
USA
Tel.: 1-817-868-4006
E-mail: secretariat@iamra.com
Website: www.iamra.com/

The International Association of Medical Regulatory Authorities (IAMRA) summarizes the purpose of the organization as being "to encourage best practice among medical regulatory authorities worldwide in the achievement of their mandate—to protect, promote and maintain the health and safety of the public by ensuring proper standards for the profession of medicine." Organizational goals are arranged around four areas: high standards; supporting IAMRA members; relationship building; innovation and dissemination of best practices.

International Association of Scientific Experts in Tourism (AIEST)
Dufourstrasse 40a
CH-9000 St. Gallen
Switzerland
Tel.: +41-71-224 25 30
E-Mail: aiest@unisg.ch
Website: www.aiest.org/

This association dates from 1951. As the name suggests, its interest is scientific research and education in tourism. It organizes an annual conference, publishes the *Tourism Review* journal, and provides networking and collegial opportunities for tourism professionals.

International Hospital Federation (IHF)
Immeuble JB SAY
13 Chemin du Levant
F-01210 Ferney Voltaire
France
Tel.: +33 (0) 450 42 6000
P.A. Hôpital de Loëx
Route de Loëx 151
1233 BERNEX
Switzerland
Tel.: +41 (0) 22 850 94 20
E-mail: info@ihf-fih.org
Website: www.ihf-fih.org/

This federation is a global, independent, not-for-profit, non-governmental association of health care organizations. It encourages cooperation and communication among member hospitals and health care organizations. The IHF also helps international hospitals improve their service delivery to patients of all socio-economic statuses.

International Institute of Medical Education (IIME)
750 Third Avenue, 23rd Floor
New York, New York 10017
USA
Tel.: 1-212-661-7375
E-mail: institute@iime.org
Website: www.iime.org/

Established in 1999, the Institute for International Medical Education (IIME) addresses the quality of medical education around the world. The organization helps to develop "global minimum essential (core) requirements." The IIME's activities include setting independent international standards for outcomes and ensuring common standards for medical competencies. The organization's emphasis is on specifying the knowledge, skills, professional attitudes, and behavior that medical graduates should demonstrate.

International Medical Volunteers Association (IMVA)
P.O. Box 205
Woodville, MA. 01784
USA
Tel.: 508-435-7377
E-mail: info@imva.org
Website: www.imva.org/

The nonprofit International Medical Volunteers Association (IMVA) "promotes, facilitates, and supports voluntary medical activity through education and information exchange," primarily in developing countries. The association does not send or sponsor volunteers. Rather, its task is to educate and motivate potential volunteers, and to help organizations locate volunteers when they need them.

International Monetary Fund (IMF)
Headquarters 1 (HQ1):
700 19th Street, N.W.
Washington, DC 20431
USA
Headquarters 2 (HQ2):
1900 Pennsylvania Ave NW
Washington, DC 20431
USA
Tel.: 202-623-7000
E-mail: through the contact directory at: www.imf.org/external/
    np/exr/contacts/contacts.aspx
Website: www.imf.org/

The International Monetary Fund (IMF) summarizes itself as, "an organization of 187 countries, working to foster global monetary cooperation, secure financial stability, facilitate international trade, promote high employment and sustainable economic growth, and reduce poverty around the world." Its focus is on global growth and economic stability, with an emphasis on low-income and developing nations.

International Network of Agencies for Health Technology Assessment (INAHTA)
INAHTA Secretariat
c/o SBU P.O. Box 3657

Street address: Olof Palmes gatan 17
SE-103 59,
Stockholm, Sweden
Tel.: +46 8 412 32 00
E-mail: secretariat@inahta.org
Website: www.inahta.org/

Established in 1993, the INAHTA is a nonprofit organization that facilitates the sharing of health technology assessment (HTA) between different cultures. The organization produces a range of publications, including briefs, reposts, newsletters, and informational leaflets, which are accessible through the INAHTA website. These materials are targeted toward HTA professionals rather than patients.

International Organization for Standardization (ISO)
ISO Central Secretariat
1, ch. de la Voie-Creuse
CP 56
CH-1211 Geneva 20
Switzerland
Tel.: +41 22 749 01 11
E-mail: central@iso.org
Website: www.iso.org/iso/home.htm

This nongovernmental organization identifies and develops international business standards. Its network of national standards institutes approves and accredits hospitals, clinics, and other health care institutions. The ISO mostly oversees facilities and administration. Its jurisdiction doesn't cover health care procedures, practices, and methods.

International Society for Equity in Health (ISEqH)
Department of Family and Community Medicine 256 McCaul,
    Canada
Tel: +1 (416) 978-3763
E-mail: info@iseqh.org
Website: www.iseqh.org/

The International Society for Equity in Health (ISEqH) promotes "equity in health and health services internationally through education, research, publication, communication and charitable support." The society supports an interdisciplinary approach, as well as a research and policy partnership in addressing equity. ISEqH launched the online, peer-reviewed journal *International Journal for Equity in Health* in 2002.

International Society for Quality in Health Care (ISQua)
3rd Floor
Joyce House
8–11 Lombard Street East
Dublin 2
Ireland
Tel.: +353 1 670 6750
E-mail: isqua@isqua.org
Website: www.isqua.org/

The International Society for Quality in Health Care (ISQua) is an independent, nonprofit organization that "Accredits the Accreditors" through its International Accreditation Program (IAP). It is the only international organization that performs this role and as such, is recognized by the Ministries of Health in various countries. Health professionals from almost two dozen countries act as peer reviewers to ensure that more than 30 sets of international quality standards are met. In partnership with Accreditation Canada, the ISQua has created an online collaborative forum (accessible through the ISQua website) for sharing accreditation research and best practices worldwide.

International Society for Stem Cell Research (ISSCR)
ISSCR Headquarters
111 Deer Lake Road, Suite 100
Deerfield, IL 60015
USA
Tel.: 1-847-509-1944
E-mail: isscr@isscr.org
Website: www.isscr.org/

As the name suggests, the focus of this independent, nonprofit organization is on fostering information exchange and education on stem sell research. The International Society for Stem Cell Research (ISSCR) organizes an annual meeting and conference series, and its website provides information targeted to medical professionals and scientists, the media, and the general public. Resources for patients, their families, and doctors are provided as decision-making aids to stem sell treatments.

International Society of Aesthetic Plastic Surgery (ISAPS)
ISAPS Executive Office
45 Lyme Road, Suite 304
Hanover, NH 03755
USA
Tel.: 1-603-643-2325
E-mail: isaps@conmx.net
Website: www.isaps.org/

The International Society of Aesthetic Plastic Surgery (ISAPS) membership includes qualified and certified plastic surgeons in almost 100 countries around the globe. The organization's mission is to provide ongoing education for member surgeons; offer helpful, accurate, and current information on aesthetic or cosmetic medicine and surgery; and promote safe surgery. The ISAPS maintains a directory of surgeons in other countries who meet U.S. standards.

International Society of Travel Medicine (ISTM)
315 W. Ponce de Leon Avenue
Suite 245
Decatur, Georgia 30030
USA
Tel.: 1-404-373-8282
E-mail: istm@istm.org
Website: www.istm.org

Dedicated to promoting healthy and safe travel, the International Society of Travel Medicine (ISTM) was the first international society to be focused solely on travel medicine. It has now grown into the largest organization of professionals in its industry. For these professionals, ISTM activities include education and networking opportunities, as well as research. For international travelers, the ISTM offers the only worldwide database of clinics that provide both pre- and post-travel care.

International Spa Association (ISPA)
2365 Harrodsburg Road, Suite A325

Lexington, KY 40504
USA
Tel.: 1-888-651-4772
E-mail: ispa@ispastaff.com
Website: www.experienceispa.com/

Attracting medical tourists and other consumers, spas are one of the oldest destinations for travelers who are interested in health. Launched in 1991 as the International Spa and Fitness Association, today's ISPA bills itself as being "recognized worldwide as the professional organization and voice of the spa industry." The ISPA issues Global Best Practices for the Spa Industry. Members agree to abide by the organization's code of ethics, as well as its standards and practices addressing staff, safety, guest relations, and services. Additionally, the ISPA encourages a deeper "industry-wide natural" connection with the planet, its people, and prosperity.

Joint Commission
One Renaissance Blvd.
Oakbrook Terrace, IL 60181
USA
Washington, DC, Office:
601 13th Street, NW
Suite 560 South
Washington, DC 20005
USA
Tel.: 1-630-792-5000
E-mail: through the contact directory at:
www.jointcommission.org/contact_directory/default.aspx
Website: www.jointcommission.org/

The Joint Commission is the largest and most respected accreditation agency for U.S. hospitals—evaluating hospitals, clinics, home health care, and other facilities. More than 19,000 U.S. health care organizations and programs are accredited through this independent, not-for-profit organization. Its mission is to "continuously improve health care for the public, in collaboration with other stakeholders, by evaluating health care organizations and inspiring them to excel in providing safe and effective care of the highest quality and value."

Joint Commission International (JCI)
Headquarters
1515 West 22nd Street
Suite 1300W
Oak Brook, Illinois 60523
USA
Tel.: 1-630-268-4800 (regarding accreditation) or 1-630-268-2900 (regarding consulting)
E-mail: jciaccreditation@jcrinc.com
Website: www.jointcommissioninternational.org

The Joint Commission (above) launched its international affiliate agency in 1999. To be accredited by JCI, an international health care provider must meet the same rigorous standards set by the Joint Commission. JCI staff travel to inspect hospitals, applying similar but culturally adjusted standards to the ones used in the United States. The American Medical Association advises anyone traveling overseas for care to select a JCI-accredited facility.

Medical Tourism Association (MTA) (also known as the Medical Travel Association)
10130 Northlake Blvd.
Suite 214-315
West Palm Beach, Florida, 33412
USA
Tel.: 1-561-791-2000
E-mail: Info@MedicalTourismAssociation.com
Website: www.medicaltravelauthority.com

Founded by attorney Jonathan Edelheit, who is also CEO, the Medical Tourism Association provides a forum for industry communication. It is the first membership-based international non-profit trade organization dedicated to medical tourism and health care worldwide. The MTA's goal is to raise awareness of the quality health care available overseas. It does this by focusing on transparency in quality, pricing, and patient safety, as well as through educational efforts. The MTA seeks to be an unbiased source of information for patients, insurance companies, and employers.

National Committee for Quality Assurance (NCQA)
1100 13th Street, NW

Suite 1000
Washington, DC 20005
USA
Tel.: 1-202-955-3500
E-mail: customersupport@ncqa.org
Website: www.ncqa.org/

Founded in 1990, this organization reports on NCQA-accredited health plans in every state, the District of Columbia, and Puerto Rico. According to their data, more than 1 million Americans are covered under these plans. That works out to 70.5 percent of all Americans enrolled in accredited health plans.

Netherlands Institute for Accreditation of Hospitals (NIAZ)
Postbus 4045
3502 HA Utrecht
The Netherlands
Office:
Churchilllaan 11, 14e
3527 GV Utrecht
The Netherlands
Tel.: +31 30 2330380
E-mail: through the online form at: http://en.niaz.nl/contact-info
Website: http://en.niaz.nl/

The Netherlands Institute for Accreditation of Hospitals (NIAZ) was formed in 1998. It develops quality standards and conducts compliance assessments based on those standards. The letter "Z" in the organization's acronym stands for *zorginstellingen,* which means health care organizations. NIAZ is accredited by the International Society for Quality in Health Care (ISQua).

Office of American Citizens Services and Crisis Management (ACS)
Bureau of Consular Affairs (CA), Consular Information Program
U.S. Department of State
Main address:
U.S. Department of State
2201 C Street NW
Washington, DC 20520
USA

Main Switchboard:
202-647-4000
Hotline for American Travelers:
1-888-407-4747 (within the US); 1-202-501-4444 (from outside the US)
Passport Information:
1-877-487-2778
Visa Information:
202-663-1225
E-mail: through the online form at: http://travel.state.gov/about/contact/contact_4745.html
Website: http://travel.state.gov/travel/travel_1744.html

The Bureau of Consular Affairs (CA) protects the lives and interests of American citizens abroad. The CA website provides information on handling crises while traveling (e.g., arrest, death), dealing with international travel (e.g., spring breaks abroad), and securing visas and passports, as well as a range of other topics.

One World Healthcare
One World Healthcare USA, Inc
7737 Southwest Freeway, Suite 819
Houston, Texas 77074
USA
Tel.: 1-713-504-1173; 1-713-773-0003
E-mail: Oneworldhealthcareusainc@gmail.com; Kanayo.ubesiemd@gmail.com
Website: www.oneworldhealthcareusa.org/

Medical and nonmedical volunteer opportunities are available through One World Healthcare. This nonprofit organization conducts medical missions in developing countries, especially in Africa.

Operation Giving Back (OGB)
American College of Surgeons
633 N Saint Clair Street
Chicago, IL 60611-3211
USA
Tel.: 312-202-5000 or 800-621-4111 (toll free)
E-mail: postmaster@facs.org
Website: www.operationgivingback.facs.org/

Operation Giving Back (OGB) is the surgical volunteerism initiative of the American College of Surgeons. The organization's mission offers a twist on medical tourism, in that the focus is not on the traveling patient. Rather, OGB's focus is on providing informational resources and programs for health care workers who travel to provide medical care. Specifically, it seeks to facilitate volunteerism among surgeons to meet the needs of medically underserved areas.

Organisation for Economic Cooperation and Development (OECD)

Headquarters
2, rue André Pascal
75775 Paris Cedex 16
France
Tel.: +33 1 45 24 82 00
E-mail: cynthia.coutu@oecd.org (for questions about OECD)
Website: www.oecd.org/

The Organisation for Economic Cooperation and Development (OECD) was established in 1961, but is actually rooted in post–World War II efforts to support reconstruction through the Marshall Plan. The organization's mission is to promote economic and social well-being policies for the 34 member nations and beyond. As part of this effort, the OECD compiles comparison data, including data on health care economics, which are available through its online databases.

Organization for Safety, Asepsis and Prevention (OSAP)

1997 Annapolis Exchange Parkway, Ste. 300
Post Office Box 6297
Annapolis, Maryland 21401
USA
Tel.: 410-571-0003
E-mail: office@OSAP.org
Website: www.osap.org/

The mission of this nonprofit organization, which is composed of dental care providers and other industry insiders, is "to be the world's leading advocate for the safe and infection-free delivery of oral care." The OSAP site is an informative safety resource. Two specific resources from OSAP that are helpful to medical tourists are available in print and online.

Organization of American States (OAS)
Main Building:
17th Street and Constitution Ave., N.W.
Washington, DC 20006,
USA
General Secretariat Building:
1889 F Street, N.W.
Washington, DC 20006
USA
Administration Building:
19th Street and Constitution Ave., N.W.
Washington, DC 20006
USA
Tel.: 1-202-458-3000
E-mail: through the online form at: www.oas.org/en/contactus.
    asp
Website: www.oas.org/en/

This organization brings together all 35 independent states of the Americas (which include Antigua and Barbuda, Barbados, Belize, Grenada, and Panama). Its essential purposes include: strengthening peace and security; promoting economic, social, and cultural development; and eradicating poverty. OAS is based in the "pillars" of democracy, human rights, security, and development.

Overseas Security Advisory Council (OSAC)
U.S. Department of State, Bureau of Diplomatic Security
Washington, DC 20522-2008
USA
Tel.: 1-571-345-2223
E-mail: for general correspondence, through the online form at:
    www.osac.gov/Pages/ContactUs.aspx
Emergency Duty Officer
Phone: 202-309-5056
E-mail: osac_risc@state.gov
Website: www.osac.gov/

Through the Bureau of Diplomatic Security, the OSAC establishes a liaison to exchange information and assist security cooperation between the State Department and the private sector. The site provides daily news and reports on items related to global security interests.

Pan American Health Organization (PAHO)
Regional Office of the World Health Organization
525 Twenty-third Street, N.W.
Washington, DC 20037
USA
Tel.: 202-974-3000
E-mail: through the online form at: http://new.paho.org/hq/
    index.php?option = com_contact&Itemid = 137
Website: http://new.paho.org/

This international health organization is the regional Office
for the Americas of the World Health Organization, and is part
of the United Nations system. As the name implies, the focus of
the organization is on Latin American and Caribbean countries.
Pan American Health Organization (PAHO) scientific and technical experts work at the Washington, DC, headquarters, in its
27 country offices, and its nine scientific centers.

QHA Trent Accreditation
QHA Ltd
Office 20
BMI Thornbury Hospital
312 Fulwood Road
Sheffield S10 3BR
United Kingdom
Tel.: + 44 1142674477
E-mail: qha.international@googlemail.com
Website: www.qha-international.co.uk/

QHA ("Quality Healthcare Advice") began its operation in
2010, after the former Trent Accreditation Scheme (TAS) stopped
providing hospital accreditation. The "QHA Trent" arm of the QHA
Group provides surveying and accreditation for hospitals, clinics,
and residential care homes globally. The "QHA Global" arm offers
various consulting services related to accreditation and medical
tourism.

Quality Improvement Council (QIC)
5th Floor
Health Sciences 2
La Trobe University
Victoria 3086, Australia

Tel.: +61394795630
E-mail: qic@qic.org.au
Website: www.qic.org.au/

This International Society for Quality in Health Care (ISQua) member organization is an Australian not-for-profit that has been serving the health and community services sectors for two decades. Their program includes more than 450 organizations, representing more than 30 service types, in all Australian states and territories, as well as New Zealand.

Quality Resources International (QRIntl)
5 Revere Drive
One Northbrook Place, Suite 200
Northbrook, IL 60062-1500
USA
Tel.: 1-847-205-5510
E-mail: www.qrintl.com/contact.aspx (contact through the online
    form at this URL)
Website: www.qrintl.com/

Quality Resources International (QRIntl) provides international consulting services, education, and technical assistance to health care organizations globally. QRIntl's emphasis is on health care performance improvement and patient safety, accreditation preparation, and comprehensive educational programs. Dr. David Jaimovich founded the organization in 2009, bringing with him significant previous experience in international health care accreditation. QRIntl helps health care organizations prepare for JCI accreditation and select their national accreditations.

**Simon Fraser University (SFU) Medical Tourism Research
    Group**
University Main Address:
Simon Fraser University
8888 University Drive
Burnaby, B.C. Canada V5A 1S6
Tel.: 778-782-3111 (main switchboard, Burnaby campus)
E-mail: medtour@sfu.ca (directly to the SFU Medical Tourism
    Research Group)
Website: www.sfu.ca/medicaltourism/index.html

Based at Simon Fraser University (SFU) near Vancouver, Canada, this research group consists of team members across several disciplines, including public health, geography, and philosophy. Much of its ongoing research is funded by the Canadian Institutes of Health Research. Many of the team's publications are available online through links on the research group's website.

Spa Quality
1024 Oriente Avenue
Wilmington, Delaware 19807
USA
Tel.: 302-426-0274
E-mail: Info@SpaQuality.com
Website: www.spaquality.org/

This organization offers certification for spa facilities "to create effective and efficient spa operations that result in consistent delivery." Certification involves two annual on-site assessments of the spa's operations and is based on the organization's International Standards of Spa Excellence. The standards book is used in an online course offered in partnership with the University of California—Irvine Extension's Spa and Hospitality Management Certificate Program.

Taiwan Joint Commission on Hospital Accreditation (TJCHA)
5F, No. 31, Sec. 2
Sanmin Road
Banqiao Dist.
New Taipei City 22069
Taiwan (R.O.C.)
Tel.: +886229634055
E-mail: service@tjcha.org.tw
Website: www.tjcha.org.tw/FrontStage/aboutus_en.html

The Taiwan Joint Commission on Hospital Accreditation (TJCHA) was established in 1999 for the purpose of promoting, executing, and certifying the nation's health care quality policies. It is certified by the International Society for Quality in Health Care (ISQua).

TEMOS
TEMOS GmbH
Friedrich-Ebert-Str.

TechnologiePark Bergisch Gladbach, Geb. 56
51429 Bergisch Gladbach
Germany
Tel.: +49 2204 42648-0
E-mail: info@temos-international.com
Website: www.temos-worldwide.com/

This organization states as its mission, "to optimize medical care for travelers and expatriates worldwide." Among its services, TEMOS provides worldwide quality assessment and certification of hospitals and dental clinics, validates telemedicine applications, and organizes an international conference on "Healthcare Abroad and Health Tourism." Additional services include providing hospital and dental directories and Continuous Medical Education (CME).

Tourist Research Center (TRC)
Secretariate:
WES
Baron Ruzettelaan 33
B-8310 Assebroek/Brugge
Belgium
Tel.: +3250367136
E-mail: info@wes.be
Website: http://trc.aiest.org/

Members of the Tourist Research Center (TRC) include academics and independent researchers who are interested in networking, collaboration, and exchanging experiences on tourism research. Researchers share findings at TRC annual meetings. The Center's General Assembly accepts new members based on their record of "significant involvement in research in tourism."

United Nations (UN)
UN Headquarters
First Avenue at 46th Street
New York, NY 10017, USA
USA
Public Inquiries, Visitors Services
United Nations Headquarters
Room GA-0305
New York, NY 10017, USA
Tel.: 212-963-4475

E-mail: inquiries@un.org
Website: www.un.org/en/

The United Nations (UN) was founded in 1945, and given its name by then-U.S. president Franklin D. Roosevelt. The UN lists its main four purposes as: keeping peace throughout the world; developing friendly relations among nations; helping nations work together to address poverty, hunger, disease, and illiteracy, and encouraging respect for each other's rights and freedoms; and assisting nations in achieving these goals.

United Nations Educational, Scientific and Cultural Organisation (UNESCO)
(UNESCO Headquarters Offices are at two locations in Paris.)
7, place de Fontenoy 75352 Paris 07 SP France
1, rue Miollis 75732 Paris Cedex 15 France
Tel.: +33 (0)1 45 68 10 00
E-mail: through the online form at: www.unesco.org/new/en/
    unesco/about-us/where-we-are/contact-us/
Website: www.unesco.org/

Comprised of 193 member states and 7 associate member states, the United Nations Educational, Scientific and Cultural Organisation's (UNESCO) mission is "to contribute to the building of peace, the eradication of poverty, sustainable development and intercultural dialogue through education, the sciences, culture, communication and information." It works to encourage sustainable development through international dialogue. The Millennium Development Goals (MDGs) (see below) are also central to UNESCO's mission and activities.

United Nations Millennium Campaign
Global Office
Address: 220 East 42nd Street
New York, New York 10017
USA
E-mail: www.endpoverty2015.org/en/contact-us
Website: www.endpoverty2015.org

In 2000, 189 world leaders signed the Millennium Declaration, agreeing to the Millennium Development Goals (MDGs). The MDGs provide a roadmap of measurable milestones for ending poverty and addressing other problems of the world's poorest areas. The target date for achieving the MDGs is 2015.

The eight MDGs are:

- Eradicate extreme poverty and hunger
- Achieve primary universal education
- Promote gender equality and empower women
- Reduce child mortality
- Improve maternal health
- Combat HIV/AIDS, malaria, and other diseases
- Ensure environmental sustainability
- Create a global partnership for development

United Network for Organ Sharing (UNOS)
Postal mail:
Post Office Box 2484
Richmond, Virginia 23218
USA
Street address:
700 North 4th Street
Richmond, Virginia 23219
USA
Tel.: 1-804-782-4800
E-mail: through the online forms at: www.unos.org/contact/
    index.php
Website: www.unos.org/

The United Network for Organ Sharing (UNOS) contracts with the federal government to manage the U.S. organ transplant system. UNOS is a private, nonprofit organization. Among its many responsibilities, UNOS manages the national transplant waiting list and matches donors with recipients, maintains the national organ transplant database, addresses policies and monitors policy adherence, and provides education to medical professionals and the public. It also provides assistance to transplant patients, their family members, and their friends.

United States Agency for International Development Information Center (USAID)
Ronald Reagan Building
Washington, DC 20523-1000

USA
Tel.: 1-202-712-4810
E-mail: through the online contact directory at: www.usaid.gov/
contact.html
Website: www.usaid.gov

In support of U.S. foreign policy goals, this independent agency provides economic, development, and humanitarian assistance in more than 100 countries around the world. Its overall foreign policy guidance comes from the U.S. Secretary of State. USAID undertakes projects related to medical tourism, most specifically under the following areas:

- Global Health Bureau: www.usaid.gov/our_work/
  global_health/
- Office of American Schools and Hospitals Abroad
  (ASHA): www.usaid.gov/our_work/cross-cutting_
  programs/asha/

United States Commercial Service
U.S. Department of Commerce
International Trade Administration
1401 Constitution Ave NW
Washington, DC 20230
USA
Tel.: 1-800-USA-TRAD (1-800-872-8723)
Website: http://trade.gov/cs/

The purpose of the U.S. Commercial Service (CS) is to "help U.S. companies get started in exporting or increase sales to new global markets." CS trade promotion activities are conducted through trade counseling, market intelligence, business matchmaking, advocacy and commercial diplomacy, and trade promotion programs.

U.S. Travel Insurance Association (UStiA)
Administrative Offices
US Travel Insurance Association c/o Empire Travel
The 20 Mall
2080 Western Avenue
Guilderland, NY 12084, USA
Headquarters

US Travel Insurance Association
1333 H Street, N.W.
Suite 820
Washington, DC 20005, USA
Tel.: 1-212-877-2798
E-mail: information@ustia.org
Website: www.ustia.org/

The U.S. Travel Insurance Association (UStiA) helps travelers learn about travel insurance, decide if they need it, and know what questions to ask when buying it. The association represents travel insurance organizations, promoting ethical and professional industry standards, government relations, member information and assistance, and consumer education.

World Alliance for Patient Safety
WHO Patient Safety
Information, Evidence and Research (IER/PSP)
World Health Organization
Avenue Appia 20
CH-1211 Geneva 27
Switzerland
E-mail: patientsafety@who.int
Website: www.who.int/patientsafety/en/

A 2002 World Health Assembly Resolution urging global attention to patient safety led to the 2004 launch of the World Health Organization's World Alliance for Patient Safety. The alliance facilitates international collaboration on behalf of patient safety, and provides a range of programs to that end. In October 2011, it released the *Multi-professional Patient Safety Curriculum Guide*, which was designed to train health care professionals on patient safety priorities.

World Bank
The World Bank
1818 H Street, NW
Washington, DC 20433
USA
Tel.: 202-473-1000
E-mail: through the online form at: http://go.worldbank.org/
     EROS2XNAG0
Website: www.worldbank.org/

The World Bank is not a bank in the traditional sense of the word. Rather, it is comprised of two development institutions that are owned by their 187 member countries: the International Bank for Reconstruction and Development (IBRD) and the International Development Association (IDA). The organization provides low-interest loans, interest-free credits, and grants to developing countries to support inclusive and sustainable globalization and poverty reduction.

World Economic Forum
US Office:
3 East 54th Street
18th Floor
New York, NY 10022
USA
Tel.: 1-212-703-2300
E-mail: forumusa@weforum.org
Website: www.weforum.org/

The World Economic Forum is an independent international organization with the mission of "improving the state of the world." The goals of its projects are to find solutions to global challenges such as HIV/AIDS, and facilitate dialogue among various entities.

World Federation For Medical Education (WFME)
University of Copenhagen
Faculty of Health Sciences
Blegdamsvej 3
DK-2200 Copenhagen N, Denmark
Phone: + 45 353 27103
E-mail: wfme@wfme.org
Website: www.wfme.org/

The World Federation For Medical Education (WFME) represents medical teachers and medical teaching institutions around the world. The focus of the organization is on quality improvement in medical education. The WFME's efforts cover basic medical education, postgraduate medical education, and continuing professional development.

World Health Organization (WHO)
Headquarters
Avenue Appia 20

1211 Geneva 27
Switzerland
Tel.: + 41 22 791 21 11
E-mail: info@who.int (for general information)
Website: www.who.int/en/

The World Health Organization (WHO) is an entity within the United Nations system. It is the world's foremost global health organization, providing leadership on epidemiology and surveillance, medical research, international standards, and policy, and offering technical support on health matters. Addressing international public health issues is an important facet of the WHO's responsibility. The WHO undertakes projects on a wide variety of health topics related to medical tourism, which include but are not limited to:

- Food safety: www.who.int/ith/chapters/en/index.html
- Health systems: www.who.int/topics/health_systems/en/
- Health workforce: www.who.int/topics/health_workforce/en/
- Poverty (including development and health): www.who.int/topics/poverty/en/
- Trade, foreign policy, diplomacy, and health: www.who.int/trade/en/
- Travel and health: www.who.int/topics/travel/en/

World Health Organization (WHO) Food Safety
Department of Food Safety and Zoonoses (FOS)
World Health Organization
Avenue Appia 20
CH-1211 Geneva 27, Switzerland
E-mail: foodsafety@who.int
Website: www.who.int/foodsafety/en/

The WHO Food Safety program recognizes the growing health problem caused by foodborne illnesses and threats to food safety. The WHO helps its members improve food safety throughout the entire production chain, from the production process through consumption. In doing so, the WHO works with the Food and Agriculture Organization of the United Nations, the

World Organisation for Animal Health, and other international organizations that share interests and goals.

World Health Professions Alliance (WHPA)
WHPA Secretariat
c/o World Medical Association
BP 63
01210 Ferney Voltaire, France
Tel.: +33 450 40 7575
E-mail: whpa@wma.net
Website: www.whpa.org

The mission of the World Health Professions Alliance (WHPA) is to "improve global health and the quality of patient care." WHPA partners include more than 600 member organizations representing more than 26 million dentists, nurses, pharmacists, physical therapists, and physicians in more than 130 countries. Areas of organizational activity include public health, patient safety, counterfeit medicines, human rights in health, regulation of the health professions and collaborative practice, health human resources and workforce issues, and health care systems.

World Medical Association (WMA)
13, ch. du Levant
CIB—Bâtiment A
01210 Ferney-Voltaire
France
Tel.: +33 4 50 40 75 75
E-mail: wma@wma.net
Website: www.wma.net/

This international organization that represents physicians was founded in 1947. The World Medical Association's (WMA) mission statement cites that its purpose is "to serve humanity by endeavoring to achieve the highest international standards in Medical Education, Medical Science, Medical Art and Medical Ethics, and Health Care for all people in the world." Medical ethics information and links are provided on the WMA website.

World Medical Tourism and Global Health Congress
10130 Northlake Blvd.
Suites 214-289

West Palm Beach, FL 33412
USA
Tel.: 561-792-6676
E-mail: info@medicaltourismcongress.com
Website: www.medicaltourismcongress.com/

This annual conference brings together medical travel industry professionals to share industry knowledge. In addition to hosting a variety of key speakers, workshops, exhibits, and educational sessions, much of the conference is focused on networking opportunities.

World Tourism Organization (UNWTO)
Headquarters
World Tourism Organization
Capitán Haya 42
28020 Madrid
Spain
Tel.: +34 91 567 81 00
E-mail: omt@unwto.org
Website: http://unwto.org/en

The World Tourism Organization (UNWTO/OMT) is a specialized United Nations agency which, as the name implies, is dedicated to tourism. In 2011, the organization was comprised of 154 countries, 7 territories, and more than 400 affiliate members. (Affiliate members include those from the private sector, educational institutions, tourism associations, and local tourism authorities.) As a forum for international tourism policy issues, the UNWTO works to promote sustainable tourism through the Global Code of Ethics for Tourism. Tourism as promoted by the UNWTO allows countries, and particularly developing countries, to maximize their economic, social, and cultural benefits while minimizing their risks. Through its commitment to the United Nations Millennium Development Goals (MDGs), the organization also seeks to use tourism as a means to address poverty.

World Trade Organization (WTO)
Centre William Rappard,
Rue de Lausanne 154,
CH-1211 Geneva 21,
Switzerland
Tel.: +41 (0)22 739 51 11

E-mail: enquiries@wto.org
Website: www.wto.org/

The WTO was established in 1995, and bills itself as "the international organization whose primary purpose is to open trade for the benefit of all." It is the only international organization that deals with global trade rules. Additionally, it provides a forum for negotiating trade agreements that reduce trade barriers, implementing and monitoring agreements, and settling disputes surrounding those agreements. As of 2008, the WTO had 153 member countries. The WTO's trading system is comprised of 16 multilateral and two plurilateral trade agreements. These agreements include the General Agreement on Trade in Services (GATS), the Sanitary and Phytosanitary Measures Agreement (SPS), the Technical Barriers to Trade Agreement (TBT), and the Trade Related Aspects of Intellectual Property Rights (TRIPS) Agreement.

World Travel and Tourism Council (WTTC)
1–2 Queen Victoria Terrace
Sovereign Court
London E1W 3HA
United Kingdom
Tel.: +44 (0)870 727 9882 or +44 (0)20 7481 8007
E-mail: enquiries@wttc.org
WTTC India Initiative
A-228, Sushant Lok
Phase I, Gurgaon
Haryana—122 002
India
Tel.: +91 124 426 1874,
E-mail: wttcii@gmail.com
Website: www.wttc.org/

Established in 1990, WTTC states as its mission to "raise the awareness of the full economic and social impact and potential of the Travel & Tourism industry." The organization grew out of an identified need by travel and tourism executives to provide both consolidated data and a voice for the industry that did not previously exist, even though travel and tourism was one of the world's largest industries. Since its formation, the WTTC has worked with governments and other entities to support the growth and development of the global tourism industry.

8

Resources

T his selected bibliography provides an array of materials extending the content of this volume and representing the range of current scholarship and perspectives on medical tourism. Because the extensive body of literature on the topic is constantly evolving, this listing is not offered as an exhaustive directory of available materials.

Books

Research Focus

Bookman, Milica Z., and Karla R. Bookman. *Medical Tourism in Developing Countries.* New York, NY: Palgrave Macmillan, 2007.

Writing from their backgrounds in economics and law, the authors of this book focus on the economic and developmental impacts of medical tourism on destination locations. Their research is well done and the book is accessible to academics and non-academics alike.

Connell, John. *Medical Tourism.* Cambridge, MA: CABI, 2011.

This well-researched book covers a range of topics in medical tourism, from the history of travel for medical care, to the impacts of medical tourism on current health systems. The author's attention to media and advertising serves as an informative focus of the volume.

Hall, C. Michael. *The Ethics, Regulation, and Marketing of Health Mobility.* New York: Routledge, 2012.

This edited volume bills itself as being one of the first books "to critically address the substantial political, philosophical, and ethical issues that arise out of the transnational practices of medical tourism." Regulatory and policy structures are examined by looking at a range of destinations, medical systems, and economic perspectives.

Kumar, Rajesh. *Global Trends in Health and Medical Tourism.* New Delhi: SBS Publishers and Distributors Pvt. Ltd., 2009.

This volume provides an international perspective on medical tourism. It makes extensive use of documents from international bodies, and includes a discussion of health care systems in the United States, India, and Barbados.

Reisman, David. *Health Tourism: Social Welfare Through International Trade.* Cheltenham, UK, Edward Elgar, 2010.

True to the title, Reisman's book focuses on medical tourism through international trade regulations. Opening with a discussion of the World Trade Organization's General Agreement of Trade in Services (GATS), the book moves through discussions of the benefits and costs of medical tourism, including public health issues. Singapore and Asian destinations are addressed in separate chapters.

Patient Guides

Frankum, Scott. *The Well Report-Cosmetic, Plastic & Reconstructive Surgery in India and Malaysia.* [Kindle Edition.] West Hollywood, CA: The Well Report, 2010.

Written for a U.S. audience, this book is divided into three sections. The first section addresses "The Case for Health Travel." The second section is "Where to Go for Care Now." The third section, "Resources," contains lists and check sheets about pricing, finding quality providers, and more. The author also edits The Well List website (see p. 295).

Gahlinger, Paul. *The Medical Tourism Travel Guide: Your Complete Reference to Top-Quality, Low-Cost Dental, Cosmetic, Medical Care & Surgery Overseas.* North Branch, MN: Sunrise River, 2008.

This guide begins with an overview of medical tourism in a section titled, "What Your Doctor Doesn't Know About Medical Tourism." It covers some of the basic "whats" and "whys" of medical tourism, and discusses some procedures (e.g., cosmetic surgery, dental care) medical tourists often seek. The second section, "A Global Guide to Medical Tourism Facilities," offers country-specific information on more than 40 countries around the world.

Hancock, David. *The Complete Medical Tourist: Your Guide to Inexpensive and Safe Cosmetic, Medical and Dental Surgery Overseas.* London: John Blake, 2006.

Section one of this guide covers procedures that are popular with medical tourists: various types of surgery, dental care, sex reassignment, transplants, and scans and health checks. The second section focuses on destinations for these procedures. The "tourism" aspect of medical tourism is also included in these discussions.

Marsek, Patrick W., and Frances Sharpe. *The Complete Idiot's Guide to Medical Travel.* Royersford, PA: Alpha, 2009.

Part of "The Complete Idiot's Guide to" series, this book offers a variety of information for potential medical tourists, discussed in an uncomplicated manner. It starts with the basics of medical tourism, as well as cost and safety considerations. It then offers information on location, decision-making, trip planning, financial planning, and recovering after returning home.

Schult, Jeff, Curtis Schroeder, and John Corey. *Beauty from Afar: A Medical Tourist's Guide to Affordable and Quality Cosmetic Care Outside the U.S.* New York: Stewart, Tabori and Chang, 2006.

Beauty From Afar derives from the American journalist's personal experience with dental work abroad. The book provides consumer information and emphasizes the importance of doing research before going abroad for a medical procedure, offering guidance on how to do so.

Woodman, Josef. *Patients Beyond Borders: Everybody's Guide to Affordable, World-Class Medical Travel.* Chapel Hill, NC: Healthy Travel Media, 2008.

Currently in its second edition, this popular and easily readable guidebook covers a range of information for the prospective medical tourist. The book offers sections on background information, step-by-step guidance for planning the trip (including a chapter written specifically for travel companions), destinations, and further resources.

Spas

Spas are one of the oldest forms of medical tourism. Today, the global spa industry is a fast-growing segment of both the leisure and medical tourism industries. Selected books specifically targeting the spa industry are included here.

Bodeker, Gerry, and Marc Cohen. *Understanding the Global Spa Industry: Spa Management.* Oxford: Butterworth-Heinemann, 2008.

This volume has chapters on planning, profit, product, planet, and people. The chapters cover a range of considerations that are important in spa management, including financial performance, regulatory guidance, cultural, social, and environmental responsibilities, technology, and future trending.

Burt, Bernard, and Pamela Joy Price. *100 Best Spas of the World, 3rd (100 Best Series).* Guilford, CT: GPP Travel, 2006.

Looking for a spa destination? If so, this book (in its third edition at this writing) covers top-rated spas in more than 30 countries.

Chapman, Judy, and Luca Invernizzi Tettoni. *Ultimate Spa: Asia's Best Spas and Spa Treatments.* United Kingdom: Periplus Editions/Berkeley Books Pte Ltd., 2006.

This book discusses Asian spas and their various treatments, and contains photographs that accentuate the material.

Erfurt-Cooper, Patricia, and Malcom Cooper. *Health and Wellness Tourism: Spas and Hot Springs.* Bristol, UK: Channel View Publications, 2009.

As the title suggests, this book focuses on natural geothermal hot spring spas. It includes information on the history of the spa industry, geology, cultural and environmental issues, technology, and the business aspects of spa management, and it provides case studies of various spas.

Smith, Melanie, and Laszlo Puczko. *Health and Wellness Tourism.* Oxford: Butterworth-Heinemann, 2009.

This comprehensive book provides an in-depth look at the spa industry. It covers the history and varieties of spas, retreats, health-oriented festivals, and more. The content is useful to those interested in traveling; however, much of the book's content is targeted to spa operations and management. Several destinations are covered in detail.

Other

Carabello, Laura. *Medical Travel Today: Opinions and Perspectives on an Industry in the Making.* Elmwood Park, NJ: CPR Strategic Marketing Corporation, 2011.

This book compiles more than 40 interviews from *Medical Travel Today.* The interviewees are experts from many different facets of the medical tourism industry, including academicians, attorneys, health executives, insurers, policy makers, physicians, and more.

Goldberg, James R. *The American Medical Money Machine: The Destruction of Health Care in America and the Rise of Medical Tourism.* London: Homunculus Press, 2009.

Written by the father of an adult son who died in a Thai hospital, this book offers a critical look at systemic issues in health care, including the Obama Health Care Plan.

Academically Focused Resources

Selected Journals (Academic)

These selected journals generally include content that either addresses medical tourism issues directly, or has significant connections with medical tourism. Because of the interdisciplinary interests in medical tourism, articles appear in a wide variety of journals in diverse fields, and may also be published in a journal that is not contained in this list.

Developing World Bioethics

North American Office:
John Wiley & Sons, Inc.
350 Main Street
Malden, MA 02148
USA
Tel: +1 781 388 8598; (toll free) +1 800 835 6770
E-mail: cs-journals@wiley.com
Website: http://onlinelibrary.wiley.com/journal/10.1111/(ISSN)
   1471-8847

Developing World Bioethics, the peer-reviewed companion journal to *Bioethics*, is dedicated exclusively to the bioethics of developing countries. It provides case studies, teaching materials, news briefs, and legal backgrounds.
   A 2012 special volume is devoted to medical tourism.

Globalization and Health

Postal address:
c/o BioMed Central Ltd
Floor 6 236 Gray's Inn Road
London WC1X 8HB
United Kingdom
Tel: +442031922009
E-mail: globalizationandhealth@lse.ac.uk
Website: www.globalizationandhealth.com/

   This open-access, peer-reviewed online journal is associated with the London School of Economics. The journal's focus is on the globalization of health care, and its effects (whether positive or negative) on health.

International Journal for Equity in Health (IJEqH)

c/o BioMed Central Ltd
Floor 6 236 Gray's Inn Road
London WC1X 8HB
United Kingdom
Tel: +44 (0) 20 3192 2009
E-mail: editorial@equityhealthj.com
Website: www.equityhealthj.com/

The IJEqH is the journal of the International Society for Equity in Health (ISEqH). It focuses on health equity across and within countries. The journal is peer-reviewed, and is available online.

International Journal for Quality in Health Care (IJQHC)

Oxford University Press
2001 Evans Road
Cary, NC 27513
USA
Tel: + 1 919-677-0977; (toll free from US and Canada) + 1-800-852-7323
Editorial address:
Eric Schneider, M.D., M.Sc.
Senior Scientist and Director
RAND Boston
20 Park Plaza
7th Floor, Suite 720
Boston, MA 02116
USA
E-mail: eschneid@rand.org
Website: http://intqhc.oxfordjournals.org/

Published by the International Society for Quality in Health Care (ISQua), this interdisciplinary peer-reviewed journal contains ISQua news, as well as research, policy, and implementation related to the quality of global health care and health outcomes.

International Journal of Behavioural and Healthcare Research (IJBHR)

Inderscience Publishers
General editorial matters:
The Editor-in-Chief
Editorial Office
P O Box 735
Olney, Bucks., MK46 5WB
UK.
E-mail: editor@inderscience.com
IJHBR Editor:
Demetri Kantarelis
Professor of Economics
Assumption College

Department of Economics & Global Studies
500 Salisbury Street
Worcester, MA 01609-1296
USA
E-mail: dkan@besiweb.com
Website: www.inderscience.com/browse/index.php?journalID=274

The content of this journal includes original papers, review papers, case studies, notes, commentaries, reports relating to technology and education, and book reviews on behavioral and health care concerns.

The IJBHR published a "Special Issue on Medical Tourism" in its volume 2, number 1, 2010. www.inderscience.com/browse/index.php?journalID=274&year=2010&vol=2&issue=1 (accessed October 15, 2011).

International Journal of Health Services (IJHS)

Baywood Publishing Company, Inc.
26 Austin Avenue
Box 337
Amityville, NY 11701
USA
Tel: +16316911270
E-mail: info@baywood.com
Website: http://baywood.com/journals/PreviewJournals.asp?Id=
    0020-7314

The widely cited *International Journal of Health Services (IJHS)* examines developments in global health and social sectors. Content includes academic articles, position papers, and topical debates.

International Journal of Pharmaceutical and Healthcare Marketing

Emerald Group Publishing Limited
Howard House
Wagon Lane
Bingley BD16 1WA
United Kingdom
Tel: +441274777700

E-mail: Publisher, Martyn Lawrence, mlawrence@emeraldinsight.
   com; Editor, Professor Avinandan Mukherjee, editor-IJPHC@
   mail.montclair.edu
Website: www.emeraldinsight.com/products/journals/journals.
   htm?id=IJPHM

A specialist reference, this journal ties together pharmaceutical and healthcare marketing through empirical research, concep-
tual papers, literature reviews, case studies, quantitative models,
qualitative studies, pedagogical innovations (syllabus development), and book reviews.

International Journal of Technology Assessment in Health Care

Cambridge University Press
(For USA editorial, marketing, production, publicity, sales)
32 Avenue of the Americas
New York, NY 10013-2473
USA
Tel: +441223326070
E-mail: journals@cambridge.org
(For USA orders, customer service)
100 Brook Hill Drive
West Nyack, NY 10994-2133
USA
Tel: +18453537500
E-mail: subscriptions_newyork@cambridge.org
Editor-in-Chief
Dr Marjukka Mäkelä
FINOHTA (Finnish Office for Health Technology Assessment)
THL (National Institute for Health and Welfare)
P.O.Box 30
00271 Helsinki
Finland
Website: http://journals.cambridge.org/action/displayJournal?jid=
   THC

As this journal's title suggests, it addresses health technology
from economic, social, ethical, medical, and public health perspectives. It is the official journal of Health Technology Assessment
International (HTAi).

Journal of Travel Medicine

John Wiley & Sons, Inc.
350 Main Street
Malden, MA 02148
USA
Tel: +1 781 388 8598; (toll free) +1 800 835 6770
E-mail: cs-journals@wiley.com
Website: http://onlinelibrary.wiley.com/journal/10.1111/(ISSN)
1708-8305

The *Journal of Travel Medicine* is the official, peer-reviewed journal of the International Society of Travel Medicine (ISTM). Among other topics, the journal covers prevention and treatment, clinic management, education, immunization, refugees, impact on destination countries, military medicine, and specific diseases.

The Lancet

North American Offices and Customer Service:
360 Park Avenue South
New York, NY 10010-1710 USA
Tel: (Toll Free) +1 (800) 462 6198; (Direct) +1 (314) 447 8057
E-mail: USLancetCS@elsevier.com
Publisher and website operator:
Elsevier Inc.
1600 John F. Kennedy Boulevard, Suite 1800
Philadelphia, PA 19103-2899
USA
Website: www.thelancet.com/

This prestigious international general medical journal, founded in 1823, publishes a weekly journal and three monthly specialty journals in the fields of oncology, neurology, and infectious diseases. Much of the content is available online. In January 2009, *The Lancet* published a series on "Trade and Health" that included medical tourism. The series content is available online at: www.thelancet.com/series/trade-and-health.

Tourism Management

Elsevier B.V. (Corporate Office)
Radarweg 29, Amsterdam 1043

Netherlands
Tel: +31 20 485 3911
Editor
Chris Ryan
Centre for Management Studies
University of Waikato
Hillcrest Road Private Bag 3015
3216 Hillcrest, Hamilton, New Zealand
E-mail: through the online form at: www.journals.elsevier.com/
    tourism-management/editorial-board/chris-ryan/
Website: www.journals.elsevier.com/tourism-management/

Taking an interdisciplinary and integrative approach, this journal addresses tourism policy and planning for academics and practitioners through primary research, and a discussion of current issues, case studies, reports, book reviews, and forthcoming meetings.

Tourism Review

Emerald Group Publishing Limited
Howard House
Wagon Lane
Bingley BD16 1WA
United Kingdom
Tel: +441274777700
E-mail: Publisher, Martyn Lawrence, mlawrence@emeraldinsight.
    com; Editor, Dr. Christian Laesser, christian.laesser@unisg.ch
Website: www.emeraldinsight.com/products/journals/journals.
    htm?id=tr

From the International Association of Scientific Experts in Tourism (AEIST), this journal is targeted to scientists, policymakers, and managers. Its articles examine scientific concepts and research on developments, issues, and methods in tourism research.

World Medical and Health Policy (WHMP)

Berkeley Electronic Press
2809 Telegraph Avenue, Suite 202
Berkeley, California, 94705

USA
PSOCommons—The Policy Studies Organization
1527 New Hampshire Avenue
NW Washington DC, 20036
USA
Tel: (202) 483-2512
GMU—George Mason University, School of Public Policy
4400 University Drive, MS 3C6
Fairfax, Virginia, 22030
USA
Phone: (703) 993-8217
Website: www.psocommons.org/wmhp/

This journal of the Policy Studies Organization publishes evidence-based research on the ways in which public policy affects the practice of medicine. In particular, it focuses on the intersection of public policy and medical practice, and its translation into policy implications and recommendations.

World Medical Journal

Website: www.wma.net/en/30publications/20journal/

Published by the World Medical Association (WMA), this journal is available in PDF format at the WMA website.

Medical Journal Finder Directories

Free Medical Journals

Website: www.freemedicaljournals.com/

This site was created "to promote the free availability of full text medical journals on the Internet."

Medical-Journals.com

Website: www.medical-journals.com/

This website links to both free and subscription medical journals from all over the world. Other links include editorials, medical-legal journals, news, and related classifieds. Registration is required.

Selected Journal Articles, Essays, and Book Chapters

Cohen, I. Glenn. "Protecting Patients with Passports: Medical Tourism and the Patient-Protective Argument." *Iowa Law Review* 95, no. 5 (2010): 1476–1567.

Crooks, Valorie A., Paul Kingsbury, Jeremy Snyder, and Rory Johnston. "What Is Known about the Patient's Experience of Medical Tourism? A Scoping Review." *BMC Health Services Research* 10 (2010): 266–278. www.biomedcentral.com/1472-6963/10/266 (accessed July 3, 2011).

Crooks, Valorie A., and Jeremy Snyder. "Regulating Medical Tourism." *The Lancet* 376, no. 9751 (2010): 1465–1466.

Goodrich, J. "Socialist Cuba: A Study in Health Tourism." *Journal of Travel Research* 32 (1993): 36–41.

Hall, C. Michael. "Health and Medical Tourism: Kill or Cure for Global Public Health?" *Tourism Review* 66, no. 1/2 (2011): 4–15.

Hopkins L., R. Labonté, V. Runnels, and C. Packer. "Medical Tourism Today: What Is the State of Existing Knowledge?" *Public Health Policy* 31, no. 2 (July 2010): 185–198.

Horowitz, Michael D., and Jeffrey A. Rosensweig. "Medical Tourism—Health Care in the Global Economy." *Physician Executive* 33, no. 6 (2007): 24–29.

Johnston, Rory, Valorie A. Crooks, Jeremy Snyder, and Paul Kingsbury. "What Is Known about the Effects of Medical Tourism in Destination and Departure Countries? A Scoping Review." *International Journal for Equity in Health* 9 (2010): 24–37.

Lee, Kelley, Devi Sridhar, and Mayur Patel. "Bridging the Divide: Global Governance of Trade and Health." *The Lancet* 373 (January 31, 2009): 416–422.

Lundy, Douglas W. "The Liability Implications of Medical Tourism." AAOS *Now*. February 2008. www.aaos.org/news/aaos-now/feb08/managing7.asp (accessed October 1, 2011).

Menvielle, Loick. "Medical Tourism: Paradoxes of Globalisation and Ethical Issues." In *The Paradoxes of Globalisation,* edited by Eric Millinot and Nadine Tournois. New York: Palgrave/MacMillan, 2010, 145–165.

Milstein, Arnold, and Mark Smith. "Will the Surgical World Become Flat?" *Health Affairs* 26, no. 1 (2007): 137–141.

Nahrstedt, W. "Wellness: A New Perspective for Leisure Centers, Health Tourism, and Spas in Europe on the Global Health Market." In *The Tourism and Leisure Industry: Shaping the Future,* edited by K. Weiermair and C. Mathies. Binghamton, NY: Haworth Hospitality, 2004: 181–198.

NaRanong, Anchana, and Viroj NaRanong. "The Effects of Medical Tourism: Thailand's Experience." *Bulletin of the World Health Organization* 89 (2011): 336–344. doi: 10.2471/BLT.09.072249. www.who.int/bulletin/volumes/89/5/09–072249/en/index.html (accessed October 1, 2011).

Page, S. J. "The Evolution of Travel Medicine Research: A New Research Agenda for Tourism?" *Tourism Management* 30, no. 2 (2009): 149–157.

Pennings, G., G. de Wert, F. Shenfield, J. Cohen, B. Tarlatzis, and P. Devroey. "ESHRE Task Force on Ethics and Law 15: Cross-border Reproductive Care." *Human Reproduction* 23, no. 10 (2008): 2182–2184. www.eshre.eu/binarydata.aspx?type=doc&sessionId=34unxn45sf25cl55ivin2o45/Task_force_XV_cross_border.pdf (accessed October 20, 2011).

Snyder, Jeremy, Valorie A. Crooks, Krystyna Adams, Paul Kingsbury, and Rory Johnston. "The 'Patient's Physician One-Step Removed': The Evolving Roles of Medical Tourism Facilitators." *Journal of Medical Ethics.* (2011). Published Online First: 8 April 2011 doi:10.1136/jme.2011.042374. http://jme.bmj.com/content/early/2011/04/06/jme.2011.042374.full.pdf (accessed July 3, 2011).

Snyder, Jeremy, Valorie Crooks, and Leigh Turner. "Issues and Challenges in Research on the Ethics of Medical Tourism: Reflections from a Conference." *Bioethical Inquiry* 8 (2011): 3–6.

Turner, Leigh G. "Quality in Health Care and Globalization of Health Services: Accreditation and Regulatory Oversight of Medical Tourism Companies." *International Journal for Quality in Health Care* 23, no. 1 (2011): 1–7.

Unti, James A. "Medical and Surgical Tourism: The New World of Health Care Globalization and What It Means for the Practicing Surgeon." www.surgicalpatientsafety.facs.org/news/medicaltourism.html (accessed December 17, 2010).

York, D. "Medical Tourism: The Trend Toward Outsourcing Medical Procedures to Foreign Countries." *Journal of Continuing Education in the Health Professions* 28, no. 2 (2008): 99.

Reports

American Medical Association (AMA). *Medical Care Outside the United States.* Resolutions 711 and 732, A-07. www.ama-assn.org/ama1/pub/upload/mm/372/a-08cms1.pdf (accessed October 20, 2011).

Asian Medical Tourism Analysis (2008–2012). *New Delhi: RNCOS Industry Research Solutions;* 2009. Available from: www.rncos.com/Market-Analysis-Reports/Asian-Medical-Tourism-Analysis-2008–2012-IM105.htm (accessed October 1, 2011).

Deloitte Center for Health Solutions. *2011 Survey of Health Care Consumers in the United States: Key Findings, Strategic Implications.* 2011. www.deloitte.com/assets/Dcom-UnitedStates/Local%20Assets/Documents/US_CHS_2011ConsumerSurveyinUS_062111.pdf (accessed September 28, 2011).

Deloitte Center for Health Solutions. *Medical Tourism: Consumers in Search of Value.* October 2, 2008. www.deloitte.com/view/en_HR/hr/industries/lifescienceshealthcare/article/964710a8b410e110Vgn VCM100000ba42f00aRCRD.htm (accessed November 20, 2009).

Deloitte Center for Health Solutions. *Medical Tourism: Update and Implications—2009 Report.* www.deloitte.com/assets/Dcom-UnitedStates/Local%20Assets/Documents/us_chs_Medical Tourism_111209_web.pdf (accessed February 27, 2010).

Gallup Organization. "Cross-Border Health Services in the EU: Analytical Report." *Flash Eurobarometer 210.* June 2007. http://ec.europa.eu/public_opinion/flash/fl_210_en.pdf (accessed January 22, 2012).

Helble, Matthias. "The Movement of Patients Across Borders: Challenges and Opportunities for Public Health." *Bulletin of the World Health Organization* 89 (2011): 68–72.

Herrick, Devon M. *Medical Tourism: Global Competition in Health Care.* National Center for Policy Analysis. NCPA Policy Report No. 304, November 2007.

Leng, C. H. *Medical Tourism in Malaysia: International Movement of Healthcare Consumers and the Commodification of Healthcare.* (Working Paper Series No. 83). 2007. Singapore: Asia Research Institute. www.ari.nus.edu.sg/showfile.asp?pubid=642&type=2 (accessed September 1, 2011).

Renub Research. *Asia Medical Tourism Analysis (2008–2013).* September 2009. www.researchandmarkets.com/research/5b1fd2/asia_medical_touri (accessed December 7, 2009).

Organisation for Economic Co-operation and Development (OECD), Eurostat, World Health Organization (WHO). *A System of Health Accounts, 2011 Edition.* OECD Publishing. doi: 10.1787/9789264116016-en.   www.who.int/nha/sha_revision/sha_2011_final1.pdf (accessed September 28, 2011).

United Nations Economic Commission for Latin America and the Caribbean (ECLAC). *Medical Tourism: A Survey.* March 2010. Washington, DC: ECLAC. www.eclac.cl/publicaciones/xml/7/39397/Medical_Tourism_A_Survey_L111_final.pdf (accessed October 15, 2011).

United Nations Environment Programme. *World Tourism Organisation. Global Code of Ethics for Tourism.* www.unep.org/bpsp/Tourism/WTO%20Code%20of%20Conduct.pdf (accessed March 16, 2010).

Wellness Tourism Worldwide. *4WR: Wellness: for Whom, Where, and What? Research Report. Phase 1: Wellness Tourism—Present. July 2011.* www.wellnesstourismworldwide.com/uploads/7/2/1/6/7216110/wtw_4wr_phase1_web_2.pdf (accessed October 1, 2011).

Wellness Tourism Worldwide. *4WR: Wellness: for Whom, Where, and What? Research Report. Phase 2: Wellness Tourism—2020.* July 2011. www.wellnesstourismworldwide.com/uploads/7/2/1/6/7216110/wtw_4wr_phase2_web.pdf (accessed October 1, 2011).

YourSurgeryAbroad.com, in association with the International Medical Travel Association. Medical Tourism Report: United States of America. July 2009. www.yoursurgeryabroad.com/pdf/medical_tourism_report_usa.pdf (accessed September 20, 2011).

Medical Society Positions and Statements

American College of Obstetricians and Gynecologists (ACOG). *Ethical Considerations for Performing Gynecologic Surgery in Low-Resource Settings Abroad. Committee Opinion.* Number 466. September 2010. www.acog.org/from_home/publications/ethics/co466.pdf (accessed October 27, 2011).

American College of Surgeons (ACS). [ST-65] "Statement on Medical and Surgical Tourism." *Bulletin of the American College of Surgeons* 94, no. 4 (April 2009). www.facs.org/fellows_info/statements/st-65.html (accessed October 15, 2011).

American Dental Association (ADA). *Tourism (Dental Care Away from Home).* www.ada.org/3029.aspx?currentTab=1 (accessed October 1, 2011).

American Medical Association (AMA). *New Guidelines on Medical Tourism.* www.ama-assn.org/ama1/pub/upload/mm/31/medicaltourism.pdf (accessed March 15, 2010).

American Society of Plastic Surgeons. *Medical Tourism: Plastic Surgery Is Real Surgery. Do You Have the Facts You Need?* www.plasticsurgery.org/articles-and-galleries/patient-and-consumer-information/patient-safety/medical-tourism.html (accessed October 27, 2011).

Infectious Disease Society of America: Hill, David R., Charles D. Ericsson, Richard D. Pearson, Jay S. Keystone, David O. Freedman, Phyllis E. Kozarsky, Herbert L. DuPont, Frank J. Bia, Philip R. Fischer, and Edward T. Ryan. "The Practice of Travel Medicine: Guidelines by the Infectious Diseases Society of America." *Clinical Infectious Diseases* 43, no. 12 (2006): 1499–1539.

Regulations and Legislation

United States

Colorado General Assembly Bill 07–1143. www.statebillinfo.com/bills/bills/07/1143_01.pdf (accessed October 27, 2011).

This bill would have established "incentives for state employees who are covered under a state self-insured group benefits plan who elect to obtain medical care in an accredited foreign health care facility when the cost of such care is lower in the foreign facility than in a covered U.S. facility." The bill was postponed indefinitely.

Health Insurance Portability and Accountability Act of 1996 (HIPAA)

U.S. Department of Health and Human Services. Understanding Health Information Privacy. www.hhs.gov/ocr/privacy/hipaa/understanding/index.html (accessed October 25, 2011).

This act addresses health information privacy concerns that pertain to all patients. Medical tourists are advised to be especially attentive to how their medical privacy will be handled abroad.

Healthcare.gov

Website: www.healthcare.gov/

This site, which is provided by the U.S. federal government, offers information about the Affordable Care Act (ACA). The site explains insurance options, offers consumers help in using insurance and finding health care providers, provides the laws and tools needed to better understand health care issues, and includes covered preventive and wellness services. It also contains a blog written by members of the current administration.

U.S. Senate Special Committee on Aging. *The Globalization of Health Care: Can Medical Tourism Reduce Health Care Costs?* Senate Hearing 109–659. 109th Congress, Second Session. June 27, 2006. Washington, DC. Government Printing Office. http://frwebgate.access.gpo.gov/cgi-bin/getdoc.cgi?dbname=109_senate_hearings&docid=f:30618.pdf (accessed August 30, 2011).

This special hearing addressed medical tourism and health care cost control. It raised concerns, including lack of affordable insurance and quality, and also recognized the growth of medical tourism and its potential role in cost control.

West Virginia State Legislature House Bill 4359. www.legis.state. wv.us/Bill_Text_HTML/2006_SESSIONS/RS/Bills/hb4359%20intr.htm (accessed October 1, 2011).

"A BILL to amend the Code of West Virginia, 1931, as amended, by adding thereto a new section, designated §5–16–28, relating to establishing a system to reduce the cost of medical care paid by the Public Employees Insurance Agency by providing incentives to covered employees to obtain treatment in low cost foreign health care facilities accredited by the Joint Commission International." The bill was not passed, but it is notable because it was the first such bill to ever be introduced in a U.S. state legislature.

International
The European Union (EU)
(See chapter 7.)

Council of the European Union. Directive on Cross-border Healthcare Adopted. February 28, 2011. www.consilium.europa. eu/uedocs/cms_data/docs/pressdata/en/lsa/119514.pdf (accessed September 28, 2011).

World Tourism Organization (UNWTO)
(See chapter 7.)

UNWTO Agreements

Blouin, C., N. Drager, and R. Smith. *International Trade in Health Services and the GATS—Current Issues and Debates.* 2006. World Bank: Washington, DC.

General Agreement on Trade in Services (GATS) www.wto.org/english/docs_e/legal_e/26-gats_01_e.htm.

Pan American Health Organization. *Trade in Health Services: Global, Regional and Country Perspectives.* Pan American Health Organization, Program on Public Policy and Health, Division of Health and Human Development, Washington, DC, 2002. www.who.int/trade/resource/THS/en/ (accessed October 20, 2011).

Sanitary and Phytosanitary Measures Agreement (SPS) www.wto.org/english/docs_e/legal_e/15sps_01_e.htm

Technical Barriers to Trade Agreement (TBT). www.wto.org/english/docs_e/legal_e/17-tbt_e.htm

Trade Related Aspects of Intellectual Property Rights (TRIPS) www.wto.org/english/docs_e/legal_e/27-trips_01_e.htm

World Health Organization (WHO)
(See chapter 7.)

World Health Organization (WHO). *International Health Regulations 2005,* 2nd ed. 2008. whqlibdoc.who.int/publications/2008/9789241580410_eng.pdf (accessed September 15, 2011).

Workforce Issues

Global Health Workforce Alliance. *Adding Values to Health: The Global Health Workforce Alliance 2010 Annual Report.* Global Health Workforce Alliance. Switzerland: World Health Organization. www.who.int/workforcealliance/knowledge/resources/ghwa_annualreport2010_web.pdf (accessed October 10, 2011).

Frenk, Julio, Lincoln Chen, Zulfi qar A Bhutta, Jordan Cohen, Nigel Crisp, Timothy Evans, Harvey Fineberg, Patricia Garcia, Yang Ke, Patrick Kelley, Barry Kistnasamy, Afaf Meleis, David Naylor, Ariel Pablos-Mendez, Srinath Reddy, Susan Scrimshaw, Jaime Sepulveda, David Serwadda, and Huda Zurayk. "Health Professionals for a New Century: Transforming Education to Strengthen Health Systems in an Interdependent World." *The Lancet* 376 (2010): 1923–1958.

Hazarika, Indrajit. *The Potential Effect of Medical Tourism on Health Workforce and Health Systems in India.* Asia Pacific Action Alliance on Human Resources for Health; 2008. www.hrhresourcecenter.org/node/2281 (accessed September 11, 2011).

Organisation for Economic Cooperation and Development (OECD). "International Migration of Health Workers: Improving International Co-Operation to Address the Global Health Workforce Crisis." Policy Brief. February 2010. www.oecd.org/dataoecd/8/1/44783473.pdf (accessed September 15, 2011).

Organization for Safety, Asepsis and Prevention (OSAP). *Guide for Safety and Infection Control for Oral Healthcare Missions.* http://osap.site-ym.com/?page=ICOralHCMissions (accessed October 31, 2011).

World Health Organization (WHO). "The WHO Global Code of Practice on the International Recruitment of Health Personnel." WHO 63, no. 16 (2010). www.who.int/hrh/migration/code/practice/en/index.html (accessed September 15, 2011).

Issues in Medical Ethics

Bioethics.com
Medical Tourism Issues
E-mail: info@bioethics.com
Website: http://bioethics.com/?cat=51

This website, which is dedicated to global issues in medical ethics, includes medical tourism as a specific topic. It includes recent annotated links to a variety of news items.

Birch, Daniel W., Lan Vu, Shahzeer Karmali, Carlene Johnson Stoklossa, and Arya M. Sharma. "Medical Tourism in Bariatric Surgery." *American Journal of Surgery* 199, no. 5 (2010): 604–608.

Ethics Committee of the Transplantation Society. "The Consensus Statement of the Amsterdam Forum on the Care of the Live Kidney Donor." *Transplantation* 78, no. 4 (August 27, 2004): 491–492.

Gill, J., B. Madhira, D. Gjertson, G. Lipshutz, J. M. Cecka, P. Pham et al. "Transplant Tourism in the United States: A Single-Center Experience." *Clinical Journal of the American Society of Nephrology* 3, no. 6 (2008):1820–1828.

International Society for Stem Cell Research (ISSCR). *Guidelines for the Clinical Translation of Stem Cells.* December 3, 2008. www.isscr.org/clinical_trans/pdfs/ISSCRGLClinicalTrans.pdf (accessed March 16, 2010).

International Society for Stem Cell Research (ISSCR). *Patient Handbook on Stem Cell Therapies.* December 3, 2008. www.isscr.org/PatientHandbook.htm (accessed July 22, 2011).

Mladovsky, Philipa. "IVF and Reproductive Tourism." *EuroObserver* 8, no. 4 (2006): 5. www.euro.who.int/__data/assets/pdf_file/0019/80371/EuroObserver8_4.pdf (accessed July 10, 2011).

National Institutes of Health (NIH) Stem Cell Information Home Page. *Stem Cell Information.* 2011. Bethesda, MD: National Institutes of Health, U.S. Department of Health and Human Services. http://stemcells.nih.gov/index (accessed October 28, 2011).

Roy, Nilanjana S. "Protecting the Rights of Surrogate Mothers in India." *The New York Times.* www.nytimes.com/2011/10/05/world/asia/05iht-letter05.html?_r=3 (accessed October 28, 2011).

Shimazono, Y. "The State of the International Organ Trade: A Provisional Picture Based on Integration of Available Information." *Bulletin of the World Health Organization* 85, no. 12 (2007): 955–962.

United Network for Organ Sharing. "What Every Patient Needs to Know." 2009. UNOS. www.unos.org/docs/WEPNTK.pdf (accessed July 5, 2011).

Trade Associations/Industry Resources

Certificate in Medical Tourism Studies

University of Richmond, School of Professional & Continuing Studies.

Website: spcs.richmond.edu/professional/medical-tourism.html (accessed October 10, 2011)

As of the fall semester of 2012, the University of Richmond in Richmond, VA, and the Medical Tourism Association are partnering to offer a Certificate in Medical Tourism Studies. The certification is offered through the School of Professional & Continuing Studies. Six courses are required and students earn continuing education units (CEUs) for their coursework. Students can complete courses online, while attending the annual World Medical Tourism and Global Healthcare Congress, or a combination of both.

Code of Practice for Medical Tourism

Website: www.treatmentabroad.net/medical-tourism/code-of-practice/

Treatment Abroad has launched a voluntary "Code of Practice for Medical Tourism." The objectives of the code are to drive quality by encouraging best practices among facilitators and health care providers, reassure patients about foreign health services they find promoted on the web, and combat negative views about the medical tourism industry.

Directory of Industry Associations

Website: www.imtj.com/marketplace/industry-associations/directory/

This list of medical tourism-related industry associations around the world is provided by the *International Medical Travel Journal (IMTJ)*.

Health Care Strategy, International (HCSI)
Graefelfing Office:
Lenbachstr. 8
82166 Graefelfing
Germany
Munich Office:
LENBACHPLATZ 1
80333 Munich
Germany
Tel: +49-89-1011 9222; (cell) +49-177-325 2968
E-mail: hcsi@healthcsi.de; seebacher@healthcsi.de
Website: www.healthcsi.de/

Among its activities, this consulting company conducts feasibility studies for governments, medical suppliers, investors, and health care providers, as well as offering training and workshops.

HealthCare Tourism International and HealthCare Trip
(See chapter 7.)

healthCare cybernetics *(hCc)*
Constantine Constantinides M.D., Ph.D.
(Chief Executive, healthCare cybernetics)
10 Amerikis Street
Syntagma (Constitution / Parliament) Square
ATHENS 106 71
Greece
Tel: (cell) +30 6945 8576 42
E-mail: constantinides@healthcarecybernetics.com
Website: www.healthcarecybernetics.com/

healthCare cybernetics (*hCc*) identifies itself as a "self-funded, unaffiliated private sector think and do tank." This is the "mother site" for a number of websites addressing various aspects of medical tourism. These sites are indexed on a directory page at: www.healthtourismdomain.com/Our-Health-Tourism-Sites/Our-Health-Tourism-Sites.htm.

The organization also advances *ht8*—"the concept, strategy and practice of integrating 8 Health-related Tourism Segments into Health Tourism." These are identified as: Medical Tourism; Dental Tourism; Spa Tourism; Wellness Tourism; Culinary Tourism; Sports Tourism; Accessible Tourism; and Assisted Residential Tourism (Ambient Assisted Living Abroad). Links to these eight segments can be found at the www.healthtourism8.com/ website.

Medical Tourism Association (MTA) (also known as the Medical Travel Association)
(See chapter 7.)

Medical Travel Quality Alliance (MTQUA)
E-mail: through the online form at: www.mtqua.org/contact/
Website: www.mtqua.org/

The Medical Travel Quality Alliance (MTQUA), initiated in 2009, has a mission of advancing patient safety and promoting medical excellence for medical tourists. It pursues this mission by focusing on professionalism in medical travel and health tourism. Additionally, the MTQUA is interested in defining quality in medical tourism and successful medical journeys, and addressing the unique needs and concerns of medical tourists.

Todd, Maria K. *Handbook of Medical Tourism Program Development: Developing Globally Integrated Health Systems.* New York: Productivity Press, 2011.

This book, written by an industry insider with decades of experience, offers a plan for facilities that are interested in developing a patient-centered program in medical tourism. Topics include internationally integrated health care systems, facilitation, patient privacy and security, case management, and the insurance and financing aspects of medical tourism.

Todd, Maria K. *Medical Tourism Facilitator's Handbook.* New York: Productivity Press, 2011.

This book provides a resource of "hard-to-find tools, checklists, terminology, and other helpful information for hospital-based, lay facilitators, travel agents, and even retired physicians and nurses." It deals with safety, service, and case studies that help facilitators prepare to meet their clients' needs.

Medical Tourism Magazine
10130 Northlake Blvd Suite 214-315
West Palm Beach, Florida, 33412
USA
Tel: 001-561-791-2000
E-mail: Info@MedicalTourismMagazine.com
Website: www.medicaltourismmag.com/

Published by the nonprofit Medical Tourism Association (MTA), *Medical Tourism Magazine* bills itself as the "voice" of the medical tourism industry. The magazine is available both in print and online versions. Targeted at MTA members and industry experts, *Medical Tourism* readership is estimated at more than 120,000 annually.

Medical Tourism Training, Inc.
1018 Beacon Street, Suite 201
Brookline, MA 02446-4084
USA
Tel: +18573661315
E-mail: contact@medicaltourismtraining.com
Website: www.medicaltourismtraining.com

This company provides online and onsite training programs. Five online courses are categorized as "essential" courses: "Introduction to Medical Tourism," "Basic Medical Terminology," "Telephone Skills for Professionals," "E-mail Etiquette—Netiquette," and "Working with the Upset Customer." "Caring for the Medical Tourist: Training for Hotel and Resort Employees" is offered as an onsite course.

Premier Medical Travel
6303 Owensmouth Avenue
10th Floor
Woodland Hills, CA 91367
USA
Tel: 1-818-936-3313
E-mail: info@premieremedicaltravel.com
Website: www.premieremedicaltravel.com/

This organization specializes in offering U.S. medical travel and consumer health care research to clients who want to better understand travelers and the medical tourism market. The company provides clients with information on medical travel opportunities, health care needs (current and future), business challenges, and U.S. medical traveler perceptions and choices.

Travel Market Report
71 Audrey Ave
Oyster Bay, NY, 11771
USA
Tel: +15167303097
E-mail: comments@travelmarketreport.com
Website: www.travelmarketreport.com/content/publiccontent.as
px?pageid=1362

The Travel Market Report links to various topics of interest to travel industry professionals, including medical travel. Items keep readers abreast of current news and upcoming events, such as conferences. Potential patients may also find some of the overview information of interest.

Wellness Tourism Worldwide
Tel: +13107201755
E-mail: through the form at: www.wellnesstourismworldwide.
com/contact.html
Website: www.wellnesstourismworldwide.com/

This international trade alliance, which has offices in Los Angeles, California, and Budapest, Hungary, launched in 2010 with the goal of supporting the worldwide development and promotion of wellness tourism. It brings together an alliance of government agencies, tourism organizations and related businesses, business interests, and higher education institutions to accomplish this goal.

General Audience Resources

Magazines

Health Tourism Magazine

10130 Northlake Blvd #214-315

West Palm Beach FL 33412
USA
Tel: 561-791-2000
E-mail: info@healthtourismmagazine.com
Website: www.healthtourismmagazine.com/

This bi-monthly magazine launched in 2009 with a business-to-consumer approach to its topic. It covers complementary treatments and quality-of-life improvements, with topics such as integrative, alternative, homeopathic and preventive medicines, spas, and wellness. *Health Tourism Magazine* is the "sister" magazine to *Medical Tourism Magazine.* Both are published by the Medical Tourism Association (MTA).

International Medical Travel Journal (IMTJ)

Intuition Communication Ltd
3 Churchgates
Wilderness
Berkhamsted
Herts HP4 2UB
United Kingdom
Tel: +441442817817
Website: www.imtjonline.com

Established in 2007, the *International Medical Travel Journal (IMTJ)* is owned and managed by the United Kingdom-based online publisher, Intuition Communication. In addition to offering extensive news and articles on its website, the *IMTJ* also includes directories, patient information, a blog, and a forum.

Medical Travel Today

CPR Communications
Attn: Medical Travel Today
475 Market Street, 2nd Floor
Elmwood Park, NJ 07407
USA
Telephone: (201) 641-1911
E-mail: info@medicaltraveltoday.com
Website: www.medicaltraveltoday.com/

This twice-monthly newsletter calls itself "the authoritative newsletter for medical tourism." It is e-mailed free to subscribers.

The target audience of the newsletter includes decision makers, managed care leaders, employers, international health care destinations, and potential medical tourists.

Selected News Articles (Print and Video)

A search of the Internet will return numerous marketing materials that, without closer inspection, may appear to be news items. Many sites (including facilitation agencies) also provide video patient testimonials for marketing purposes. The articles and video links provided here are to actual news reports on medical tourism.

Appleby, Julie. "Latest Destination For Medical Tourism: The U.S." *Kaiser Health News.* July 27, 2010. www.kaiserhealthnews. org/Stories/2010/July/07/domestic-medical-tourism.aspx (accessed July 29, 2011).

"*'Beauty From Afar'* Author Tackles Medical Tourism." *ABC News* (video). August 29, 2006. http://abcnews.go.com/Business/video?id=2370634 (accessed October 15, 2011).

Kher, Unmesh. "Outsourcing Your Heart." *Time.* May 21, 2006. www.time.com/time/magazine/article/0,9171,1196429,00.html (accessed July 30, 2011).

"Medical Tourism: Pros and Cons of Plastic Surgery Abroad" *Fox News.* (video) April 28, 2011. http://video.foxnews.com/v/4667707/medical-tourism/ (accessed October 15, 2011).

Norton, Leslie P. "Medical Tourism Takes Flight." *Barron's* 9, no. 36 (September 7, 2009): 24–25.

Prashad, Sharda. "The World is Your Hospital." *Canadian Business.* August 18, 2008. Vol. 81, Issue 12/13, pp 62–64.

Rahim, Saqib. "Q&A: Preparing for a Surgery Abroad." NPR. org. November 14, 2007. www.npr.org/templates/story/story. php?storyId=16296677 (accessed September 28, 2011).

Riczo, Steve, and Sarah Riczo. "Globalizing Health Care Through Medical Tourism." *USA Today* 138, no 2772 (September 2009): 26–28.

Sicko. Dir. Michael Moore. Dog Eat Dog Films. 2007. Documentary.

This documentary offers a critical view of American for-profit health care, compared with the health care systems of other countries. It features a traveler obtaining care in Cuba.

Sweeney, Camille. "More Fun Than Root Canals? It's the Dental Vacation." *The New York Times.* February 7, 2008. www.nytimes.com/2008/02/07/fashion/07SKIN.html (accessed October 20, 2011).

Tae-hoon, Lee. "Major Hospitals Overcharge Foreigners." *The Korea Times.* February 15, 2010. www.koreatimes.co.kr/www/news/nation/2010/02/116_60838.html (accessed October 20, 2011).

"Thailand's Medical Tourism." *CBS News.* (video) August 16, 2005. www.cbsnews.com/video/watch/?id=781417n (accessed October 15, 2011).

Van Dusen, Allison. "U.S. Hospitals Worth The Trip." Forbes.com. May 29, 2008. www.forbes.com/2008/05/25/health-hospitals-care-forbeslife-cx_avd_outsourcing08_0529healthoutsourcing.html (accessed October 20, 2011).

Patient Information

Facilitators/Medical Tourism Companies

There are a large and constantly changing number of companies (estimated at 1,000 or more) offering medical tourism services. The directory here is for informational purposes only, to represent the general range of service providers around the world. The list is primarily comprised of the medical travel providers that most frequently appeared in the medical tourism literature and Internet searches used when compiling this volume. The inclusion or exclusion of any company in this listing should not be considered a reflection on, endorsement of, or recommendation regarding the company or its business practices.

Aziza Travel
35 Lingard House
E14 3HH London
United Kingdom
Tel: 0775 647 2 432

E-mail: info@youraziza.co.uk
Website: www.youraziza.co.uk/

This London-based medical and health spa tour facilitator specializes in packaging spa holidays to Poland. They advertise 17- and 7-day respiratory-focused holidays to the Wieliczka Salt Mine. The destination is listed on UNESCO's First World List of Cultural and Natural Heritage.

BridgeHealth Medical
5299 DTC Blvd Suite 800
Greenwood Village CO 80111
USA
Tel: (US) +18006801366; (outside US) +13034575745
E-mail: through the online form at: www.bridgehealthmedical.com/contact-us
Website: www.bridgehealthmedical.com/

BridgeHealth Medical provides Surgery Benefit Management, including medical travel services, both within the United States and internationally. The company also offers *Early Indicators*, which allows employers to identify plan members before they need surgery, to provide them with more time and quality/cost options.

China Medical Tourism, Inc.
#1202, Building 17
55 Changyi Road, Pudong New Area
Shanghai, China
Zip: 200120
Tel: +86-21-58773798; (toll free) 4008-836-070
E-mail:info@shmtppp.com
Website: www.shmtppp.com

The Shanghai Medical Tourism Products and Promotion Platform (SHMTPPP) is China Medical Tourism Inc.'s online website for medical tourism. It is supported by several government agencies and, as the name indicates, is focused on advancing medical tourism in Shanghai. It also includes information for Chinese people seeking medical care in the United States, Korea, or Switzerland.

Companion Global Healthcare

E-mail: through the online forms at: www.companionglobal-healthcare.com/contact.aspx

Website: www.companionglobalhealthcare.com

Based in Columbia, South Carolina, Companion Global Healthcare coordinates medical tourism trips to multiple destinations. It also connects clients with insurance providers and offers a discount card that can also be used domestically. An online chat with an agent is also available on the site.

Croatian Medical Tourism

Peti kantun d.o.o.

Vukovarska 1a

23000 Zadar, Croatia

Tel: +385 98 276 880

E-mail: cmt@peti-kantun.hr

Website: www.croatianmedicaltourism.com/

This Croatian company emphasizes quality of care, service, medical education, level of technology, and number of tourism destinations as reasons for medical tourists to choose Croatia. Regenerative medicine—stem cell therapies—is one of the specialties offered in this eastern European country.

Dignitas

P.O. Box 9

8127 Forch

Switzerland

Tel: +41 43 366 10 70

E-mail: dignitas@dignitas.ch

Website: http://www.dignitas.ch/index.php?lang=en

"DIGNITAS—To live with dignity—to die with dignity" was founded in Switzerland in 1998. The association provides a range of end-of-life services, including "accompaniment of dying patients and assistance with a self-determined end of life."

Euromedical Tours

Tel: 020 7619 3838

E-mail: info@euromedicaltours.com

Based in the United Kingdom, this medical tourism facilitator specializes in trips to seven different countries: Belgium, Croatia, Greece, Hungary, India, Pakistan, and Turkey. Cosmetic surgery is an option in each of those locations.

GlobalMedTravel.com
Unimar, LLC
2899 E. Big Beaver Rd. 245
Troy, MI 48083
USA
Tel: 1-888-987-GLOBAL (toll free); 888-987-4562
E-mail: customer-service@globalmedtravel.com
Website: www.globalmedtravel.com/index.htm

This American-based company focuses on medical tourism to European destinations (i.e., Bulgaria, the Czech Republic, and Turkey). The idea is that American visitors will experience less culture shock in these countries than in other destinations. A U.S. and European case manager coordinates to assist clients through the process.

Heal in Turkey
Divanyolu Caddesi Bickiyurdu Sk: No:12-A
Sultanahmet/Istanbul Turkey
Tel.: +90 212 252 34 01
E-mail: info@fastbooktourism.com
Website: www.healinturkey.com

Based in Istanbul, this company facilitates medical tourism throughout the country of Turkey. Hospitals and doctors are advertised in Istanbul, Antalya, Kangal and Sivas, and North Cyprus. Among the procedures listed on the site are psoriasis treatments and hyperbaric oxygen therapy.

Healthbase Online
Tel: (toll free) 1-888-MY1-HLTH (1-888-691-4584); (international)
     1-617-418-3436
E-mail: info.hb@healthbase.com
Website: www.healthbase.com/

Healthbase is a Boston-based medical tourism facilitator that connects clients with health care providers in 14 countries. The company collaborates with health benefits company Wellpoint to send some non-emergency patients to India for certain procedures. The site advertises that it won the 2007 Consumer Health World Award in the category of Best Website for Accessing International Medical Information for Patients/Consumers.

Healthglobe (formerly Patients Without Borders)
304 Newbury Street
Suite 364
Boston, Massachusetts 02115
USA
Tel: 1 800 290 0197; (international) +1 617 708 4229
E-mail: info@myhealthglobe.com
Website: www.myhealthglobe.com/

Orthopedic, spinal, bariatric, cardiac, cosmetic and dental procedures, treatments for various chronic conditions, and in vitro fertilization are all advertised on the Healthglobe site. Destinations include medical facilities in 11 countries.

IndUShealth
IndUShealth, Inc.
7413 Six Forks Rd. #362
Raleigh, NC 27615
USA
Tel: +18007791314
E-mail: info@indushealth.com
Website: www.indushealth.com/

This company specializes in medical travel and medical tourism programs in India. Its program targets uninsured/underinsured American patients and U.S.-based employer health plans.

International Patient Facilitators (IPF)
Corporate Offices
Av. Tulum Lote 01 MZ 01 SM 12
Cancun, Quintana Roo, Mexico
Tel: 1 800 210 5124
E-mail: through the online form at: www.international-patient-facilitators.com/form.html
Website: www.international-patient-facilitators.com

Patient facilitators in Cancun and Tijuana, Mexico, coordinate medical care in those two cities. According to the site, a group of American, Canadian, and Mexican professionals facilitate care.

The company emphasizes lap band surgery and offers testimonials and e-mail addresses so that prospective travelers can contact former patients for references.

Malaysia Healthcare
US Offices
1165 State Park Rd.
Chipley, Florida 32428
USA
Tel: + 1 850 638 1797
E-mail: info@malaysiahealthcare.com
Website: www.malaysiahealthcare.com

This facilitator sells the tourism aspect, as well as the medical benefits of a Malaysian medical tourism trip. The website advertises several packaged tours, along with treatments. In addition to common treatment specialties, Malaysia Healthcare advertises that it offers "Medical Advisors" in aviation and occupational safety and health.

Med Journeys
120 S. Mountain Ave.
Montclair, NJ 07042
USA
Tel: 1-888-633-5769E-mail: mj-info@medjourneys.com
Website: www.medjourneys.com

Med Journeys is headquartered in New York. Through their corporate and employer programs, they act as a broker and have established partnerships and affiliations with both domestic and international health care providers. Destination countries are in Central and South America, Europe, Israel, the Caribbean, and Asia.

Medical Tourism Arizona
7825 E. Redfield Rd.
Suite #104
Scottsdale, Arizona 85260
USA
Tel: +14804208687
E-mail: steve@azmedtours.com
Website: www.azmedtours.com/

This organization provides U.S. domestic tourism, with Arizona as the destination. Their focus is on orthopedic surgery. Medical Tourism Arizona partners with J.W. Marriott and offers sightseeing trips to the Grand Canyon as part of their package.

Medical Tourism of Costa Rica

Tel: 1-267-886-3888
E-mail: through the online form at: www.medicaltourismofcos
    tarica.com/contact.php
Website: www.medicaltourismofcostarica.com

Medical Tourism of Costa Rica is a trade name of SRF Management Associates, S.R.L. The Costa Rican-based company advertises English-fluent physicians and specialties in plastic and reconstructive surgery, cosmetic and general dentistry, bariatric medicine, general surgery, addiction treatment, and general health and wellness.

Medical Tourism Partners (MTP)

1333 North Avenue, Suite A
New Rochelle, NY 10804
USA
Tel: 800-687-6110
E-mail: info@medicaltourismpartners.com
Website: http://captivatedesigns.net/clients/medicaltourism/

Founded by a Thai immigrant, this company primarily serves as a facilitator for medical tourists traveling to Thailand for procedures. The list of procedures the company handles includes Lasik surgery, as well as sex reassignment surgery (a specialty for which Thailand has become well known).

Medical Tourist Vacations

530 E Patriot Blvd. #172
Reno NV 89511
USA
Tel: 1 775 852 5105
E-mail: contact@poshjourneys.com
Website: www.medicaltouristvacations.com

As a subsidiary of Posh Journeys, which is owned by upscale tour providers, this company advertises medical vacations, rather than just medical packages. They have a partnership with Med Access India, an Indian medical tourism facilitator (www. medaccessindia.com/). Vacation packages include a Taj Mahal overnight excursion and a post-surgical package to a Himalayan spa.

MedRetreat
MedRetreat, LLC
2042 Laurel Valley Drive
Vernon Hills, IL 60061
USA
Tel: 1 443-451-9996; (toll free) 1-877-876-3373; (outside of U.S.) 001-443-451-9996
E-mail: customerservice@medretreat.com
Website: www.medretreat.com/

This company was founded in 2003 with the goal of "providing a safe, affordable, and timely option to healthcare in North America." MedRetreat offers a low-risk guarantee. If patients arrive at their destination country and find that conditions are unacceptable, they have the option to cancel their surgery. According to MedRetreat, they are the only company offering such a guarantee.

Medtral New Zealand
PO Box 99-894
Newmarket
Auckland 1149
New Zealand
Tel: +64-9- 6236588
E-mail: info@medtral.com
Website: www.medtral.com/

This company promotes New Zealand's natural scenery and temperate climate, Auckland's cosmopolitan city life, and an English-speaking population. The site also gives attention to the accreditation standards of its partner hospitals.

MedTrava Group
US Headquarters
8716 Mendocino Drive
Austin, TX 78735
USA
Tel: 1.512.732.0478; (toll free) 1.877.My.Medtrava

Fax: 1.800.296.0145
E-mail: info@medtrava.com
Website: www.medtrava.com/

This company advertises Costa Rica, India, Mexico, and Thailand as its destinations. It also includes an Ayurvedic resort, located in Kerala, in addition to more traditional "Western" medical procedures.

Placid Way
Tel: +1.303.578.0719
E-mail: info@placidway.com
Website: www.placidway.com

Placid Way is based in Denver, Colorado. This organization works with more than 125 healthcare providers based in more than 25 countries worldwide.

PlanetHospital
Tel: 1.800.243.0172; (outside the U.S +1.818.665.4801
E-mail: info@planethospital.com
Website: www.planethospital.info/

PlanetHospital began in 2002, after the founder fell while traveling and had a positive experience in a Thai hospital. The company advertises that it has been a member of the Better Business Bureau since that year, with no unresolved complaints and an "A" rating. Destinations in 16 countries around the world are featured on its website.

Prime Medical Concierge
R. Comendador Miguel Calfat, 128, cj.207
São Paulo—SP—Brasil
Tel: +55 11 3528-4545
E-mail:throughtheonlineformat:www.primemc.com.br/english/
    contato/
Website: www.primemedicalconcierge.com.br

Founded in 2006, this company promotes medical tourism in Sao Paulo, Brazil. Users of the website can view the content in several different languages.

SafeMedTrip
Tel: U.S. and Canada toll free +18887716965; outside U.S. and
  Canada +919899993637
E-mail: help@safemedtrip.com; safemedtrip@gmail.com
Website: www.safemedtrip.com

This medical tourism facilitator offers a wide variety of procedures in India. Packages for kidney transplants, brain tumor surgery, and knee replacements are described on the site, along with their costs in U.S. dollars.

Satori World Medical
Global Headquarters
591 Camino de la Reina, suite 407
San Diego, CA 92108
USA
Tel: (866) 613-9686; (619) 704-2000
E-mail: info@satoriworldmedical.com
Website: www.satoriworldmedical.com

Satori's unique Business & Care Model is set up such that payors can share savings with employers, plan sponsors, and patients. To do this, Satori utilizes a Health Reimbursement Account (HRA). This is an employer-funded benefit plan that reimburses employees for qualified medical expenses. The specialized Satori Global Transgender Network advertises cost-savings on sex reassignment surgeries at 30–50 percent less than procedures performed in U.S. hospitals. Satori even provides a Gender Transition Advocate (GTA) to help shepherd the patient through the process.

Solis
Tel: +902122756971; (toll free in U.S. and Canada) +18888747822
E-mail: info@solisturkey.com
Website: www.solisturkey.com

Solis Health and Wellness, LLC, is an Internet-based medical tourism facilitator. Its health care providers are based in Turkey. The company provides medical treatment packages for cosmetic surgery and dentistry, orthopedic and cardiac surgery, eye care, in vitro fertilization, weight loss, and hair restoration.

Surgeon and Safari
Head Office

Postal Address:
PO Box 97646
Petervale, 2151
South Africa
Street Address:
158 Mount Street
Bryanston, Johannesburg
Tel: (27 11) 463 3154
E-mail: through the online form at: www.surgeon-and-safari.
co.za/forms/contacts_form.cfm
Website: www.surgeon-and-safari.co.za

Established in 1999, Surgeon and Safari advertises itself as South Africa's original medical tourism company. Several consultation options are provided, and the company's consultation pages indicate that live video consultations are "soon to be implemented" but are not yet active at the time of this writing.

SurgeryPlanet
2280 Diamond Blvd
Ste: 300–304
Concord, CA 94523
USA
Tel: +1 (925) 429 4422; (toll free) 1-800-780-8460
E-mail: info@surgeryplanet
Website: www.surgeryplanet.com/

Headquartered in California, SurgeryPlanet has regional offices in the United Kingdom, India, and Guatemala. Their organization advertises 122 destinations and services that not all medical tourism providers offer.

Surgical Attractions
45 Bristol Road
Parkwood
Johannesburg 2193
South Africa
Tel: + 27 11 880 5122
E-mail: info@surgicalattractions.com
Website: www.surgicalattractions.com

Specializing in cosmetic surgery, this company invites medical tourists to "embark on a private journey of personal renewal."

"Rejuvenation holiday" packages include bush safaris and other sightseeing tours, visits to Singita and Thornybush, golfing, and winery visits. The site also lists exchange rates for the South African Rand against several world currencies.

Surgical Bliss
Unit A 315 Sandown Crescent
Grand National Boulevard
Milnerton Ridge
7441
Western Cape, South Africa
Tel: +27 (0) 82 857 4414
E-mail: denise@surgicalbliss.com
Website: www.surgicalbliss.com

This medical tourism company is based in South Africa. For travelers who want to take advantage of the country's unique tourism opportunities in addition to its medical expertise, Surgical Bliss offers spa, golf, safari, and garden route medical tourism packages.

Travel For Care
E-mail: contact this company through the online form to receive a
    return telephone call: www.travelforcare.com/call-me-button
Website: www.travelforcare.com

This organization specializes in arranging care for medical tourists who travel to Mexico, in particular Monterrey. Travel For Care emphasizes that medical tourism in Mexico is world-class, affordable, and closer to home for Americans.

WorldMedAssist
Tel: +18669993848
E-mail: through the online form at: www.worldmedassist.com/
    #free_box_bot
Website: www.worldmedassist.com

Destination countries for this medical tourism company are Belgium, Costa Rica, India, Korea, Mexico, and Turkey. The site provides a description of its partner hospitals and physicians. WorldMed

Assist has also joined with Wells Fargo Insurance Services to promote Medical Travel programs to Wells Fargo's self-funded employers.

Information Portals (Medical Tourism)

AllMedicalTourism.org
E-mail: Info@AllMedicalTourism.com
Website: www.allmedicaltourism.com/

This information portal seeks to help prospective medical tourists sift through the extraordinary amount of information available online. The site provides standardized information on price and quality of care.

Arabmedicare.com
(A service of Davis HealthPartners)
4401-203 Green Road
Raleigh, North Carolina 27604
USA
Tel: +1-919-862-3444
E-mail: contact@arabmedicare.com
Website: www.arabmedicare.com/

This site provides information on health care services in the Middle East & North Africa.

Discover Medical Tourism
E-mail: admin@discovermedicaltourism.com
Website: www.discovermedicaltourism.com/

This website serves as an information portal to help prospective travelers conduct research on medical tourism. Discover Medical Tourism contains information on destinations, treatments, alternative therapies, health spas, healthy living, and general medical tourism information.

Dr. Prem
Website: www.DrPrem.com

This website is written by medical doctor, businessman, and health consultant, Dr. Prem Jagyasi. Among the information on the website are a number of excerpts from Dr. Prem's guidebooks that address medical tourism.

Healism.com

E-mail: through the online form at: www.healism.com/contact_
us/
Website: www.healism.com/medical_tourism/overview/medical_
tourism/

With a tag line that reads "universal health care through medical tourism," this site has content created by providers from across the medical tourism spectrum. Patient testimonials are also posted. From healism.com, "Our goal...our mission statement is to educate the world about medical tourism."

MedicalNomad, LLC

5551 Ridgewood Drive
Suite 101
Naples, FL 34108
USA
E-mail: info@medicalnomad.com
Website: www.medicalnomad.com

MedicalNomad seeks to be a comprehensive site for researching medical and dental travel choices. Articles on the site contain general information regarding medical travel, and links are included to help medical travelers locate providers and learn about destinations.

OnlineMedicalTourism.com

E-mail: through the online form at http://www.onlinemedical-
tourism.com/contact.html
Website: www.onlinemedicaltourism.com/

Established in 2008 with offices in New York and Nevada, this information portal provides information searchable in a variety of different ways. Search headings include facilities, procedures, location, insurance, accreditation organizations, medical spas, and more.

Patients Beyond Borders

Tel: +18008835740; (outside US) +19199290634

E-mail: connect@patientsbeyondborders
Website: www.patientsbeyondborders.com/

As the name indicates, this resource is associated with the popular *Patients Beyond Borders* medical travel guidebooks. The mission of the site is to connect patients with the best medical choices and quality care available abroad. The site also aims to reduce the stress and uncertainties patients, families, and loved ones feel when undergoing medical procedures.

Treatment Abroad
Intuition Communication Ltd
3 Churchgates
Wilderness
Berkhamsted
Herts
HP4 2UB
England
Tel: +441442817817
E-mail: through the online form at: www.treatmentabroad.net/
about/aboutus-contacts/
Website: www.treatmentabroad.com/

This medical tourism information portal site lists its philosophy as, "helping you make the right choice." The extensive site includes an overview of medical tourism guides that address a number of topics (e.g., how to compare providers, how to check out clinics), and information on destinations and treatments. Patient testimonials and a blog are also part of the website.

The Well List
8581 Santa Monica Blvd, #535
West Hollywood, CA 90069
E-mail: through the online site at: http://wl.drupalgardens.com/
contact
Website: http://wl.drupalgardens.com/content/medical-research-
websites

The Well List is a partner site with *The Well Report* (see Patient Guides above). Author Scott Frankum, whose background includes a Masters of Business Administration in Global Management, edits the list. Among the resources the site provides is a Medical Research Website Directory, which is a series of handy links to credible online sources for general medical information.

YourSurgeryAbroad.com
c/o Operations Worldwide Ltd
Trans-World House
100 City Road
London
EC1Y 2BP
E-mail: info@yoursurgeryabroad.com
Website: www.yoursurgeryabroad.com

This website says, "We've spent our time researching so you don't have to." The information on the site includes "real-life stories" of successful medical tourism trips.

Information Directories

Best Hospitals

U.S. News Health

Website: http://health.usnews.com/best-hospitals

This searchable directory includes hospital rankings by specialty (including a separate listing for children's hospitals), by metro area, and by "most connected." The final category identifies hospitals that are "significantly advanced in the adoption of electronic medical records."

ClinicalTrials.gov

Website: www.clinicaltrials.gov/ct2/home

ClinicalTrials.gov provides current information on federally and privately funded medical research trials being conducted in the United States and elsewhere. The site has been developed by the U.S. National Institutes of Health (NIH) through the National Library of Medicine (NLM), and in collaboration with the Food and Drug Administration (FDA). Its searchable database contains more than 115,000 trials in every U.S. state and more than 170 countries around the world.

Find a Plastic Surgeon Abroad

American Society of Plastic Surgeons (ASPS)

Website: www1.plasticsurgery.org/ebusiness4/patientconsumers/findintsurgeon.aspx

The American Society of Plastic Surgeons (ASPS) offers this searchable database, which includes surgeons who are ASPS Members or Candidates for Membership. All are board-certified by the American Board of Plastic Surgery and/or The Royal College of Physicians and Surgeons of Canada.

Joint Commission International

Joint Commission International (JCI)-Accredited Organizations. www.jointcommissioninternational.org/JCI-Accredited-Organizations/ (accessed March 15, 2010) (See chapter 7.).

Medical Tourism Reviews

http://reviews.treatmentabroad.com/

This website, which is managed by Treatment Abroad, allows patients to get reviews from other medical tourists before making their travel plans. Searchable categories include health care providers, health care facilities, destination countries, and medical tourism agencies.

QualityCareFinder

Medicare.gov

Website; www.medicare.gov/quality-care-finder/

The United States federal government's official site for Medicare provides this QualityCareFinder tool. Users can use it to compare information about the quality of care and services different providers and plans offer, and to get contact information for hospitals, doctors, nursing homes, home health agencies, dialysis facilities, and drug and health plans. The site also provides tips for comparing providers and plans.

Blogs

An Internet search will find a number of blogs, many of which were inactive for some time (perhaps two or three years) before this list was compiled. Although those entries may contain useful information, only currently active blogs are included in this listing.

Searching the Internet will also turn up a wide variety of patient discussion forums. A number of these forums and patient reviews are associated with information portals, or are provided on the homepages of medical tourism companies or the providers themselves.

Aziza Travel

www.youraziza.co.uk/blog.html

Focused primarily on respiratory and pulmonary issues, this blog is housed on the website of a London-based medical and health spa tour facilitator that specializes in packaging spa holidays to Poland.

Healthbase

http://blog.healthbase.com/

A team from the U.S.-based medical and dental tourism facilitator, Healthbase, writes occasional posts on various topics of interest to medical tourists on this blogsite. The Healthbase website is available at: www.healthbase.com.

Healthcare Europa

www.healthcareeuropa.com/categories/healthcareblog

Journalist Max Hotopf and medical sociologist Rebecca Hotopf write blog entries as part of their Healthcare Europa website, which was established in 2008 "to provide visibility on the European private healthcare and care markets." The site also offers a newsletter that covers private health care, outsourcing, and the health care industry across Europe.

Healthglobe

http://blog.myhealthglobe.com/

This blog is part of the Healthglobe website. Blog entries cover news that is pertinent to medical tourism and related to Healthglobe's services.

International Medical Travel Journal (IMTJ) Health Tourism Blog

www.imtj.com/blog/

The Health Tourism blog focuses on news and events in medical tourism. The blog is written by Keith Pollard, Managing Director of the web publisher, Intuition Communication Ltd. Intuition's sites include the International Medical Travel Journal (IMTJ), Treatment Abroad, DoctorInternet, and Private Healthcare UK. This blog was previously housed at the Health Tourism blogspot: http://treatmentabroad.blogspot.com/.

Medical Tourism City Blogs

www.medicaltourismcity.com/profiles/blog/list

Medical Tourism City is the social network of the Medical Tourism Association (MTA). Medical Tourism City Blogs cover a variety of medical tourism news, deals, and more.

Medical Tourism Corporation

www.medicaltourismco.com/medical-tourism/

This blog is housed on the website of the Texas-based medical tourism facilitator, Medical Tourism Corporation. Its content covers popular medical tourism procedures.

Patients Crossing Oceans (PCO)

http://emedtravel.wordpress.com/

This bilingual (English and French) blog began in 2010. Authored by Amin Etemad-Rezai, posts are lengthy and illustrated with graphics. PCO has partnerships with a number of parties in the medical tourism arena.

Stanley Rubenti Medical Tourism Blog

www.healism.com/blogs/the_stanley_rubenti_medical_tourism_blog/

This blog is housed on the information portal site, Healism.com. The site seeks to be a comprehensive source of information for the range of health issues and medical concerns facing potential medical tourists.

First-Person Accounts and Individual Stories

Books

Grace, Maggie, and Howard Staab. *State of the Heart: A Medical Tourist's True Story of Lifesaving Surgery in India.* Oakland, CA: New Harbinger 2007.

This book recounts the story of North Carolinians Grace and Staab's journey to Escorts Heart Institute in New Delhi, India, where Staab underwent successful heart surgery. Uninsured, Staab could not afford the estimated cost of surgery in the United States. Publicity about his story raised interest in medical tourism among Americans.

Rose, Daniel Asa. *Larry's Kidney: Being the True Story of How I Found Myself in China with My Black Sheep Cousin and His Mail-Order Bride, Skirting the Law to Get Him a Transplant—and Save His Life.* New York: William Morrow, 2009.

Larry's Kidney shares the story of an American traveling to China for a kidney transplant. The book highlights the controversy surrounding organ procurement in China at the time, and the issues surrounding global organ demand.

News Reports

Comarow, Avery. "Saving on Surgery by Going Abroad." *U.S. News Health.* March 1, 2008. http://health.usnews.com/health-news/family-health/articles/2008/05/01/saving-on-surgery-by-going-abroad (accessed September 2, 2011).

This item profiles American Brad Barnum, who saved 80 percent on knee and hip surgery in India.

Dellorto, Danielle. "Lower Costs Lure U.S. Patients Abroad for Treatment." International CNN.com. March 27, 2009. http://edition.cnn.com/2009/HEALTH/03/27/india.medical.travel/index.html (accessed September 25, 2011).

Sandra Giustina, the feature of this story, traveled from her Las Vegas, Nevada, home to New Delhi, India, to have surgery for atrial fibrillation.

Konrad, Walecia. "Going Abroad to Find Affordable Health Care." *The New York Times.* March 20, 2009. www.nytimes.com/2009/03/21/health/21patient.html?_r=3 (accessed September 20, 2011).

This article is about retired Camden, South Carolina, executive Ben Schreiner's trip to Costa Rica for hernia repair surgery.

McDermott, Nick. "'Now I've Had My Five Babies Here, I Want to Stay,' Says Nigerian 'Health Tourism' Mother." MailOnline. July 4, 2011. www.dailymail.co.uk/news/article-2011049/Now-Ive-babies-I-want-stay-says-Nigerian-health-tourism-mother.html (accessed September 25, 2011).

This article discusses foreign use of Britain's National Health System. The specific case highlighted is Bimbo Ayelabola, a Nigerian woman who gave birth to quintuplets while in the United Kingdom.

Ramesh, Randeep. "This UK Patient Avoided the NHS List and Flew to India for a Heart Bypass. Is Health Tourism the Future?" *The Guardian.* February 1, 2005. www.guardian.co.uk/uk/2005/feb/01/health.india (accessed September 25, 2011).

This article provides an account of medical tourist George Marshall's trip to India, and details his cost savings.

Sreenivasan, Hari. "Passage to India, for Surgery." *ABC News Nightline.* October 19, 2006. http://abcnews.go.com/Nightline/story?id=2587670&page=1 (accessed October 15, 2011).

This *Nightline* report profiles the trip of Oklahoman Dodie Gilmore to India for hip surgery.

Traveler Information

Health and safety are definite concerns for any traveler. The following sites provide travel information for medical tourists and their travel companions.

Healthy Travel

CDC Health Information for International Travel 2012

Centers for Disease Control and Prevention (CDC). New York: Oxford University Press; 2012. wwwnc.cdc.gov/travel/page/yellowbook-2012-home.htm (accessed September 28, 2011).

Also known as the CDC Yellowbook, this reference book is published by the CDC every two years. It is targeted to the health professionals who advise international travelers about health risks. However, the book is also useful to others who are interested in travel health.

A Guide on Safe Food for Travelers

World Health Organization. WHO: Department of Food Safety, Zoonoses and Foodborne Diseases, 2007. www.who.int/foodsafety/publications/consumer/en/travellers_en.pdf

This brief brochure provides five keys for safer food. Its purpose is to give travelers the information they need to avoid illnesses caused by unsafe foods or drinks, and to let them know what to do if they get diarrhea.

International Travel and Health Pages

Website: www.who.int/ith/en/

WHO information on this website includes disease distribution maps; traveler updates; links to yellow fever, malaria, and rabies information; and links to other travel health-related information. The site also hosts the *International Travel and Health* book, which includes content ranging from general health risks and precautions, to the needs of special groups of travelers (such as those who are HIV-positive).

Medical Guidelines for Airline Travel, 2nd edition.

These guidelines are provided by the Aerospace Medical Association's Medical Guidelines Task Force, and were published in *Aviation, Space, and Environmental Medicine.* May 2003, 74, 5 (Section II Supplement): A1-A19. www.asma.org/pdf/publications/medguid.pdf (accessed October 27, 2011).

Multi-Professional Patient Safety Curriculum Guide

www.who.int/patientsafety/education/curriculum/Curriculum_Tools/en/index.html

This guide, released by WHO Patient Safety, was published in October 2011. It consists of input from international organizations representing physicians, dental providers, the pharmaceutical industry, midwives, nurses, health care students, and patients. It serves as an educational guide for faculty on patient safety, including ready-to-use basic safety programs.

Travel Medicine
369 Pleasant Street
Northampton, Massachusetts, 01060
Tel: 1 800 872 8633
E-mail: travmed@travmed.com
Website: www.travmed.com/index.htm

This site provides a variety of general travel safety information, such as destination advisories, links to additional information, and commercial products including insurance and supplies. The website also hosts the following online traveler's guide, which contains a wealth of information on obtaining health care while traveling.

Rose, Stuart R., and Jay S. Keystone (with Peter Hackett). *International Travel Health Guide*. Updated Online Edition. www.travmed.com/health_guide.htm (accessed October 15, 2011).

Travel Medicine also maintains guides to infectious disease and travel medicine specialists who are experts in travel risks. These experts can advise on various aspects of travel safety, administer vaccines (including yellow fever), and prescribe preventive drugs for malaria and travelers' diarrhea. Regional directories are available for:

The United States: www.travmed.com/clinics/index.html?mode=reg&r=US

Canada:www.travmed.com/clinics/index.html?mode=reg&r=Canada

International (countries around the world): www.travmed.com/clinics/index.html?mode=reg&r=International

Traveler's Guide to Safe Dental Care.

Organization for Safety, Asepsis and Prevention (OSAP). http://www.osap.org/?page=TravelersGuide (accessed February 21, 2012).

This document covers information on avoiding dental emergencies, getting vaccinations, finding a dentist abroad, and assessing infection control in dental offices. It concludes with a checklist for obtaining safe dental care.

Travelers' Health Pages
Centers for Disease Control and Prevention (CDC)
Website: www.cdc.gov/travel/

The Centers provide information on a range of topics, including traveler's health. The CDC recommends that all travelers stay up-to-date with routine immunizations, including influenza, chickenpox (varicella), polio, measles/mumps/rubella (MMR), diphtheria/pertussis/tetanus (DPT), and hepatitis B. Many of these diseases are uncommon in the United States, but are still prevalent in other parts of the world.

TravelWell Handbook for Travel Health

TravelWell, Emory Healthcare: www.emoryhealthcare.org/travel Well/pdf/Patient%20Education%20Booklet.pdf

This brief handbook advises patients on how to have a healthy trip. It discusses planning ahead, offers advice regarding several potential travel hazards, and provides information on various immunizations.

World Health Organization (WHO) Collaborating Centres on Travel and Health
Travel Health Centre, Royal Free Travel Health Centre
The Royal Free Travel Health Centre
The Royal Free Hospital
Pond Street, London NW3 2QG
Tel: (+44) 020 7830 2885
E-mail: admin@travelclinicroyalfree.com
Website: www.travelclinicroyalfree.com/

This centre provides comprehensive health services for travelers, including vaccines (e.g., for yellow fever and other diseases), malaria prevention, and diarrhea kits, among other products. The clinic operates under the auspices of University College London Medical School, and is a designated WHO Collaborating Centre for Reference, Research and Training in Travel Medicine, and the Department of Infectious and Tropical Diseases.

TravelWell, Emory Healthcare
550 Peachtree Street, NE, 7th floor
Atlanta, Georgia 30308
Tel: 404-686-5885
E-mail: through the online form at: www.emoryhealthcare.org/
    connecting/ask-nurse.html
Website: www.emoryhealthcare.org/TravelWell/

Affiliated with Emory Healthcare of Emory University, Travel-Well provides health services to international travelers. TravelWell services include pre-trip advice and planning, as well as post-trip care when needed.

Information on Specific Countries

CIA World Factbook

Hard copies can be purchased through the U.S. Government Printing Office at the following address:

732 N. Capitol St.
Washington, DC 20401
USA
Tel: 1-202-512-1800; toll free: 1-866-512-1800
http://bookstore.gpo.gov/

This resource provides various maps and a wealth of information (including historic, cultural, political, economic, geographic, military, and transnational issues) on 267 world entities. The Factbook can be accessed free online at: www.cia.gov/library/publications/the-world-factbook/index.html

Country Reports
P.O. Box 430
Pleasant Grove, UT 84062-0430
USA
Tel: 1.801.208.5635; 1.866.689.0542 (toll free)
E-mail: through the online form at: www.countryreports.org/feed
    back.htm
Website: www.countryreports.org/index.htm

This resource, established in 1997, provides more than 35,000 pages of culturally rich content useful to travelers, educators, students, researchers, and businesses. Activities on the site make it an interactive learning experience and a good resource for teachers.

Country Studies
Library of Congress
Federal Research Division
101 Independence Ave. SE
John Adams Building, LA 5281
Washington, DC 20540-4840
USA
Tel: 1-202-707-3900
E-mail: frds@loc.gov
Website: http://lcweb2.loc.gov/frd/cs/cshome.html

The Federal Research Division of the Library of Congress provides descriptions and analyses of the historical, social, economic, political, and security systems, as well as the interrelationships of those systems and cultures, for countries worldwide.

Country Watch
Two Riverway, Suite 725
Houston, TX 77056
USA
Tel: 1-713-355-6500; toll free 1-800-879-3885
E-mail: support@countrywatch.com
Website: www.countrywatch.com

CountryWatch is an information provider of "country-specific intelligence" for each of the world's recognized countries. Intelligence and data are provided to more than 4,000 corporate, governmental, educational, and individual clients.

Lonely Planet
150 Linden Street
Oakland, CA 94607
USA
Tel: 1-510-250-6400; toll free 1-800-275-8555

E-mail: select the appropriate contact link for your needs at: www. lonelyplanet.com/contact/
Website: www.lonelyplanet.com/us

For three decades, Lonely Planet (owned by BBC Worldwide) has provided travel information written by expert travel writers for independent travelers. The site offers a wide variety of travel guides, phrasebooks, and other resources for travelers, and focuses on responsible, sustainable travel practices.

World Travel Guide
Tel: +19057531017, extension 223
E-mail: through the online form at: www.worldtravelguide.com/ about/contact.html
Website: www.worldtravelguide.com

The *World Travel Guide* was co-founded by college professor and literary travel guide Wade Rowland. This online travel magazine offers firsthand, detailed information for global travelers.

Travel Documents

Website: http://travel.state.gov/travel/cis_pa_tw/cis/cis_4965.html Passports — U.S. Department of State: http://travel.state.gov/passport/

Visas — U.S. Department of State: http://travel.state.gov/visa/

Travel Warnings

Office of American Citizens Services and Crisis Management (ACS)

(See chapter 7.)
In addition to handling travel documents, part of the CA's responsibility includes issuing travel warnings and travel alerts. Travel alerts address short-term conditions (e.g., natural disasters, anniversaries of terrorist events, etc.) that pose significant risks to the security of U.S. citizens.

Travel Alerts: http://travel.state.gov/travel/cis_pa_tw/pa/pa_1766.html

Travel warnings are issued when the CA wants citizens to consider very carefully whether to travel to a particular country.

Travel Warnings: http://travel.state.gov/travel/cis_pa_tw/tw/tw_p1764.html
Additionally, the CA oversees the Smart Traveler Enrollment Program (STEP) program.

Through this free service, U.S. citizens who travel or live abroad can record their trip information, so the Department of State can provide them with emergency assistance if needed. The program also allows Americans living in other countries to receive information from the nearest U.S. embassy or consulate. Subscribers to STEP also receive Travel Alerts, Travel Warnings, and other country-specific information. Information on STEP is available at:

E-mail: CAIBRS@state.gov
Website: https://travelregistration.state.gov/ibrs/ui/index.aspx

Overseas Security Advisory Council (OSAC)
U.S. Department of State, Bureau of Diplomatic Security
Washington, DC 20522-2008
USA
Tel: 1-571-345-2223
E-mail: for general correspondence, through the online form at:
    www.osac.gov/Pages/ContactUs.aspx
Website: www.osac.gov/
Emergency Duty Officer
Phone: 202-309-5056
E-mail: osac_risc@state.gov

Through the Bureau of Diplomatic Security, the OSAC provides a liaison for the State Department and the private sector to exchange information and cooperate on security issues. This site provides daily news and reports on items of global security interest.

U.S. Customs and Border Protection (CPB)
U.S. Department of Homeland Security
300 Pennsylvania Avenue, N.W.
Washington, DC 20229
USA

Tel: 1-877-227-5511 (for U.S. callers); 703-526-4200 (for international callers)

E-mail: through the online forms at: help.cbp.gov/app/answers/detail/a_id/1207

Website: www.customs.gov/xp/cgov/travel/

U.S. Customs and Border Protection (CBP) is responsible for the safety of the approximately 1 million travelers who cross U.S. borders daily. The CPB site provides information of use to travelers before departing and upon re-entering the U.S.

Travel Tools

Language Tools

These online language tools can be used to search and find resources in languages other than English, and to translate web pages.

Language Tools—Google

www.google.com/language_tools?hl=en

These Google tools allow users to search a phrase, translate text that they type or cut and paste into a text box, translate a webpage by entering the URL, use the Google interface in more than 100 languages, and visit the Google site in the user's local domain.

Yahoo! Babel Fish

http://babelfish.yahoo.com/

This Yahoo! site allows users to translate text that they either type or cut and paste into a text box. Other features translate a webpage when the URL is entered, and enable translation directly from a browser.

Currency Converters

Medical tourists need accurate financial information to make informed decisions about their care and travel arrangements. These tools provide currency exchange rates, and one even offers an interactive worksheet for comparing the costs of medical procedures globally.

Country Reports

Currency Converter: www.countryreports.org/currency-converter. htm

This is a basic currency converter, provided on an uncluttered page. Users can click through other resources on the site if they want additional information about specific countries.

World Budget Estimator

U.S. News and World Report Health: http://health.usnews. com/health-news/family-health/articles/2008/05/01/ world-budget-estimator

This interactive site provides a printable worksheet that allows users to compare the cost of surgery at U.S. hospitals and at hospitals outside of the United States. The estimator comes from the *Patients Beyond Borders* series.

XE: http://www.xe.com/

In addition to offering conversion rates, this site answers a variety of questions about currency conversion. It has an extensive offering of online Internet foreign exchange tools and services.

World Clocks

Travelers must consider time differences between their home and destination when making travel plans, considering jet lag issues, and communicating with family and friends at home. The following sites make these calculations simple.

Timeanddate.com: www.timeanddate.com/worldclock/

This site allows users to quickly find current local time zones around the world. It also includes a handy Time Zone Converter—Time Difference Calculator. Visitors to the site can set up a personal world clock, and use the Event Time Announcer to convert the time of scheduled events to local times all over the world.

Worldtimeserver.com: www.worldtimeserver.com/

With the motto, "Any time, anywhere," the World Time Server includes the current time and date for cities large and small worldwide. It also provides a mobile version for iPhones and other devices.

Weather Tools

World Weather

The Weather Channel: www.weather.com/common/welcome-page/world.html

Weather reports for thousands of cities around the globe are accessible here. The site also offers daily video weather forecasts for locations around the world. In addition to English, weather information is accessible in Portuguese, French, German, and Spanish.

Glossary

Ayurveda the ancient traditional Indian holistic healing practice that seeks harmony and balance of the mind, body, and spirit. Prevention and treatment practices include lifestyle modifications and natural therapies. One of the oldest medical systems in the world, Ayurveda is still widely practiced in India and other nearby countries. Ayurvedic medicine is also practiced in other countries, including the United States, often as a complementary approach to Western medicine.

bariatric surgery surgical procedures performed on the stomach or intestines, aimed at reducing weight. This is sometimes referred to as obesity surgery, because it is generally only performed on people who are considered dangerously overweight.

circumvention tourism an emerging term for medical travel that is undertaken to intentionally bypass (i.e., circumvent) laws or restrictions in place in the traveler's home country. Traveling to obtain abortions, fertility treatments, or for euthanasia may all be reasons for circumvention tourism. The legal aspects of this type of travel are still being worked out.

conference tourism travel to attend events targeting special issues or interests such as a disease or healing approach. This is also known as MICE tourism, an acronym that stands for "meetings, incentives, conferences, and exhibitions."

cosmetic surgery surgery performed to improve appearance and sometimes self-esteem, rather than for medically necessary reasons. Cosmetic surgery is sometimes referred to as plastic surgery, or cosmetic plastic surgery. Because it is elective surgery, it is generally not covered under medical insurance policies.

delocalization activities that were once conducted locally are conducted across distances. Rather than using face-to-face interactions, social and economic changes require more impersonal systems (such as business

313

entities headquartered in another country or through online transactions). Delocalization is a facet of globalization.

dental tourism   travel to receive dental care abroad. Dental care is one of the easiest medical services to receive abroad, because it is usually performed on an outpatient basis and the recovery is quick. Perhaps 40 percent of medical tourists go abroad for dental work.

elective procedures   medical procedures not seen as medically necessary by a doctor or insurer. Elective procedures are undertaken by choice (i.e., elected) and planned, rather than being emergency procedures. Cosmetic surgeries, infertility treatments, and laser eye surgery are all examples of elective procedures pursued by medical tourists.

euthanasia   the intentional killing of a human being who is terminally ill, or experiencing great pain or suffering. Because of the emphasis on ending pain and suffering, euthanasia is sometimes referred to as "mercy killing." More exacting definitions of the term vary based on whether death was caused by an action (e.g., giving a lethal overdose of pain medicine) or omission (e.g., withholding nutrition), was requested by a consenting patient, or was assisted by someone who knowingly provided the means for committing suicide (e.g., a physician who writes a prescription for a potentially lethal drug).

expatriate   a person whose country of residence is other than their native country. An unknown percentage of medical tourists are actually expatriates returning home to receive medical care in familiar surroundings, or in the company of family.

facilitators, medical tourism   entities that assist travelers in connecting with the care they are seeking. Medical tourism facilitators function as specialized travel agents. They help clients find appropriate and high-quality medical care, and they arrange trip details, from booking accommodations to transportation and leisure activities during the recuperation phase after medical procedures.

globalization   the increasing interconnectedness of the world's economic, social, and cultural systems. The rapid growth of technologies (including communications and social media), multinational corporations, and the diffusion of cultures around the world as people travel between countries are all factors behind increasing globalization. Globalization has, in turn, facilitated the rapid expansion of medical tourism, which has become one facet of the more general globalization of health care and biotechnology.

holistic medicine   a system of health care that treats the "whole patient." Holistic medicine addresses balances in physical, mental, emotional, and spiritual health. A variety of treatments are encompassed under the umbrella of holistic medicine, including Ayurveda, herbal remedies, and lifestyle factors such as eating a natural diet and exercising. Holistic therapies may be used independently, or in conjunction with, Western "scientific" medicine.

hymenoplasty a form of cosmetic surgery that reconstructs the hymen. The hymen is a thin membrane that partially covers the opening of the vagina. This membrane is torn during sexual intercourse, and sometimes during strenuous physical activity and by tampon use. Hymenoplasty is performed for religious and cultural reasons, particularly in cultures that value a woman's virginity. It is variously referred to as hymen repair, hymen restoration surgery, hymen reconstruction, revirgination, or restoring virginity.

inbound medical tourism travelers coming into a country from abroad to receive health care. Americans may also sometimes be considered inbound medical tourists when they travel from their home state to a hospital in another state.

informed consent a legal procedure required in the United States and by many other medical systems to ensure that patients fully understand the potential benefits, risks, and alternative options before undergoing any procedure. Competent patients should have all the information they need (i.e., be "informed") about the procedure and legally agree ("consent") to undergoing that procedure. There is no mechanism in place to ensure that the information prospective medical tourists receive before their treatment is accurate, applicable, or thoroughly understood.

lifestyle tourism traveling to spas and resorts for health and rejuvenation. The practice of lifestyle tourism also includes massage, yoga, anti-aging, meditation, weight loss, stress reduction, and many other pampering services. Additionally, patients sometimes travel not to receive a medical procedure, but to recover from a treatment they have already had at home.

MICE tourism an acronym that stands for "meetings, incentives, conferences, and exhibitions" and involves travel to attend such events. These events target special issues or interests, such as a disease or healing approach. This is also known as conference tourism.

organ trafficking buying and selling human body parts, usually for transplantation. This practice is tied to transplant commercialism and transplant tourism. It is often illegal, conducted on the black market, and involves significant ethical and human rights concerns.

outbound medical tourism travelers leaving one country, or location, to obtain health care elsewhere. American patients who travel to another country to receive medical care are considered outbound tourists. Americans may also sometimes be considered outbound medical tourists when they travel to a hospital in another state.

outsourcing   contracting or transferring work to third parties or outside suppliers, rather than having employees perform the work "in house." Outsourcing may be used as a cost-saving measure. This is a growing trend in areas such as manufacturing, human resources, and information technology, as well as in some medical procedures, such as having radiologists in India read American patients' test results. Medical tourism is viewed by some as a form of outsourcing health care. Outsourcing is tied to globalization, delocalization, and supraterritoriality.

public health   the field of medicine that deals with protecting and improving the health of entire communities. To accomplish these tasks, public health incorporates preventive medicine, sanitation, health monitoring, and the identification of, and intervention in, emerging problems. The impacts of medical tourism on public health systems are still a matter of debate.

reproductive tourism   travel to receive fertility treatments, conceive, or terminate a pregnancy, and which may involve surrogacy. Reproductive medical tourism has been nicknamed the "procreation vacation."

science tourism   traveling to a location to undertake scientific research that is not allowed in the researcher's home country. For example, science tourists sometimes research medical therapies using stem cells.

sex reassignment surgery   surgically changing a person's external anatomy to appear as that of the opposite sex. Hormonal treatments are also used in this process. Sex reassignment surgery can be conducted for a person who wishes to be reassigned from male to female, or from female to male. Sex reassignment surgery is variously known as gender reassignment surgery, genital reconstruction surgery, sex affirmation surgery, sex re-alignment surgery, and sex change surgery, among other terms.

stem cell   cells that are able to "self-renew," in other words, divide and produce more stem cells. They can also "differentiate" into various types of specialized cells with specific functions in the body (e.g., blood or muscle cells). Because of their unique properties, stem cells are the subject of medical research on a variety of diseases and conditions. Although some proven stem cell therapies exist, much of the stem cell research sought by medical tourists is experimental and potentially dangerous. Stem cell research and treatments are also topics of ongoing ethical debates.

suicide tourism   travel for the purpose of ending one's life. This controversial form of medical tourism is intertwined with various legal, moral, and ethical interpretations of euthanasia.

supraterritoriality   social and economic exchanges occur across borders, or are controlled elsewhere in the world. Activities occur cross-border, or outside of traditionally defined "territories" (e.g., outsourcing the reading of medical test results). Supraterritoriality is a facet of globalization.

telemedicine   exchanging medical information electronically to improve a patient's health. This form of distance care covers a range of services, such as conducting medical consultations via the Internet, sending X-rays or laboratory tests to another country to be read, hosting online patient support groups, and remotely monitoring a patient's condition, among others.

transplant commercialism   a term referring to organs that are bought and sold like any other commodity. This practice has led to exploitation and illegal trafficking in organs purchased by transplant tourists.

transplant tourism   traveling to a country with less stringent rules about organ distribution to receive a transplant organ more quickly. Organs from foreign donors sometimes become available through organ trafficking and may be obtained illegally on the black market. This is a serious ethical concern in medical tourism that has been condemned by the World Health Organization (WHO) and other entities.

xenotransplantation   transplanting organs or other living cellular matter or tissue from one species to another species. The term refers to transplanting nonhuman animal tissue into humans. Chimpanzees, baboons, and pigs have all been sources of xenotransplant materials. Xenotransplantation shows promise for treating conditions including neurodegenerative disorders and diabetes. In addition to ethical concerns, concerns have also been raised about the possibility of viral transfer between species and subsequent human-to-human transmission.

Index

319

About the Authors

KATHY STOLLEY is Batten Associate Professor of Sociology at Virginia Wesleyan College in Norfolk, Virginia. Her emphasis is applied sociology—using sociological tools and perspectives to bring about positive social change. She has worked in various sociological practice positions outside of academics, including policing, organizational consulting, freelance writing, and social science research. Stolley holds a Ph.D. in Sociology from The George Washington University in Washington, DC. Her previously published books are *The Basics of Sociology* (Greenwood, 2005), *The Praeger Handbook of Adoption* co-edited with Vern L. Bullough (Praeger, 2006), and *HIV/AIDS*, co-authored with John E. Glass (Greenwood, 2009).

STEPHANIE WATSON has been a freelance writer and editor specializing in health and science for more than 12 years. Her clients have included WebMD, A.D.A.M. (MedlinePlus), Sharecare, Rosen Publishing, and Thomson Gale. Prior to launching her freelance writing career, she was a producer for The Travel Channel, and a writer/producer for Weather.com. Watson holds a B.S. in Mass Communications from Boston University in Boston, Massachusetts, with a minor in English. Her previously published works include *Understanding Obesity: The Genetics of Obesity* (Rosen Publishing, 2008), *Genetic Diseases and Disorders: Spina Bifida* (Rosen Publishing, 2008), and (as a contributor) *Biotechnology: Changing Life Through Science* (UXL, 2007).